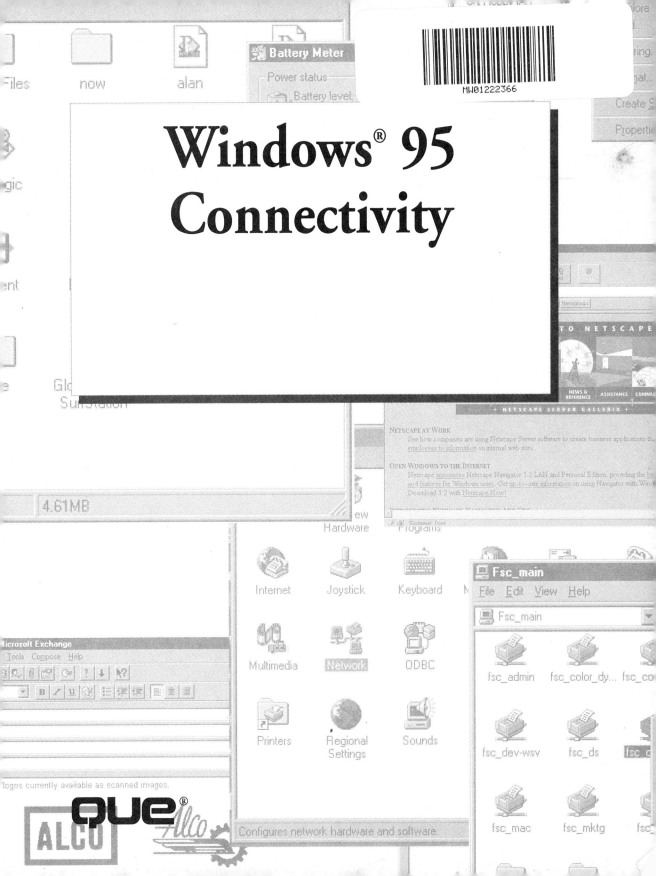

Windows® 95 Connectivity

MW01222366

Windows® 95 Connectivity

Written by

Rob Cima
Gregory J. Root
John W. Nelsen
Michael Marchuk
Mark Davidson
Alan Westenbroek

que®

Windows 95 Connectivity

Copyright© 1995 by Que® Corporation.

Library of Congress Catalog No.: 95-78891

ISBN: 0-7897-0183-9

97 96 95   6 5 4 3 2 1

Interpretation of the printing code: the rightmost double-digit number is the year of the book's printing; the rightmost single-digit number, the number of the book's printing. For example, a printing code of 95-1 shows that the first printing of the book occurred in 1995.

Screen reproductions in this book were created using Collage Plus from Inner Media, Inc., Hollis, NH.

Credits

President and Publisher
Roland Elgey

Associate Publisher
Joseph B. Wikert

Editorial Services Director
Elizabeth Keaffaber

Managing Editor
Sandy Doell

Director of Marketing
Lynn E. Zingraf

Senior Series Editor
Chris Nelson

Publishing Manager
Bryan Gambrel

Acquisitions Editors
Lori A. Jordan
Fred Slone

Product Director
Stephen L. Miller

Production Editor
Patrick Kanouse

Editors
Kelli Brooks
Douglas Wayne Bowers
Thomas Cirtin
Mike La Bonne
Jeanne Terheide Lemen
Lynn Northrup
Caroline Roop
Mary Anne Sharbaugh

Assistant Product Marketing Manager
Kim Margolius

Technical Editors
David Shinn
Russell L. Jacobs

Technical Specialist
Cari Skaggs

Acquisitions Coordinator
Angela Kozlowski

Operations Coordinator
Patty Brooks

Editorial Assistant
Michelle R. Newcomb

Book Designer
Barbara Kordesh

Cover Designer
Dan Armstrong

Production Team
Steve Adams
Chad Dressler
John Hulse
Damon Jordan
Brian-Kent Proffitt
Julie Quinn
Kaylene Riemen
Michael Thomas
Scott Tullis
Colleen Williams
Jody York

Indexers
Debra A. Myers
Kathy Venable

Composed in *Stone* and *MCPdigital* by Que Corporation.

Dedication

To Mom and Dad, whose love and support make all things possible.

About the Authors

Rob Cima has worked as a computer network engineer with the University of Missouri–Columbia for the last four years. Currently, he is also involved as the Chief Technologist for Global Image, Inc., an Internet company providing cutting-edge Internet design services.

Gregory J. Root started his work with computers when TRS-80s were in style and 16K of RAM was equivalent to infinity. He has worked for Northern Trust Bank and Follett Software Company. He also has made part of his living as a computing consultant for lawyers, churches, and a government contract. Throughout his career he has administered and installed peer-to-peer and server-based networks, developed applications using Fortran and Visual Basic, and managed software development projects. He lives in Lake in the Hills, Illinois, with his beautiful wife and lifelong companion, Tracy.

John W. Nelsen is Vice President-Operations for Local Cable News, Inc., in Albany, New York, and a co-author of Que's *Insider's Guide to Windows 95 Programming*.

A veteran broadcast journalist, including 16 years' service with CBS, John has been working with personal computers since the early 80s. He is now active, professionally, in the design and planning of digital audio and video facilities for broadcast and cable television applications.

John also makes wide use of PCs at home and in his volunteer work as archivist for The ALCo Collections. He is directly responsible for creating and maintaining the computerized indexes and catalogues to the organization's extensive archival holdings relating to the 121-year history of the American Locomotive Company and its constituent predecessors.

John can be reached electronically at CompuServe—**73410,1253**.

Michael Marchuk has been working in the computer industry since 1979 when he started as a part-time BASIC programming instructor. Along with his bachelor's degree in Finance from the University of Illinois, he has received certification as a NetWare CNE and a Compaq Advanced Systems Engineer.

He has designed and built an international multi-protocol wide area network for a Fortune 500 company and now serves as an Integration Engineer and as the Network Security Chairman for a Forbes 400 corporation.

Mark Davidson has been developing with Borland products since Turbo Pascal for CP/M and has been using Borland C++ since it was Turbo C 1.0. He has been writing Windows applications since the days of Windows 2.0. Currently, he works for Sony Electronic Publishing, where he develops Windows as well as Macintosh applications.

Alan Westenbroek is a technical instructor and developer for Datastorm Technologies, Inc. in Columbia, Missouri. By day, he teaches support technicians about communications and troubleshooting and catches bugs. By night, he loses sleep surfing the Internet and writing books about the Internet and connectivity with Windows 95.

We'd Like To Hear from You!

As part of our continuing effort to produce books of the highest possible quality, Que would like to hear your comments. To stay competitive, we *really* want you, as a computer book reader and user, to let us know what you like or dislike most about this book or other Que products.

You can mail comments, ideas, or suggestions for improving future editions to the address below, or send us a fax at (317) 581-4663. For the online inclined, Macmillan Computer Publishing has a forum on CompuServe (type **GO QUEBOOKS** at any prompt) through which our staff and authors are available for questions and comments. The address of our Internet site is **http://www.mcp.com** (World Wide Web).

In addition to exploring our forum, please feel free to contact me personally to discuss your opinions of this book: I'm **76103,1334** on CompuServe, and I'm **smiller@que.mcp.com** on the Internet.

Thanks in advance—your comments will help us to continue publishing the best books available on computer topics in today's market.

Stephen L. Miller
Product Development Specialist
Que Corporation
201 W. 103rd Street
Indianapolis, Indiana 46290
USA

Contents at a Glance

Learning Your Way Around

Getting Started

Using Your New Network

Communicating

Windows on the Internet

Connecting to Networks

Appendixes

Contents

9 Sharing Network Hardware — 137

10 Setting Up for Remote Access — 153

11 Using Remote Access — 169

17 Connecting to the Internet   289

18 Using Internet Services in Windows   307

Introduction

When computers are networked, they can do more work for people. People accomplish entire projects, consisting of many tasks, when they work in teams. You can think of a network as a team of computers, designed to support a team of people.

Networking computers, like managing a team of people, is a challenge. The vocabulary of local area networks is full of acronyms. The products that you can buy sometimes operate well together and sometimes do not (things have gotten better, though—Windows 95 comes with support for more hardware products than any other operating system in history). The prices you pay can range from less than a hundred dollars per computer to several thousand. The benefits you realize from networking computers may be nothing at all (or in some instances, you may be even worse off with the network than without it), or the benefits may give you a tool whose usefulness transcends the functionality of the individual computers you have networked. Mindful of the potential rewards and benefits and despite the risks, businesses are networking their computers at a rapid pace.

Setting up a team of people, coordinating tasks, managing problems, and monitoring progress are overhead jobs that must be done to help the team work together effectively. Networking computers is an overhead job too, and although the end result is worth the effort, the process has traditionally been a major headache. Networks were difficult to set up and configure, not to mention expensive. In many cases, a network specialist had to be hired to get the computers connected, and hiring a specialist was never an inexpensive proposition. Not only that, but the cost of the software required to operate the network could be thousands of dollars itself.

Enter the new operating system from Microsoft, Windows 95. Windows 95 comes with powerful networking support built right into the operating system. It works well with other networks, such as Novell's NetWare. It also contains a complete networking system for Windows computers. This built-in networking system allows you to connect all your Windows 95 computers without adding any additional software. All you need to do is buy the hardware and you are ready to begin. (Don't worry, this book will tell you everything you need to have to get your computers networked. See chapter 6, "The Pieces of a Network," for more information.)

The built-in Windows 95 networking has some advantages over traditional networks. As already mentioned, you don't have to buy any additional software. Another advantage is that setting up the network is much easier. Since the networking is built in to Windows 95, you can use the easy Windows 95 interface to set up and configure a network. And with the help of this book, you will be able to do all this yourself.

Perhaps you run an office, small or large, and you have wondered whether a local area network would help people get their jobs done in your office. You may have purchased Windows 95 and noticed some of the networking features that are built in and want to know how they work. Or you may have been given the job of recommending a local area network or even installing one. Or perhaps you are just curious about how a network works or what a network can do for you. For these and similar situations, you will need an introduction to local area networks, an introduction to the networking features of Windows 95, and a guide to setting up your Windows 95 network. This book is for you.

Why Network Computers?

The first use for networks, and the first use to which you probably will put a local area network, is the sharing of costly computer disk drives and printers. Early in the 1980s, Apple Computer's very popular Apple II computer was expensive. Large-capacity disk drives for the Apple II were likewise expensive. Local school systems wanted to purchase Apple II computers to help schoolchildren learn, but the cost of the disk drives—even small ones—was prohibitive. And the computers were not nearly as useful without disk drives. A company named Corvus saw a need and began selling one of the first local area networks to local boards of education. The school system could purchase a single large-capacity disk drive, purchase Apple II computers without disk drives, connect the computers and the disk drive through a local area network, and give access to the single, shared disk drive to each Apple II user. The idea caught on rapidly. School systems found a way to afford computers for their students, and Corvus grew at a fantastic rate.

High-capacity, high-speed disk drives are not as expensive as they used to be. Today, of course, *high capacity* means hundreds of millions of bytes (*megabytes*, or *M*), or even billions of bytes (*gigabytes* or *G*)—a far cry from the 5-million-byte and 10-million-byte Apple II disk drives purchased by the school systems. If you buy 10 computers at current prices, each with a 500-million-byte (500M) disk drive, the disk-drive component of each computer will cost about $250—a total of $2,500 for all 10 computers and 5,000M. If you buy a single 5,000M disk drive, you will pay about $1,200—a difference of $1,300. To network these 10 computers, you will probably spend more than $1,000 on network interface cards and software. The economics of local area networking have changed considerably since the days of Apple II computers and Corvus. So why would you network these ten computers?

There are three answers to this question. The first says that you can save money by sharing devices over the network. For example, rather than buy all ten people on the network a laser printer, you can buy one and let them all use it. Or rather than add an extra 500M disk drive to every computer to meet expanding storage needs, you could add one 5,000M to the network and let everyone use it.

The second answer points to the people costs associated with personal computer use. If you use a local area network to share a single disk drive, you centralize the administration of the information on the disk. You can easily make backup copies of all the information on the shared disk—for example, for all 10 people. If each person were responsible for making their own backup copies, you would quickly find that some people would ignore the guidelines and not back up their disk drives. The department of 10 people (or perhaps an entire business) would run the risk of losing some of its valuable information. Along these same lines, the 10 people could use the local area network to share files and information. Without the network, a person would share files by copying those files to a floppy disk and walking the disk over to another person. (This is sometimes referred to as *sneakernet*.) With a LAN, people can give files of information to each other simply and easily.

The third answer contains the most sophisticated and complex reason for using a LAN. A growing number of personal computer software products recognize the presence of the local area network and are multiuser. These products are *LAN-aware*: the software coordinates the updates to a central file and enables many people to access the same information at the same time.

Local area networks can save a business money, but the savings in terms of computer hardware costs is a smaller part of the overall picture. The savings in people expense is the larger part.

Many times, using a local area network to run its business is a necessity for a company. The network enables the company to function because the enterprise absolutely needs to share information. Stores that rent videotapes are a prime example. The store needs to keep an accurate record of which videotapes are rented and which ones are on the shelf. A minicomputer or mainframe computer, with a terminal for each sales clerk, would be an expensive solution. Instead, the store uses PCs, networked behind the counter, to keep track of the whereabouts of each videotape. Two or three clerks can keep each other informed by simply operating two or three personal computers and recording the rentals and returns. The common database of rentals and returns is kept on a single computer on the network. Each time a clerk enters information, the clerk's PC updates the common database file on the file server.

Perhaps your company needs to share a CD-ROM disk drive, a plotter, or a fax modem. Windows 95 has everything you need to share these devices.

What Is the Purpose of This Book?

By using illustrations, photographs, and clear, simple explanations, this book introduces you to local area networks, teaches you how to set up your own network using Windows 95 and shows you how to use the various features of your Windows 95 network. As you read further, you will learn about the new features of the Windows 95 operating system. You will learn what a network is, what the different types of networks are, and how they work. You will learn what pieces you need to have to build your network, and what pitfalls to avoid when you are purchasing them. You will find out how to assemble your Windows 95 network and how to use it effectively to share hard drives and printers, send e-mail, and work on the Internet. Finally, you will learn how to connect your Windows 95 computers to other networks, such as Novell's NetWare.

Who Should Read This Book?

You will find this book useful and informative if you are curious about networking computers with Windows 95. You do not have to have a network now. In fact, if you are in the process of selecting a local area network, you can use this book as a comprehensive guide during the selection process.

Perhaps you are getting a Windows 95 network in the office and want to know how it will affect your work. This book will provide you with the information you need to make the transition to the network as smooth as possible. It will also show you how to make the most of the features of the Windows 95 network to make you more productive in your job.

If your computer is already connected to others with a local area network, you can use this book to understand how to integrate you Windows 95 with the existing LAN. Or perhaps you want to know how to connect Windows 95 to the Internet so that you can find sports information and statistics, new software, or send e-mail. This book is for you.

What Is in This Book?

Part I of this book, "Learning Your Way Around Windows," provides a brief introduction to Windows 95. Chapter 1, "Getting Used to a Brand New Face," tells you about the Windows 95's new look and feel. Chapter 2, "Taking Inventory of New Applications and Accessories," tells you about the many small applications that come with Windows 95 and introduces you to some of the new functions of Windows 95, such as built-in networking capabilities and hardware support.

Part II, "Getting Started with Networks," gives you nuts-and-bolts information about how networks function and how to set up your Windows 95 network. Chapter 3, "Welcome to the World of Networks," explains what a network is and how you can benefit from having one. In chapter 4, "Understanding How Networks Work," you learn some of the terminology of networks and how computers work on a network. Chapter 5, "Selecting the Right Network," lets you explore what your options are when selecting a network and helps you determine which type of network is right for you. Chapter 6, "The Pieces of a Network," provides you with a shopping list of components you will need to build your network. Finally, chapter 7, "Setting Up a Windows Network," shows you how to build a network using Windows 95.

Part III, "Using Your New Network," explains how to work with your Windows 95 network once you have it set up. Chapter 8, "Using the Network Neighborhood," shows you how to use the Network Neighborhood to find out what resources are available on your network. In chapter 9, "Sharing Network Hardware," you learn how set up hard disks, printers, and fax modems so everyone on the network can use them. Chapter 10, "Setting Up for Remote Access," describes how to set your Windows 95 network up so it can be accessed from other locations by modem. Chapter 11, "Using Remote Access," tells how to use your computer on the network when you are not at the office, such as at night when you are at home. Lastly, chapter 12, "Networking with a Notebook," is a thorough discussion of the special considerations of using notebooks.

Part IV, "Communicating by Computer," gives an overview of e-mail and demonstrates how to use e-mail with Windows 95. Chapter 13, "Introduction to Electronic Mail," leads off with an explanation of what electronic mail is and how it works. Chapter 14, "Using Electronic Mail with Windows," explores how e-mail works with Windows 95. And chapter 15, "Working with Microsoft Exchange," shows you how to use Exchange, which comes with Windows 95, to send and receive mail.

In part V, "Windows 95 on the Internet," you learn what the Internet is and how to connect to it using Windows 95. Chapter 16, "Introduction to the Internet," brings you up-to-date on what the Internet is and what it can be used for. Chapter 17, "Connecting to the Internet," continues by explaining how you can connect your Windows 95 computer to the Internet. Then chapter 18, "Using Internet Services in Windows," finishes with a look at the various Internet services and what you need to do to access them.

In some cases, you may be integrating your Windows 95 computer into an existing network. Part VI, "Connecting Windows to Other Networks," tells you how to do this painlessly. Chapter 19, "Connecting to Other Networks," describes how to set up your Windows 95 computer to work with networks such as Novell's NetWare. Chapter 20, "Using Windows with Corporate Networks," explores how to perform network tasks with Windows running in a Windows NT, Novell NetWare, and UNIX networks. Finally, chapter 21, "Using the Built-In Network Tools," explains how to use the tools that come with Windows 95 to manage your network.

Appendix A, "Technical Specifications of Network Protocols," provides a more in-depth look at computer networking for those who want to know more about how it works. Appendix B, "Registry Entries for Networking," introduces you to the entries in the Windows Registry that control networking functions. Appendix C, "Glossary of Networking Terms," is a resource to explain words you may encounter as you learn more about networks. Finally, appendix D, "Internet Access Providers," tells you who to contact to get your Windows 95 computer connected to the Internet.

What Should You Already Know?

This book is not a primer on personal computers. You should already have some familiarity with computers to get the most out of this book. In particular, you should know what a personal computer is, how to start and use an application on a personal computer, and what a disk file is. Experience with Windows 95 will be helpful but not necessary. You do not need to know anything about networks themselves.

The first chapter, "Getting Used to a Brand New Face," and chapter 2, "Taking Inventory of New Applications and Accessories," provide a brief introduction to Windows 95 for those who may be new to the operating system. Let's get started!

Part I

Learning Your Way Around Windows

Chapter 1

Getting Used to a New Face

If you're used to using Windows 3.x, chances are that your first look at Windows 95 will leave you feeling a little disoriented. Microsoft has extensively studied the way people interact with their computers, trying to determine how to make working with a computer easier and more intuitive. This is great for new users but can involve some habit-changing on the part of experienced Windows people.

The largest difference is the shift to an object-oriented way of looking at things. This means that everything in your computer is treated as an object. An *object* is a self-contained item with which you can interact. Text, pictures, sound clips, entire documents, and printers are all examples of objects. As you become more familiar with Windows, you will see references to the *desktop*. Think about the real-life desktop where you work. It probably contains several objects, such as documents (letters and expense reports), tools (stapler, phone, and a nearby trash can), and places to store certain items (file folders and a bin for work). The screen that you work with in Windows is referred to as a desktop and, similar to the physical one, it can contain documents, tools, and places to store items.

When you work in an object-oriented manner, you edit the contents of an object or manipulate groups of objects to perform tasks. To help you focus on the task at hand, Windows keeps track of which object needs which tool or application. For example, you need to edit a document. To do this, you drag it out of a folder and onto the desktop. When you double-click the document, Windows starts the word processor that can edit the object. In Windows 3.x, you had to know which application could edit the document. Once you remembered that, you could start the word processor and open the document.

Each of these is a different type of object. As in real life, these objects have different characteristics that describe how they look and work. These are known as *properties*. The phone on your desk, for example, has a number of properties that define it. It has a color, a certain number of buttons, can handle calls from a certain number of phone lines, is connected, is on or off the hook, and has a certain loudness and type of ring. These properties specify the way the phone looks and behaves.

The same holds true for objects on your Windows desktop. A word-processing document has properties like title, author, length, and content. Windows treats all items as objects to give you a consistent way to interact with them.

Networking falls under the same object-orientation. You can create a shortcut object to a folder on a network drive that you frequently access. You can also create a shortcut object to a network printer on which you can drop objects to be printed. The icons for these objects don't look any different and they act like all the other icons for drives and printers.

This chapter introduces you to the new look and feel of Windows by exploring the following:

- Using object properties
- The desktop
- Icons and folders
- The taskbar
- My Computer
- The Network Neighborhood

Understanding Objects

One of the best advantages of working in an object-oriented operating system such as Windows is the consistency of operation as you move from one task to another.

For example, moving a folder is accomplished in exactly the same way as moving a document. Accessing the properties of a printer is the same as accessing the properties for a shared network disk drive.

Object Properties

An object's properties make it unique and define the way it looks and acts. In Windows, you can access any object's properties by clicking the object with the right mouse button. This displays a *pop-up menu*. This menu contains all the defined actions for an object (such as <u>D</u>elete, Se<u>n</u>d To, <u>O</u>pen, and so on). It also gives you access to the object's *Properties sheet.* Figure 1.1 shows the pop-up menu for the Projects folder.

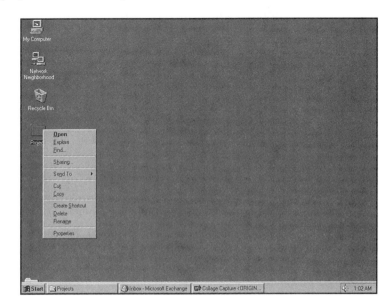

Fig. 1.1
The Projects folder's pop-up menu contains all the defined actions for the folder.

A Properties sheet gives you access to all of an object's properties. You can change some properties; you can only examine others. Figure 1.2 shows the Projects Properties sheet. The Type, Location, and Created properties are all read-only; you cannot change them. You can, however, change the Hi<u>d</u>den, Ar<u>c</u>hive, and <u>R</u>ead-Only attributes.

For example, selecting the Ar<u>c</u>hive attribute forces this folder to be archived the next time the backup program runs, even if its contents haven't changed. In a network environment, you'll have sharing properties for a folder you've shared for others to access. These define to whom you give access and what kind of access they have to the folder. You'll see a Sharing tab (refer to fig. 1.2) to access these properties.

Fig. 1.2
The Projects
Properties sheet
contains proper-
ties that you can
change and some
that you cannot.

When you have made changes to an object's properties, you can click Apply to make the changes without dismissing the Properties sheet. Alternatively, you can click OK to apply and dismiss at the same time.

Copying, Moving, and Deleting Objects

You can copy or move objects from one place to another using several methods. If the object and its destination are both easily accessible on your screen, you can simply drag-and-drop the object to the destination. The object is then copied or moved to the new location. If the destination is on the same disk drive, the object is moved. If you drag-and-drop the object to a different drive, the file is copied.

If you want to control whether an object is moved or copied, drag-and-drop it using the right mouse button. When you drop the object, a menu pops up, letting you choose whether to copy or move the object.

If the destination is not on the screen where you can see it, you can make use of Windows' advanced Clipboard to simplify the procedure. In Windows 3.x, the Clipboard could only handle pieces of data from one application to another. The Windows 95 Clipboard can handle any type of object, including entire documents or folders.

As an example, we'll copy a document object from the desktop into the Projects folder. These steps can be applied to work with any object, not just copying documents:

1. Click the right mouse button on the document on the desktop. This displays the document's pop-up menu.

2. Choose Cut or Copy. Cut places the document on the Clipboard and deletes the original. Copy creates a duplicate of the document on the Clipboard, leaving the original intact.

3. Click the right mouse button on the Projects folder to display the pop-up menu.

4. Choose Paste to place the document in the Projects folder.

Tip
You can delete an object in much the same manner. Instead of choosing cut or copy, select Delete from the pop-up menu.

Printing Objects

Any document that you have created in an application can be printed the old-fashioned way by starting the application, opening the document, and printing it. With Windows, you can also simply drag-and-drop the document to a printer object's icon. Windows prints the document automatically.

You can also print a document by opening its pop-up menu and choosing Print. Windows then prints the document.

Opening Objects

Opening an object is known as the default action for most objects. This means that when you double-click an object's icon, Windows opens it. For documents, this means that the application that created the document is started and the document opened in it. For an application object, Windows starts the application. For folders, Windows opens a window displaying the contents of the folder.

There are other ways to open an object. If you want to open a document file in a particular application, you can drag-and-drop it to that application's icon. Windows starts the application and loads the document.

If you just want a quick look at the contents of a document, you might be able to use *Quick View* instead of opening the document. Quick View lets you look at a document. You cannot change or print it. However, it's a lot faster than loading a word processor or graphics application. To see if you can Quick View a document, display its pop-up menu. If you see a Quick View option, choose it. Windows opens a new window showing the contents of the document.

What's All the Stuff on My Screen?

In Windows 3.x, the screen did not contain many features. The only interface between the user and the computer was Program Manager, which is just a

Learning Your Way Around

window full of icons used to start programs. There was no convenient place to put those items you needed to work with every day (unless it was a program group you created in Program Manager).

The Windows 95 desktop is more interesting and easier to use. Depending on the options installed on your system, your screen should closely resemble the one in figure 1.3.

Fig. 1.3
This is a standard Windows desktop with a typical installation.

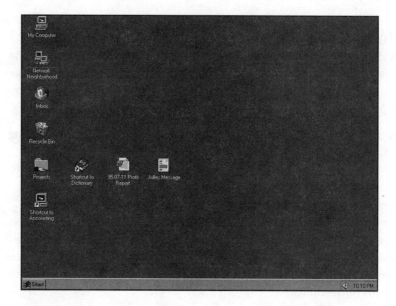

All of the standard Windows elements are present on this desktop. They include the following:

- Icons

- Folders

- Shortcuts

- The taskbar

- The desktop

Icons

Most dictionaries define an *icon* as a symbol that represents something more complex. Icons in Windows are a perfect illustration of that definition. Most of what you see on-screen are icons. The symbol of a PC in the upper left corner of the desktop (labeled My Computer) in figure 1.3 is an icon. It represents all the contents of your computer. The icon of two PCs connected together below My Computer (labeled Network Neighborhood) represents the contents of all the other computers connected to your network. Icons can also represent a special kind of object referred to as a *shortcut*. Shortcuts are a quick way for you to access an object in another place without having to move it. Shortcut icons have a small arrow in their lower left corner.

Icons can represent several things. They can stand for an application (such as Microsoft Word), a document (such as a letter or a picture), a peripheral (such as a printer or modem), or a place to store things (such as folders). Each icon represents an object; therefore, it has both properties and methods.

Folders

Folders are a convenient place for you to collect and store files and programs. Like the Projects folder in figure 1.3, they are represented by an icon that resembles a manila file folder. Think of folders as resembling a subdirectory in DOS or a directory on a network server. Windows treats existing directories as folders, as well.

One of the most convenient ways to keep your work in order is to create folders on your desktop to hold letters, expense reports, or anything else you might work with frequently.

Folders do not have to be on the desktop. They can be in any place on your computer or a network computer, including on one of its disk drives or inside another folder. Better yet, if you place them on a network drive, you can share your work with others while being archived as part of the regular backup procedures of the server.

Figure 1.4 shows the Projects folder that contains some items created using a word processor, such as documents, pictures, spreadsheets, shortcuts to network drives, and other folders.

Fig. 1.4
An icon represents a Projects folder and the folder's contents.

Windows uses some special folders to hold important system items. These are represented by different icons. The Control Panel and Printers folders are examples of these. They contain objects that affect the way your computer operates and the printers that it can send documents to. Figure 1.5 shows the Control Panel and Printers folder icons.

Fig. 1.5
The Control Panel and Printers folders have specific icons.

The Taskbar

The thin area at the bottom of the screen is referred to as *the taskbar*. Microsoft determined that one of the biggest problems people had with Windows 3.x was losing track of windows as they stacked one on top of the other. So Microsoft added the taskbar to Windows 95.

Tip
If you have many windows open, each name on the taskbar may be only a few characters long. To help you choose the window you want, Windows displays the window name in a tooltip if you pause the mouse pointer over a taskbar item.

The taskbar is used for several different purposes. One of the main functions of the taskbar is to keep the user informed as to which programs are currently running. This feature also provides an easy way to switch back and forth between windows. Figure 1.6 shows a taskbar with several programs open. To bring a window to the front, click its name on the taskbar. It becomes the front-most window and its button on the taskbar appears depressed.

The other main feature of the taskbar is the *Start button*. The Start button is a single button that displays the *Start menu*. From the Start menu, you have access to all the features and functions of Windows. With the Start menu, you can

- Run programs

- Search for files

- Search for other computers on the network

- Change the properties of objects

- Shut down your computer

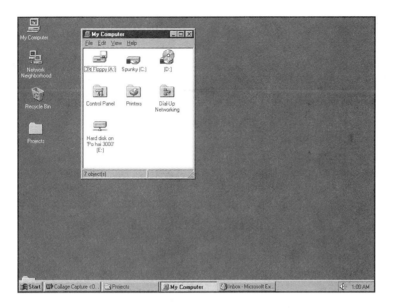

Fig. 1.6
The Windows
taskbar shows
several different
programs that are
running.

The Start menu has some default items, some have submenus, and others are
added by you. When you install new software, it is added to the Programs
submenu of the Start menu. In this way, it is always quick and easy to find.
Figure 1.7 shows the Programs submenu of the Start menu.

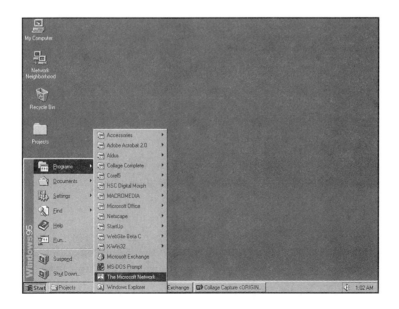

Fig. 1.7
Open the Start
menu and choose
Programs—this is
what you see.

My Computer

The My Computer icon is another kind of special folder. It represents all the objects on your computer. These include all the disk drives, drive letters mapped to network drives on other computers, the Control Panel folder, the Printers folder, and—if you installed it—the Dial-Up Networking folder.

You can access any of the files and folders on your disk drives from the My Computer folder. Figure 1.8 shows the contents of a My Computer folder with a network folder mapped to E:. You can double-click the network drive icon to see its contents. Right-clicking the network drive allows you to see its properties, start an Explorer session, or disconnect the drive.

Fig. 1.8

The contents of My Computer include all your local and network drives.

Network Neighborhood

The Network Neighborhood icon represents a folder that contains all the resources available on the network. These can be other Windows computers, file and print servers for Novell NetWare, or another corporate network. Other resources included can be other Windows networks physically connected to the same *local area network* (LAN).

When you install Windows, you identify your computer with a name and a workgroup. The name of the computer is often your name or the type of job you do. The workgroup is frequently the department in or project on which you work. You most likely work closest with the other people in the workgroup. Therefore, when you open the Network Neighborhood, you see all the computers in your own workgroup along with the Entire Network icon. This icon represents the rest of the file servers and printers available to you.

Figure 1.9 shows the Network Neighborhood with another computer in the workgroup, FAST, along with the Entire Network icon.

Fig. 1.9
The Network
Neighborhood,
the workgroup
computer(s), and
the Entire Network
make up the
Windows network.

On a computer in the Network Neighborhood, you can view many of the
same properties as your own computer. As seen in figure 1.10, the right-
mouse click of a network drive allows you to see <u>W</u>ho Am I, <u>A</u>ttach As another user, Create <u>S</u>hortcut, and <u>L</u>og Out of the server.

Fig. 1.10
The pop-up menu
of a network
computer allows
you to perform
many different
actions.

Choosing P<u>r</u>operties (refer to fig. 1.10) shows what server software is being
used, how many connections are in use, and how many total users can be
connected to it.

▶ See "Using the
Network Neigh-
borhood," p. 119

The Recycle Bin

You use the Recycle Bin icon to delete files, shortcuts, folders, and other objects from your system. Think of the Recycle Bin as a regular trash can. You
can throw items away and every week or so, the garbage truck comes to
empty it out. If you accidentally threw something away, you can go to the
trash can before the garbage truck comes. The same holds true for the Recycle
Bin on your desktop.

The easiest way to delete an object is to drag it onto the Recycle Bin. The bin accumulates many items over a long period of time. If you accidentally threw out a document, you can open the Recycle Bin, right-click the object, and select Restore from the pop-up menu to put it back where it belongs.

You can set the Recycle Bin to use only a certain percentage of drive space available. Once it reaches that point, the oldest objects are deleted to make room for the object just deleted. You can also manually empty the Recycle Bin by right-clicking it and selecting Empty Recycle Bin from the pop-up menu. This reclaims all the hard drive space used by all of the objects in the Recycle Bin.

From Here...

In this chapter you learned how Microsoft has evolved the look and feel of Windows to make it easier to use and help you be more productive. You also learned about the different elements you see on your screen and the desktop.

■ Chapter 2, "Taking Inventory of New Applications and Accessories," offers information on the different tools and utilities which make Windows easy to use.

■ Chapter 8, "Using the Network Neighborhood," discusses how to find computers, access their resources, and inspect their properties in more detail.

■ Chapter 9, "Sharing Network Hardware," talks about using shared resources on other computers in your network and mapping network drives to your local computer.

Chapter 2

Taking Inventory of New Applications and Accessories

In the beginning, there was DOS. As an operating system, DOS is pretty basic, running programs and basic diagnostics and having a rudimentary interface. DOS supports additional hardware such as sound cards by running programs known as *device drivers*. A device driver is a piece of software that tells DOS how to interact with the hardware device that you have added.

Essentially, DOS allows users to interact with the computer, and little else. Unless you are a computer professional, though, you probably don't want to interact with the computer as much as you want to write documents, schedule appointments with colleagues, draw floorplans, or send e-mail. To do these things, you need to buy additional software.

Enter Windows. Early versions of Windows were not much more than a menu program for running DOS programs with some utilities tacked on. Built into Windows is a simple calendar, a text editor, a calculator, and a painting program. These tools ship with Windows and are ready to run as soon as you start Windows. Support for additional hardware still comes from DOS's device drivers.

Windows makes it easier to get your day-to-day tasks done. Its graphical interface is more intuitive and easier to learn, and the richer set of utilities allows you to save some money on extra software.

Windows 95 takes the original Windows concept several steps further. It provides an easier-to-use interface and adds a host of great accessories that help you take care of business without buying extra software. Windows 95 also has added support for a wide variety of adapter cards and other hardware. You no longer need to worry about loading device drivers from DOS before Windows launches because Windows 95 is a complete operating system on its own, no longer requiring DOS to run, as did previous Windows versions.

Basically, Windows 95 is designed to make your computing life easier, and in this chapter you explore the operating system and discuss some of its features and benefits, such as

- How Windows 95's integrated networking can allow you to set up powerful computer networks that let you share files and printers and send e-mail messages between computers

- How Windows 95's improved hardware support can help you get your computer set up in less time and with fewer headaches

- What applications come with Windows 95, and what they allow you to do

- How you can use Windows 95's built-in accessories to speed up small everyday tasks

Integrated Networking

Pretty much any environment where more than one person works on a project or uses the same information or equipment benefits from networking. This is the real strength of Windows 95 because, although its new user interface is very functional and easy to learn, its powerful, built-in networking capabilities make setting up and running a network easy even for beginners.

A network lets you treat information, printers, fax modems, and other resources the same whether they're on your machine or on one halfway across the building. And everything you need to make it happen comes in the Windows 95 box.

The Networking Past

In the early versions of Windows, if you wanted to use Windows and a network at the same time, you had to be part engineer and part programmer (or at least it seemed that way). The problem was that the Windows and the network couldn't work together very well. Network operating systems (NOS) likeNovell NetWare and Banyan VINES didn't know anything about Windows, and Windows didn't want to know anything about the NOS. To do most network tasks, such as logging in or out, connecting to network disk drives, or attaching to network printers, it was usually easiest to exit back to DOS, make the changes you wanted, and then start Windows again. This process was frustrating.

Users asked for an easier way to use Windows and a network together. Microsoft answered with Windows for Workgroups (WFW), which added built-in networking.

WFW adds the ability to share files and printers with other people on a WFW network and, as long as all the machines on the network are Windows for Workgroups, works fine. The problem with WFW is that is doesn't work very well with other NOSs, such as Novell's NetWare.

Don't misunderstand—you can use WFW and Novell NetWare at the same time. But getting to that point is difficult. Just ask people who had to stop in the middle of a WFW installation because they had to get a file named NETWARE.DRV that didn't come with WFW. And they still had to load drivers from DOS before Windows ever started.

A Higher Standard of Networking

Windows 95 changes everything with real functional peer-to-peer networking that's built into the operating system. Gone are the days of loading drivers from DOS or editing configuration files by hand. Windows contains driver support for most common NICs and allows you to configure everything in a familiar, easy-to-use graphical environment. And not only does it include the ability to network with other Windows computers, but also with a variety of other computer network systems, such as Banyan VINES, Novell NetWare, and even the Internet, all at the same time (see fig. 2.1).

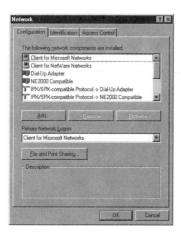

Fig. 2.1
The Network dialog box makes setting up and configuring the network much easier.

Windows also makes it easy to access your network once you have it
set up. For example, instead of having to know that the file you want is at
\\DS_FS2\VOL2:MRKTG\DATA\SALESFIG\4QTR\, you can just visit the
Network Neighborhood, go to the Marketing file server, and look in the 4th
Quarter Sales Figures folder. If you need to access the file (or even the whole
folder) often, simply drag it to your desktop or another folder to create a
shortcut, making it readily available. You don't need to worry so much about
file servers or network paths anymore.

What Can a Network Do for Me?

The networking capability built in to Windows can do a lot for you. For starters, you can share any file or folder on your computer with users on your
network. And you can protect your folders so that other users can only read
files and not change them, or you can set it up so they can do anything they
want. If you want only certain people to have access to certain files, you can
assign a password. You can also access shared files and folders on other
people's computers just as if they were on your own computer.

In fact, you can share a lot of different things, including fax modems and
printers, which means you can print to printers anywhere on the network.
There's no point in buying everyone a laser printer if you can buy only one,
attach it to the network, and let everyone use it. If you've got a choice between a laser printer, a color inkjet, and a wide-carriage dot-matrix model,
you can print to whichever one is most appropriate for the job you're doing.
All you need to do is log in to the network, which you usually have done
when you first started Windows, connect to a printer on another computer
that another user has given you access to, and print away.

With Windows and Microsoft Exchange (included with Windows), anything
you can print, you can fax right from the program you're working in, even if
the fax modem is connected to a different computer. Microsoft Exchange also
has an e-mail system, letting you send and receive mail with anyone on the
network. Exchange's e-mail in not limited to just text messages; you can send
messages that include pictures, a voice message from yourself, and even a
video clip.

There are many more functions you can do with the Windows network. For
example, you can select text in your word processor, copy it to the Clipboard,
then let someone else paste it on their computer. All this and a lot more is
possible. For more information on using the Windows network, look at chapters 8, "Using the Network Neighborhood," and 9, "Sharing Network Hardware."

Hardware Support

Windows 95 has built-in support for more hardware devices than any other computer operating system in history. What is built-in? Built-in means that all the software necessary for a given sound card, scanner, or video adapter to work with your system is included and available in the operating system.

Let's say you have a new sound card that you want to install in your computer. Under previous versions of Windows, you had to load support for the card from DOS. In many cases, this involved installing the software that came with the sound card and editing the CONFIG.SYS file, which tells the computer to load the adapter's software when the computer starts.

Windows 95 makes this much easier. You generally won't need the software that ships with your device because Windows 95 will already have everything it needs to interact with the adapter. Usually, you won't even need to know what software needs to be installed because Windows 95's Add New Hardware Wizard will automatically detect the adapter you have added to your system (see fig. 2.2). The Wizard then adds all the drivers you need to run the device.

Fig. 2.2

The Add New Hardware Wizard automatically detects your hardware and installs the appropriate software drivers.

Built-In Applications

What do you think of when you hear the term "application"? Most people envision a big, high-powered program that can do everything they need and many things they don't. Windows comes with more than just a few simple applications thrown in for good measure, it includes real applications that you can use to do real work. Included with Windows is a full-featured word processor, a graphics editing program, communications software, e-mail and groupware applications, and more. In this section, you take a look at some of these applications and their features.

WordPad

You've probably used a high-powered word processor like Word or WordPerfect before. If you're like most people, you used the program to format your document with different fonts and probably added a picture or page numbers, pretty common features for a word processor.

WordPad (see fig. 2.3) is a compromise between the features most people need in a word processor and an industrial-strength word processor that does it all. WordPad has a toolbar with buttons for the most often used functions and a formatting ribbon to choose fonts, set paragraph indent and spacing, and more. WordPad can automatically create bulleted lists and align text. WordPad can use OLE to insert a picture, sound, or video clip you download from your coworker's computer in the next office. A graph or chart from a program like Microsoft Excel or CorelDRAW! can also be inserted. You can even add custom headers and footers and change the color of text.

Fig. 2.3
WordPad is a word processor that incorporates the most commonly used functions of a full-featured word processor.

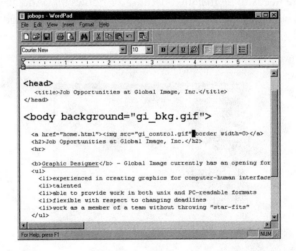

WordPad reads and writes files in the same format as Microsoft Word. This makes it easy for people with Windows to open and print Word documents by using WordPad. This, of course, works the other way around. Anyone with Word, regardless if it is running under Windows 95, can open, update, and print your WordPad documents.

WordPad is a good example of efficiency in a program. It has all the features most people need without making them wade through dialog boxes for things like revision marks and macro editing. And like all the applications in Windows, it supports drag-and-drop, so you can drag text or pictures from other programs and drop it right into your WordPad document.

Microsoft Paint

Ironically, Microsoft Paint was the same name the graphics program had back in Windows 1.0 and 2.0. It had almost no features, a hard-to-use interface, and couldn't display color. With Windows 3.0, Microsoft renamed the program Paintbrush. This version worked with colors and had a better interface. Major improvements have been added to Microsoft Paint in Windows 95.

Paint is a full-featured program for drawing and editing graphics (see fig. 2.4). Paint lets you draw maps, create illustrations for your documents, or design graphs for a report. You can also import bit-map images from other computers on the network and edit them to your heart's content. Paint can zoom in and out to various levels and edit by using all of the tools. You can type text directly on your drawing and format it by using a ribbon like the one in WordPad.

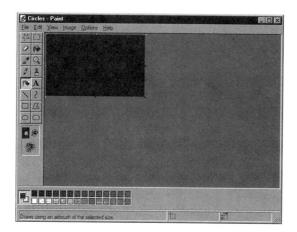

Fig. 2.4
Paint allows you to draw and edit graphic files both on your computer and over the network.

HyperTerminal

Windows 95 also includes a HyperTerminal to assist you in dial-up networking connections to remote computers (see fig. 2.5). HyperTerminal, unlike the original Terminal program that shipped with earlier versions of Windows, has a number of useful features.

While Terminal only has one or two terminal emulations and file transfer protocols, HyperTerminal supports most of the popular versions in use, including ANSI BBS, a popular full-color terminal emulation used by most computer bulletin boards, and Zmodem, one of the most popular file transfer protocols in use.

Fig. 2.5
HyperTerminal
provides dial-up
communication
capabilities.

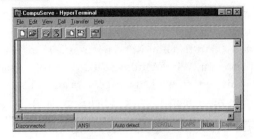

To use HyperTerminal, you create what is known as a session for each location you want to call. A *session* is a combination of the phone number, modem speed, and other modem settings that are specific to the number you are calling. After you create a session, you see an icon with the name you chose for the session. The rest is pretty painless. Double-click the icon for the session you want and HyperTerminal takes care of dialing and connecting for you.

Exchange

Once you have installed your Windows 95 network, you will want to take advantage of the ability to send electronic messages to your co-workers. To help, Microsoft has included Exchange with Windows 95. Figure 2.6 shows Exchange, which lets you communicate with other people over the network by using e-mail, interactive forms, and multimedia. You can also use it to communicate with others via CompuServe Mail. In fact, Exchange will get mail from both places and put all your messages in one easy mailbox on your desktop.

Fig. 2.6
Exchange allows
you to send e-mail
to others on your
network.

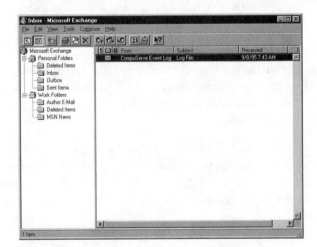

Exchange isn't limited to the version you receive with Windows. You can design electronic forms in Microsoft Visual Basic to build interactive sessions between people and departments as part of Exchange. Other companies can also develop custom "service providers" to let Exchange communicate with just about anything. It's possible for someone to give Exchange the capability to send all your voice-mail messages to your inbox or send you a message everytime someone saves a file to a particular folder on your machine.

It will be interesting to see just how far the industry takes Exchange. The possibilities are pretty limitless. Microsoft is planning on Exchange being the foundation for electronic communications in the future. They're already hard at work developing communication, online, and database applications to work with it.

For more information on Electronic Mail and Microsoft Exchange, read part IV, "Communicating by Computer."

FAX

A few years back, Microsoft decided that it wasn't enough to have just computers running Windows. If it was good for computers, it would be good for other machines too—fax machines, copiers, phones, and so on. The idea is to have a common interface for all the machines in your office. For example, you could control your copier from your computer.

Nobody (except Microsoft's ad people) got very excited about the whole prospect, and it seems to have pretty much died out, except for the FAX software in Windows, which was originally called At Work FAX, but has since been shortened to FAX or MS FAX (see fig. 2.7). It's a great concept: One person on your network has a fax modem installed on their computer, and anyone else on the network can send a FAX by using it.

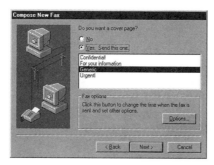

Fig. 2.7
FAX lets you send faxes over a fax modem—whether the modem is on your machine or somebody else's.

The programming and design used to accomplish this feat is pretty amazing. Basically, you tell your application you want to send a fax and Windows prints your document to a special fax-format file and then mails it to the computer with the fax modem installed by using Exchange. All this takes place in the background so that you can keep working as your fax is sent.

Fax capability built right in to Windows 95 is a very nice feature, but being able to fax over a network and save the expense and hassle of multiple modems and phone lines is tremendous. At Work Fax is one example of how Exchange can be extended to do more than just e-mail.

Built-In Accessories

Accessories are the programs that are just too small or specialized to be called applications. A lot of these have been around since early versions of Windows but have some enhancements added.

Notepad

This is the text editor you probably remember from the previous versions of Windows. Notepad is pretty much unchanged (see fig. 2.8). It's great for jotting down a quick note or editing a system file, whether that file is local on your machine or on someone else's across the network. It's also good for all those README files that seem to come with programs.

Fig. 2.8

Notepad is a simple text editor that comes with Windows 95.

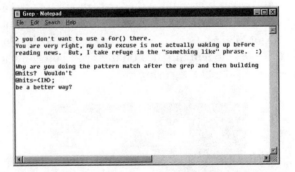

Notepad's only change is that it supports long file names. For anything more than the most basic text editing, you can use WordPad instead.

Telnet

Telnet is one of the programs you use to communicate with other computers on the Internet (see fig. 2.9). It works a lot like HyperTerminal but doesn't use a modem, using your connection to the Internet instead.

Fig. 2.9
Telnet allows you to log in to other computers on the Internet.

Telnet included with Windows 95 is one of the best versions of the program available. It loads quickly, supports multiple fonts and colors, and different terminal emulations. Telnet is an example of the best kind of accessory: simple with a very specific use.

Phone Dialer

With Windows 95, Microsoft is introducing software called the Telephony Application Programming Interface (TAPI). This software makes it easier for other programs to talk to modems and telephones. The Phone Dialer is at the core of this technology.

The Phone Dialer window is a keypad that looks like a touch-tone telephone keypad (see fig. 2.10). You type in the number you want to call and your modem dials the number for you. Then you pick up the phone and talk. There are quick-dial buttons you can use to call somebody with the click of a single button.

You can also set different dialing locations (at home, at the Columbus office, at the London office, and so on) and the dialer automatically punches in the correct codes for an outside or long distance line for you. For example, let's say you have a notebook computer that you use at home, at the office, and when you are at the lake on vacation. At home, you can simply dial the number you want, 555-2491. At work, though, you need to first dial 9 and then the number. At the lake, it is a long distance call, and you need to enter a credit card number. After you set Phone Dialer up to know that it needs to dial a 9 when you are at your office location and your credit card number when you are at the lake, it does it automatically for you. All you need to tell the program is where you are dialing from and it adds the appropriate numbers.

Fig. 2.10
The Phone Dialer remembers phone numbers for you and can dial your phone at the click of a single button.

The services of the dialer are available to any program that uses TAPI. That means you'll see a common interface every time you need to place a call.

From Here...

Well, that's a look at some of the goodies with Windows. Throughout the rest of the book, we concentrate on understanding networking, setting up a Windows network, and connecting to other networks like Novell's NetWare, and the Internet. We also take an in-depth look at using and configuring Microsoft Exchange. For more information:

- Chapter 4, "Understanding How Networks Work," describes the parts of a typical Windows network and how they fit together.

- Chapter 5, "Selecting the Right Network," helps you decide which type of network best suits your needs.

- Chapter 7, "Setting Up a Windows Network," describes the step-by-step process necessary to get your network configured and running.

- Chapter 8, "Using the Network Neighborhood," tells you how to navigate your network and see which resources, such as hard drives, printers, and fax modems are available to you.

- Chapter 17, "Connecting to the Internet," details how to get your Windows computer working on the Internet.

Part II

Getting Started with Networks

Chapter 3

Welcome to the World of Networks

We hear the word "network" used with computers all the time. It's in the advertising we read. We see it on software boxes. "This software runs over a network." "You can play this game over the network." Why does nobody ever tell us what a network is? Why do I want to play my game over the network? What does that do for me? Before you can get down to the nuts and bolts of putting a network together, you'll need answers to these questions.

In this chapter, you learn

- What a network is

- What a network does, and what you can do with it

- What sharing does for you

- What the Internet is

What Is a Network?

A network is a collection of hardware and software that allows individual computers to communicate with each other. By communicate, I mean that by using the network, computers can transfer data such as spreadsheet files and electronic messages back and forth.

Essentially a network connects users, like you, to resources, such as hard disks and fax modems. Before the advent of networks, each individual computer had to have all the resources you, as the user of the PC, wanted. Any data you needed to get your work done had to be stored on a floppy or hard disk. If you needed to send a fax, your fax modem had to be connected to the serial port.

Networking changes all of that. If your computer is networked with a variety of other computers, those resources no longer have to be local. You can easily use just about any resource attached to the network. The network hardware and software make it all possible.

What Does a Network Do?

The whole idea of a network is a lot easier if you just think of it in terms of sharing and communicating, which is what a network is all about. Everything a network does and allows you to do falls into one of those two categories.

Share Your Hardware Resources

By sharing your hardware, you allow others to use it over the network. Just about any resource connected to a network can be shared. Let's say that you are working on a spreadsheet for your boss, and she absolutely has to have it by 5:00. You finish it with plenty of time to spare at 4:45. You can sit back and relax while it prints on your printer and then run it upstairs. Then disaster strikes. The printer makes a horrible grinding noise, and your report comes out all black.

If you're on a network, this is no problem. It just so happens that your co-worker next door also has a printer connected to his computer. He can share his printer with you. With a few clicks of his mouse, he sets up his printer to be shared. You simply reprint the document to his printer.

Figure 3.1 is a representation of an office network of computers with attached devices. The network makes it possible for each device attached to each computer to be used by everyone in the office. By using the hard drive on someone else's computer, you have access to their files and programs. (Only if they let you, though. Windows comes with security features to make sure that no one goes snooping around where they shouldn't be.) You can share faxes, printers, disk drives, and CD-ROMs. All this means that networks can help keep office costs down. You don't have to have a printer for each computer. Buy one good printer, put it on a network-attached computer, and everyone can use it. The same goes for fax modems, CD-ROMs, and so on.

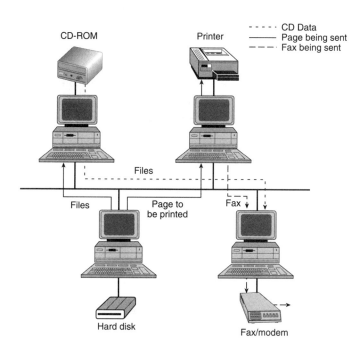

CD-ROM

Printer

- - - - CD Data
———— Page being sent
— — — Fax being sent

Files

Files   Page to
        be printed

Fax

Hard disk

Fax/modem

Fig. 3.1
A network allows
attached devices to
be shared by all
connected
workstations.

Share Your Data Files

Networks also allow you to share data. In the spreadsheet example, let's say
that your boss wanted to take a look at it on her computer instead of seeing it
on paper. How do you get this document to her if you don't have a network?
You copy to a floppy disk and walk it to her office, where she inserts the
floppy and launches her spreadsheet program to take a look at it. This doesn't
seem like too big a deal, maybe taking five minutes of your time.

What if you are updating this spreadsheet over the entire course of the day?
Your boss, ever wanting to check up on your work, needs to see it five or six
times during the course of the day. If you have to walk it to her every time
she asks to have a look at the updated info, you have now wasted a half hour
of your day. Let's say this document is extremely important to the entire
company and that you have 15 different people besides your boss who will be
working with you on it. They will all need to see a copy as you make your
revisions to check your figures against theirs, etc. Suddenly you are spending
your entire day updating files!

The data sharing of a network can help solve your problem of getting spreadsheet to all those people in a snap. All you have to do is allow all of those other users to connect to your drive over the network (see fig. 3.2). Your hard drive actually appears on their Windows desktop. You get to keep working on your project, and everyone else gets the information they need without having to take the time to call you up, ask for the information, and wait for you to arrive with it.

Fig. 3.2
A network allows you to easily share data.

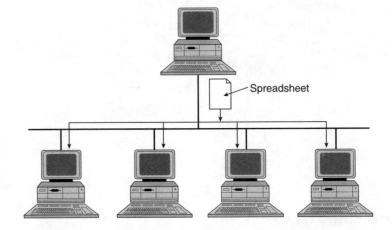

Spreadsheet

Communicating with a Network

Networks not only allow you to interact with other devices, they also allow you to talk to other people. There are a variety of applications that aid you in your communication, but they all fall into three categories: electronic mail, electronic chat, and workgroup applications.

Electronic Mail

The first category of communication is *electronic mail* (*e-mail*). As you can see in figure 3.3, e-mail is sort of the electronic equivalent of sending a letter via the U.S. postal service. However, e-mail is delivered much faster than normal mail. In fact, many regular users of e-mail now refer to paper mail as *snail mail*.

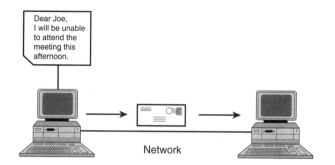

Fig. 3.3
E-mail enables you
to send messages
over the network.

E-mail can be invaluable in an office setting. In fact, many forward-thinking organizations have done away with the paper memo in favor of e-mail. E-mail provides a couple of advantages over traditional paper memos:

- E-mail can be easily stored. You can store your e-mail electronically so that it doesn't take up space in your office or get lost in the shuffle the way a paper memo can. Saved paper memos very quickly take up an unreasonable amount of space in a filing cabinet.

- E-mail is easily routed to a group of people. If you need more than one person to receive a message, just add the person's name to the recipient list. The message reaches everyone automatically. No more copying, and no more walking a memo to ten different offices.

Chatting Over Your Network

Your network allows you to chat electronically, much like you chatted in a school classroom with slips of paper. You never need to leave your office to talk to co-workers.

Both the chat and e-mail functions of the network allow you to talk to your network neighbor. The difference is that chat allows more interaction between you and the person you are talking to. Chat functions like both of you are writing on the same piece of paper. You write a line, and then the other person writes a line. With e-mail, interaction is less like a conversation. You write your whole message, and when the other person gets it, they write theirs.

Workgroup Applications

The latest communication tool to hit the networked office is the workgroup application. Workgroup applications take the cooperation and coordination that networks make possible to the next level. Some examples of workgroup applications include scheduling programs, shared whiteboards, and videoconferencing.

Scheduling Programs

Scheduling programs allow the schedules of everyone in an organization to be made automatically. For example, you are the head of the design department at an architectural firm. You need to get some people together to discuss a new project. Normally, you individually contact each of the people you need to attend and inform them that you want to have a meeting at a particular time. They check their schedules and make sure they can attend, which they then let you know. If they can't attend, you have to reschedule and go through the process of notifying everyone of the new time and so on until you find a time everyone agrees on.

With a scheduling program, though, everything is much simpler. The scheduling program keeps track of everyone's schedule. It knows when people are free and when they aren't. Using the scheduler, all you have to do is specify the time of the meeting and the people you need to attend. The scheduler automatically updates everyone else's schedule to reflect the meeting.

Shared Whiteboards

Another type of workgroup application is the shared whiteboard. This is identical to a traditional whiteboard, which is what people draw on to help express an idea—a way of thinking out loud. One person at a time can be writing and drawing, or everyone can be scribbling at the same time (depending on the number of people and the size of your whiteboard, of course).

The networked whiteboard allows you to do all of the same things, except that they get done at your computer. You don't even have to be in the same room with the people you are working with. The whiteboard application runs on each of the network computers. As you write in the white space on your computer, the things you put down show up instantly in the white spaces of the other computers. You get the same sort of interaction as if you were in the same room, and it does not matter how far apart the computers are. You could be in the next room, a couple of floors down, or even in another city, but the communication is the same.

Videoconferencing

Many of these whiteboard applications come with videoconferencing. An electronic whiteboard lacks the ability to see and talk to the person you are dealing with. Videoconferencing provides the missing human interaction. You are probably familiar with the idea of a videoconference. You've probably seen one on television—for example, around election time. When the news anchor is in the home office with one political expert, while another political expert, who is halfway across the country, can be seen on the screen, that is videoconferencing.

Videoconferencing applications on your PC allow you to do much the same thing over your network. You do need a small camera and a microphone for each of the computers involved. These are usually small and often mount on top of your computer monitor. Each computer also needs speakers. Once you start your video conference, you hear the others' voices in the speakers and see their images in a window on your screen.

Videoconferencing is not quite ready for the average office. The real problem is that the average network can't move video data fast enough. As a result, the picture in many of today's computer videoconferencing packages tends to be somewhat jerky and low-resolution. As the speed of networks increases, videoconferencing will become much more widespread.

Networked Video Games

Video games aren't exactly a workgroup application, but they deserve mention here for a couple of reasons. They are a form of interaction between humans over a network. Just as shared whiteboards and videoconferencing allow you to collaborate with your co-workers, computer games allow you to blow their ship out of the sky.

Another thing about networked video games: they are just plain fun. Apparently there is just no substitute for good old human-to-human competition. For some reason, beating the computer at a game just isn't as fun as beating your buddy from the office down the hall.

Caution

Network video games tend to require a lot of bandwidth, or network capacity. If there is a game going on between two computers down the hall, your network connections may be slower than usual.

LANs, WANs, and the Internet

There comes a point in any book about networking where you get to meet the acronyms. It's that time. Listening to someone talk computer network-speak can be painful if you are new to networking. This next section introduces you to a few of the basic terms.

The Local Area Network and the Wide Area Network

The terms *LAN* (*local area network*) and *WAN* (*wide area network*), which both sound like *can*, are interchangeable with network. The difference is that LANs are networks that cover a small geographical (local) area and WANs are networks that cover a large geographical (wide) area.

The LAN

LANs are usually physically located in just a few rooms. At their biggest, they might stretch throughout a building or two. LANs normally run over specialized cables through the building. An example of a LAN is five computers and a printer connected in the sales department.

The common characteristics of a LAN are

- Connects computers in a single building
- Runs over specialized cable
- High data transfer rate
- Small number of computers

The WAN

WANs might link computers that are thousands of miles apart. (Also, they usually have more computers than LANs.) For example, you might want to have your office in New York linked to your headquarters in Los Angeles (see fig. 3.4). Because it is probably not very practical to run your own special cable from New York to Los Angeles (not to mention expensive), WANs often rely on previously laid cable. They go through the phone company's wires, using the equivalent of high-speed modems specially designed for networks.

The common characteristics of a WAN are

- Connects computers in different cities or countries
- Runs over phone company's cable between buildings
- Usually slower data transfer rate than a LAN
- Large number of computers

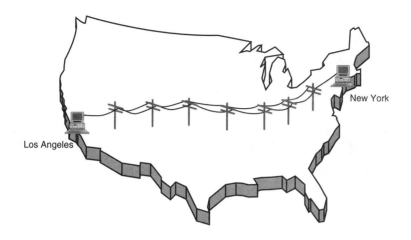

Fig. 3.4
WANs connect geographically distant computers.

The Internet

You have probably heard of the *Internet* in the past couple of years. You might not have heard it called the "Internet" necessarily because it has many names—Information Superhighway, the Net, and the Infobahn are a few other names. Figure 3.5 shows a representation of the Internet. Basically, the Internet is a giant WAN that spans the entire globe. It connects computers at universities and businesses from Los Angeles to New York, from Budapest, Hungary, to Sydney, Australia. Some people have their home computers connected. You can even connect your computer to it (to find out how, you might want to take a peek at chapter 17, "Connecting to the Internet").

II

Getting Started

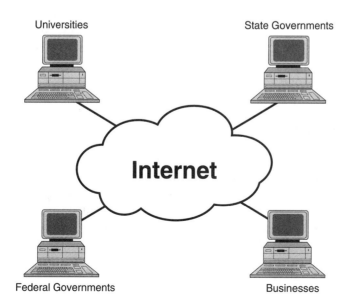

Fig. 3.5
The Internet is a collection of public networks connecting computers around the world.

The Internet is a collection of networks, containing every different type of network, and computers, connecting old IBM PCs to giant mainframes to supercomputers. The beauty of being connected to the Internet is that you have access to many of these resources. You can get the latest video driver for your computer by simply connecting to your video-card company's site on the Internet.

> **Note**
>
> When you hear talk of the Information Superhighway on the news, they are talking about the Internet.
>
> The Internet today connects many locations together, has millions of people connected, and contains plenty of information. The Information Superhighway of the future has much more aggressive plans. The plan is to connect everything. Every home, business, and school will be connected. There are even plans to allow you to be connected when you are in your car through a network based on the cellular phone system. Not only will you be connected wherever you go, but you will have access to any information you could want.

Do You Need a Network?

This is a question only you can answer. Obviously, if you have only one computer, you don't need a network. But if you work in an environment where people work together, then a network might be beneficial to you. If you are thinking of buying a CD-ROM or a printer, putting it on the network can let everyone share it. E-mail can help you get organized and get rid of some of the memos piling up on your desk. With Windows 95, you have all the software you need for a network built-in.

From Here...

In this chapter, you learned what a network is and what it can do, including sharing data and hardware resources and communicating. You also learned about the types of communication you can do with a network, such as e-mail, network chat, and workgroup applications. Finally, you found out about local area networks, wide area networks, and the mother of all networks, the Internet.

Want to find out more about networks or the Internet? Check out

- Chapter 4, "Understanding How Networks Work," describes the pieces that make up a LAN and how they fit together.

- Chapter 13, "Introduction to Electronic Mail," talks about what e-mail is and what it can do for you. You can also learn about the different types of e-mail that are out there.

- Chapter 16, "Introduction to the Internet," discusses the resources and people connected to the Internet.

II

Getting Started

Chapter 4

Understanding How Networks Work

Networks, at first glance, seem very complicated. But networks are like many things in life: once you break them into their essential components, understanding the whole is much easier.

Every network has the same three basic parts (see fig. 4.1). There are the computers and peripherals that you use to get your work done, the software that runs on your computers, and the network pieces that connect your computers and peripherals to each other. Once you break everything into more manageable pieces, networking is a snap.

This chapter introduces the three basic parts that make up a network and explains how it all works together. Once you understand the parts, you can get to work on your network in no time.

To help explain the parts, this chapter covers

- The three basic elements of computer networks

- The types of cable that are used in networks

- What a network topology is and which topologies are common

- What the difference is between a peer-to-peer network and a server-based network

Fig. 4.1
The three parts of
a network.

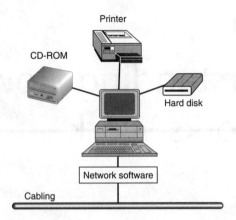

What Computers and Peripherals Should I Have To Network?

Networking is all about connecting the computers and peripherals you use every day. They are at the core of every network, and without them, there is no reason for the network to exist.

Computers

The computer on the network is where everything comes together: the network hardware is in it and the network software runs on it. The computers are where the data is kept.

What kind of computer can you network? Any kind, really. For our purposes, it should be a PC that can run Windows (this is a book about Windows networking, after all). The computer also needs an open adapter slot so that you can add your *network interface card* (NIC) to it. This can be any type of slot: ISA, MicroChannel (IBM PS/2), EISA, or PCI. NICs can be found for any of these types of slots.

Peripherals

Peripherals are another piece of your network. They include the printers, CD-ROM drives, and faxes you need to use to get your work done. Often these devices are attached to one of the computers on the network and shared with the other users on the network from there. Many new printers, though, are specially designed to be used on a network. These printers have the necessary hardware to attach directly to the network, without the aid of a computer. The software to control the printer's interaction with the network is built into the chips inside the printer.

What Software Do I Need?

The second piece of the network puzzle is the software. Think of the software as the brains of the network, while the hardware is the brawn. The software controls how the network receives and executes the commands you give it. There are two levels of software you need to know about to understand how network software works.

Your Computer Operating System

No computer can function without an operating system (OS), in this case, Windows. Windows is the piece of software that helps you control and interact with your hardware. Windows knows how to save files to your hard disk, and it knows how to send data to the printer when you have something to print.

Not only does your OS manage the interaction between you and your computer, but it also makes this interaction easy and fast. An OS that takes 15 minutes to print a file isn't a good OS. A good OS, such as Windows, makes you more productive, whether you are simply copying a file to your local hard disk or sending a fax over your network.

Your Network Operating System

A network also has an operating system, called the *network operating system* (NOS). In the past, the NOS was a separate piece of software. This software was installed on top of your existing operating system. In the same way that your OS interacts with your computer for you, your NOS interacts with your network. The NOS works with your computer's operating system to accomplish tasks over your network. Need to print a file to your network printer? Your NOS knows how to get the data there. Want to open a file on a co-worker's computer? Your NOS does the talking with the other machine to get you connected.

The easy-to-use Windows interface enables you to set up your own network in just a fraction of the time it used to take. And the best part is that you don't need a lot of network knowledge to get started. In the past, with the add-on networks, professionals were often required to get things up and running. Network professionals can be very expensive to hire. Luckily, Windows makes networking so easy that most users can set up their own network in no time.

What Do I Need To Connect It All Together?

The final pieces you need to get your network running are the connection pieces. These include the actual cables that connect your computer to the others on the network and your NIC.

Your NIC

The NIC in your computer provides the hardware to physically connect the computer to the network cabling. It fits into one of the slots in your computer and has a port on the back that connects to your network cable.

The NIC is to a conversation between two computers what a phone is to a conversation between two people. In any phone conversation, there is one item to keep in mind. You are not in the same vicinity as the person you are talking to. If you were speaking without the telephone, the other person would never hear a word you said. Fortunately, the telephone takes care of all this for us. It translates what we say onto the telephone wire, which is then transmitted to your friend's house, taken off the wire by his phone, and turned back into sound. This translation is what your NIC does for your computer. It takes the computer's commands, translates those commands, and sends them over the wire to the other computer. The NIC in the other computer then takes the signals off the network wire and translates them back into something the other computer can understand.

The Cabling

The cables that LANs use to transmit information fall into three categories: coaxial cables, twisted-pair cables, which come in shielded and unshielded varieties, and fiber-optic cables.

Coaxial Cable

Anyone who has ever installed a VCR is familiar with coaxial cable. While you can't run your LAN over the same cables you use to connect your VCR to your TV, the makeup of the cabling is similar (see fig. 4.2). One difference is in the connectors on the ends of the cable. TV cables use screw-on connectors. Network coaxial cable, on the other hand, uses a *Bayonet-Neill-Concelnan connector* or BNC connector for short (see fig. 4.3). The BNC connector is much easier to connect than the screw-on type found on television coaxial cable. For a BNC connector you simply push the male portion of the BNC connector onto the female BNC connector on the back of your NIC and give it a single half turn.

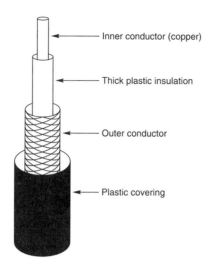

Fig. 4.2
The structure of
coaxial cable.

- Inner conductor (copper)
- Thick plastic insulation
- Outer conductor
- Plastic covering

Fig. 4.3
BNC connectors
are used with
coaxial cable.

Getting Started

II

Unshielded Twisted-Pair Cable

The most common cable used in networks is unshielded twisted-pair (UTP) cable. UTP cable is essentially the same cable that runs throughout your house for your telephone. UTP cables generally have eight wires, divided into four pairs. The two wires in each pair wind around each other—hence, twisted. The main difference between phone wires and network wires is the connector. The phone cord's type of connector is called an RJ11.

Network UTP cables use the same style of connectors you find on phone cables, only bigger. The average phone wire only has two pairs. Because computer cable has four pairs, the connector has to be wider. The connector for UTP network cable is called an RJ45 (see fig. 4.4).

Fig. 4.4
The RJ45 connector for UTP cable is similar to a standard phone connector.

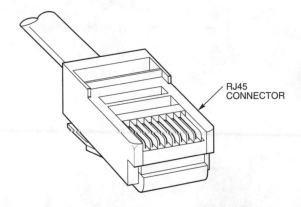

RJ45
CONNECTOR

Shielded Twisted-Pair Cable

Another common type of cable used in networking is shielded twisted-pair cable (STP), which is nearly identical to UTP cable. The difference, as shown in figure 4.5, is that STP cable has special shielding to help keep out electromagnetic interference (EMI). EMI is the interference caused by other electrical devices that may be close to your LAN cabling. Air conditioners, refrigerators, and fluorescent lights are typical examples of EMI-emitting devices. Sometimes if you run a cable too close to an EMI source, it can cause problems on your network. Connections between computers are inexplicably lost and data is corrupted. STP cable was designed to help with these potential problems.

Fig. 4.5
STP cable versus UTP cable.

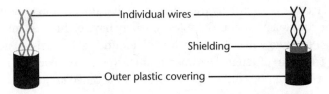

Individual wires

Shielding

Outer plastic covering

The STP cable shield consists of two pieces. First, each two-wire pair is wrapped in metal foil. Second, all of the foil-wrapped pairs are enclosed in a wire braid. This braid takes the electromagnetic waves coming from some external device and dissipates them as electricity before they can do any harm to the data flowing on the internal wire pairs.

Since STP cable has all that extra shielding inside, it isn't able to have as many pairs as UTP cable does. STP cable usually has only two pairs instead of the four found in UTP cable. Also, that extra shielding costs money, which makes STP more expensive than UTP.

Fiber-Optic Cable

Fiber-optic cable has received a lot of attention in recent years from the various long distance companies and can be used in networks. The structure of fiber-optic cable is shown in figure 4.6. Fiber-optic cable consists of thin strands of glass or plastic through which light can pass. So with fiber, light carries the information instead of electricity, which is what passes through the other types of cable you have learned about so far. In a normal copper cable, the transmitter on one end sends an electrical impulse over the wire. Electricity passes to the receiver. Fiber-optic cable does not pass electrical impulses; rather, it passes light (see fig. 4.7). Small lasers or light-emitting diodes (LED) pass a beam of light through the glass strand at the center of the cable. An optical receiver at the far end detects the presence of the light waves and decodes them.

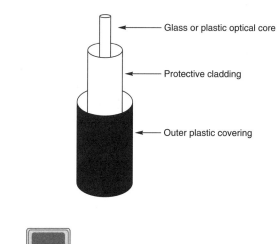

Fig. 4.6
Fiber-optic cable.

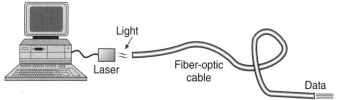

Fig. 4.7
Fiber-optic cable uses pulses of light generated by a laser or LED to transmit data.

The advantage of light over electrical impulses is that light is not subject to electromagnetic interference. This is the reason the long distance carriers like to use it. With regular copper wires, noise can be picked up from a variety of sources. Lightning storms are one very common example. Fiber-optic cable is not subject to the interference from lightning.

In networks, fiber-optic cable is more commonly used in long distance links than it is in LANs for the same reasons it is used by long distance phone carriers. With cabling inside a single room or building, it is relatively easy to keep your cables away from sources of interference such as fluorescent lighting and air conditioners. With longer links between buildings, it may be impossible to prevent your wires from coming very near to interference sources. Links between buildings may run in underground access tunnels that often also contain wiring for power, which is a major interference source. Fiber-optic cable eliminates this problem.

Another advantage of fiber-optic cable over copper cable is transmission speed. Fiber-optic cables can carry data at much higher speeds than copper.

The disadvantage of fiber-optic cable is its expense. Both the cable itself and the electronics to work with it cost many times what copper equipment does.

How the Network Fits Together— Your Network Topology

Every LAN is a little different. The distances between computers may be slightly longer or shorter. Some networks have more machines attached to them than others do. Even though networks are different physically, they are all similar—that is, all common networks fit together in the same logical way, and the way a network fits together is called the *network topology*. The three most common network topologies are the bus, ring, and star.

The Bus Topology

In a *bus topology*, all of the computers on the network are attached to a single, common wire. As you can see in figure 4.8, every computer is attached to the same cable. As information is passed on the central wire, each computer can "hear" it.

A bus network is terminated at both ends with a *resistor*. The resistor absorbs the data on the network when it reaches the end of the network cable. If the resistor was not present, some of the data could reflect back onto the wire for a second trip, which would confuse the workstations.

Fig. 4.8
Bus topology.

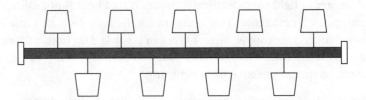

The Ring Topology

In a *ring topology*, all of the computers are attached to a single wire, just as they are in a bus topology. However, instead of being terminated at both ends, the cable in a ring topology closes around on itself to form a ring (see fig. 4.9). The data on a ring topology continues around the ring in a single direction until all of the workstations have had a chance to "hear" it, and then it is taken off the wire by the workstation that first transmitted it.

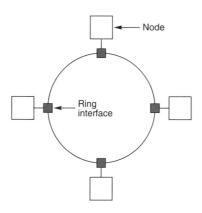

Fig. 4.9
Ring topology.

The Star Topology

The *star topology* differs from the bus and ring topologies in that the computers are not all attached to the same wire. Instead, each of the computers is attached to the end of their own, separate wire (see fig. 4.10). All of these individual wires are then connected in a central device called a *hub*, which forwards transmissions from each computer onto all of the other wires.

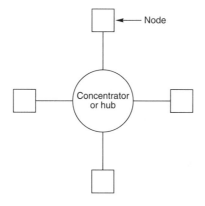

Fig. 4.10
Star topology.

II

Getting Started

The star topology has some advantages over both the bus and ring topologies. The most important is that star networks do not have what is called a *single point of failure*. With bus or ring networks, if there is a break in the main cable, the entire network goes down. If one of the cables in a star network is faulty, only one workstation is affected. If the hub goes bad, the entire network goes down, but this failure is extremely easy to diagnose because there is only one thing that can possibly be wrong if the entire network goes down—the hub. With bus and ring networks, the problem could be anywhere along the entire cable. And especially in larger installations, replacing the entire cable is no easy task.

How Do Computers Talk?

When we refer to computers "talking" to each other, what is happening is that computers are transmitting data back and forth. How this transmission actually occurs is the topic of this section, which means it's time to introduce you to some more computer networking terminology. Two conditions must be met for computers to "talk." First, the computers on the network must speak the same language. Second, there must be some rules governing the communication on the network.

The Language of Computer Networks

When you are in Paris, you speak French if you want to be understood, and when you are in Peking, you speak Mandarin Chinese. These are the languages that everyone else in the area speaks and understands.

Computer networks have their own languages, called *protocols*. In order for computers to be able to successfully communicate, they must speak the same protocol, just as humans must speak the same language if they want to communicate.

Just as there are many different languages, there are many different computer network protocols. The trick is to use the correct one at the correct time. For example, your computer needs one protocol to talk to other computers on the local Windows network and another to talk to the computers on the Internet.

Fortunately, Windows knows how to speak a wide variety of protocols, so you can set up Windows to communicate with a wide variety of other computers.

Table 4.1   Network Protocols Spoken by Windows

Abbreviation	Protocol Name	When To Use
IPX	Internetwork Packet Exchange	When connecting to Windows computers and Novell NetWare computers
NetBEUI	NetBios Extended User Interface	When connecting to Windows and Windows NT computers
TCP/IP	Transmission Control Protocol /Internet Protocol	When connecting to the Internet
NFS	Network File System	When connecting to UNIX computers

Network Data Packets

When humans speak to one another, they use words to create sentences, which convey information. Computers also must break their information into smaller pieces to get it transferred from one computer to another on the network. For computer networks, these chunks of data are called *packets* or *frames*. If you have a file you want to send to a computer down the hall over your network, to get the information there, your computer begins reading the file off of your hard disk. As it reads it, your NOS begins breaking the file into smaller pieces.

This is where your NIC comes into play. The NOS hands each of these packets off to the NIC. The NIC puts each of these packets onto the network cable and sends them to the destination workstation. At the other end, the NIC of the destination computer takes each packet off of the wire and hands it off to the NOS on that computer, which reassembles the file.

As you can see in figure 4.11, each packet that is sent from computer to computer has three basic parts: the address, the data, and the error-checking section. The addressing section is at the beginning of the packet. Each computer station has a unique number that identifies it on the network. Your NOS knows the addresses of the other stations on the network and automatically looks up this information whenever you want to send something to a particular station. Each packet contains two addresses: the address of the sending, or source, computer and the address of the receiving, or destination, computer.

Fig. 4.11
A packet contains three basic parts: addressing, data, and error-checking information.

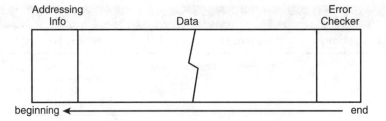

Your computer's network address is defined on your NIC. These addresses are usually six bytes long and are *burned in* to the ROM chips on your NIC, which means that the address is actually permanently stored in the silicon chips and cannot be changed. These permanent addresses are known as hardware or physical addresses because they are stored in the hardware of the NIC.

Some network protocols, such as TCP/IP, define a second type of address, the software address. This address is configured into the NOS of the computer and can be changed. The software address works together with the hardware address to make sure that data gets delivered where it needs to.

It doesn't matter what the addresses of the computers are, so long as no two addresses are the same. Each address must uniquely define a single computer. If two computers had the same address, how could you know which one was really supposed to get the data you are sending?

To help alleviate the potential for duplicate addresses, each NIC manufacturer is responsible for making sure that no two of their NICs have the same address. Furthermore, the Institute of Electrical and Electronics Engineers (IEEE) has assigned each NIC manufacturer a range of numbers that it may choose from when selecting a hardware address for an NIC. Allocating the possible hardware addresses in this manner helps ensure that no two manufacturers make an NIC with the same address.

The second part of the packet contains the data. How much data is actually encapsulated in this section of the packet depends on the type of network you have but is usually in the area of a few kilobytes.

The final part of the packet is the error-checking section. This portion of the packet contains a few bits that the receiving station can use to determine if the packet was received intact. If the packet is not received correctly, then the receiving station can ask the sender to retransmit.

Network protocols specify how a variety of functions are to be carried out. For starters, they determine exactly how the data is broken into packets, how large the packets are, and how the data is transmitted over the wire.

The Rules of Network Communication

The computers on a computer network need a set of rules to govern their communication. Many LANs today *baseband* networks. Baseband means that only one device can be communicating over the network at any one time. This type of network communication means that there must be rules in place to enable the various machines on the LAN to share the network cable. If all of the machines talk at once, nothing actually gets transmitted—the transmissions of a second machine on the network cause the signal of the first to become unintelligible.

The rules that govern computer network communication are called *access methods*. A few of the things access methods specify include

- Which computer is allowed to transmit

- How long that station is allowed to transmit

- How fast the station is allowed to transmit

- How much data can be sent over the cable at one time

- Which workstation gets to transmit next

Think of access methods as the traffic laws of networks. They are the speed limit signs that say how fast the data can travel and the stop lights that tell the data when it is its turn to travel.

The two most popular access methods today are Ethernet and token ring. There are several differences between these two, but the basic difference lies in how each method determines which computer's turn it is to transmit on the network.

According to Ethernet, the first station to start using the cable is the one who gets to transmit. The other stations must wait until that first station is done. Token ring, on the other hand, uses a round-robin system. Each station gets a chance to transmit in the order they are attached to the network.

Ethernet

The access method for Ethernet networks is known as *Carrier Sense Multiple Access with Collision Detection* (CSMA/CD). Ethernet networks can have a bus or star topology. Let's take a closer look at the rules for Ethernet conversations.

Let's say you have a spreadsheet with some yearly sales figures that you need to transfer to another computer on your network. With Ethernet, the first thing your NIC does is listen on the wire to determine if anyone is currently transmitting data on it. This is the *carrier sense* portion of CSMA/CD.

Here, one of two conditions can exist. Either the network is currently in use or it isn't. If the network is in use, your NIC keeps trying until the network is free. In fact, the NIC checks to see if transmitting is safe. Once it detects that there is no traffic on the network, your computer sends its data (see fig. 4.12). There is one problem with this approach. At any given time, there may be many workstations listening to the wire to see if it is safe to transmit. This is the *multiple access* portion of CSMA/CD, which means that more than one station has access to the LAN at the same time. Two workstations transmitting their respective data at the same time is possible; if this happens, a *collision* occurs (see fig. 4.13).

Fig. 4.12
Computers on an Ethernet network are free to transmit their data as soon as they are ready.

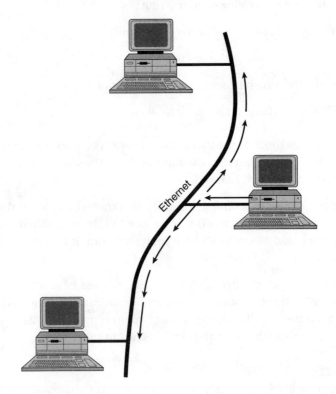

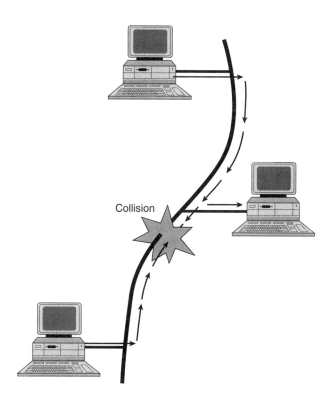

Fig. 4.13
If two worksta-
tions on an
Ethernet network
try to transmit at
the same time,
there is a collision.

Collision

Transmission Collisions

In the event of a collision, the data that both workstations were trying to
send is lost. The two competing signals on the wire destroy each other, making both unintelligible by any receiving workstations. Fortunately, every
workstation checks to see if a collision has occurred after each transmission.
This is the *collision detection* part of CSMA/CD. If the workstations detect a
collision, they try to resend the data.

But how does the data actually get resent? If both workstations detect the
collision and immediately try to resend, another collision seems likely. The
workstations then detect this collision and resend again. Nothing ever gets
transmitted.

The solution lies in a waiting period after each collision. After each computer
detects a collision on the Ethernet, it waits and then waits an additional random amount of time. Since the additional time is random, the stations are
almost guaranteed to have different waiting times before trying to resend. As
a result, the waiting period on one of the stations is shorter and the station is
able to transmit without another collision.

The problem of collisions can become serious in larger networks with many stations. As the number of stations goes up, the probability that there is another computer on the LAN that tries to transmit at the same time the initial station is trying to resend increases. If this happens, another collision occurs, and the problem starts all over again. On larger LANs with heavy traffic, the network can become so bogged down with collisions that very little data actually gets transmitted. Fortunately, the odds of this happening on a small LAN are very low. Most transmissions go through to their recipients with no delay.

Token Ring

The access method for token ring uses a round-robin method to determine which workstation is allowed to transmit. Token ring operates on a ring topology and ensures that all workstations on the network get a chance to send their data. It accomplishes this task using a specialized bit pattern known as a *token*.

> **Note**
>
> Logically, token ring has a ring topology. Physically though, it is a star topology. Each workstation is cabled back to a central hub, called a *Multistation Access Unit* (MAU). The electrical ring is implemented in the electronics of the MAU.

Let's apply the previous example to a token-ring network. You have the same file to transfer. With Ethernet, your machine starts by listening to the network and seeing if it is in use. If there is no traffic, Ethernet starts the transfer.

In a token-ring network, your computer patiently watches the network until it sees a special 24-bit pattern called the token (see fig. 4.14). Once it sees the token, it is allowed to transmit a packet of data. This packet travels around the ring once, and its recipient receives it as it passes. When the packet gets back to the workstation that originally sent it, that workstation is done talking. It must pass the token on to the next workstation, which then gets its chance to send a packet, and so on all the way around the ring until the process starts over. If a station has data to send, it does so. Otherwise, it simply passes the token along without transmitting anything.

It might seem that there is a lot of overhead in the token-passing procedure, and there is. It takes time to pass a token around a ring; time that an Ethernet network does not have to waste. But remember that these times are measured in fractions of a second. With this in mind, you can see that the total time doesn't really add up to much at all.

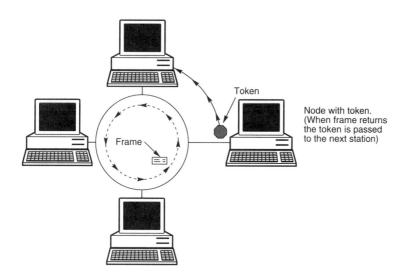

Token

Node with token.
(When frame returns
the token is passed
to the next station)

Frame

Fig. 4.14
Stations on a
token-ring
network cannot
transmit until they
have the token.

Peers and Servers

Networks can be divided into two classes: server-based and peer-to-peer networks. In the past, the traditional PC network has been the server-based network. But if you have two computers and two copies of Windows, you have
everything you need to implement a powerful peer-to-peer network.

Server-Based Networks

In a *server-based network*, all of the devices being shared among the users on
the network are attached to the same machine. There are many different hard
disks and printers attached to computers on the network, but the only ones
that can be shared are the ones attached to a machine known as the server
(see fig. 4.15).

The *file server* (or just *server*) is the most important computer in a server-based
network. This is usually a high-powered machine with a big hard disk. This is
a dedicated machine, which means it has no other function than to share its
devices and files. This is not a machine that is also sitting on someone's desk
being used for daily work. In fact, since they require so little direct contact,
you often find file servers in a room by itself for safekeeping.

The other type of machine on this type of network is called the *client*. An
example of a client is the computer on your desk. These machines are used to
get everyday work done. You see these machines running word processors
and spreadsheets. These are the computers that use the resources on the file
server.

Fig. 4.15
The resources on a server-based network are all attached to the server machine.

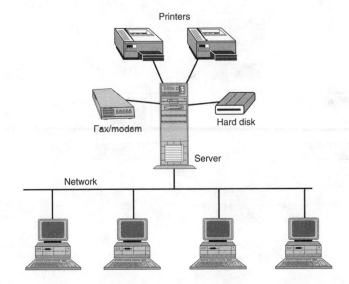

Peer-To-Peer Networks

Peer-to-peer networks differ from server-based in that every machine on the network can be either a server or a client. Figure 4.16 demonstrates that any machine can share its disks and printers. Not only can a workstation use the resources of another, but it can also share its own hard disks and faxes. The built-in networking that comes with Windows is peer-to-peer based. One of the nice things about peer-to-peer is that it does not require a special machine to run, although this is still an option.

Fig. 4.16
All computers on a peer-to-peer based network can share their resources.

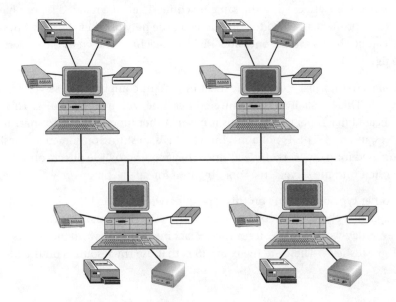

From Here...

This chapter introduced you to some of the terms and concepts of computer networking, discussing the pieces that can be found in any network and acquainting you with the ideas of network protocols and access methods.

Take a look at the following chapters to find out more about networking:

- Chapter 5, "Selecting the Right Network," contains more information about the decisions you need to make before you set up your network.

- Chapter 6, "The Pieces of a Network," tells you exactly what you need to get your network up and running.

- Chapter 7, "Setting Up a Windows Network," provides you with the information you need to put everything together and create your network.

Chapter 5

Selecting the Right Network

A wide variety of different networks are in use today. These networks differ in the software that runs them, the type of cabling they use, the speed at which they transmit data, the manner in which they transmit data, and the amount of money you have to spend to get them up and running.

Before you can get down to the work of installing your network, you need to determine what type of network you are setting up. And to decide on a network, you first need to know what you want your network to do. This chapter takes a look at some of the things you might do with your network and introduces the network options available to you.

In this chapter, you learn

- What capabilities your network needs to have

- What the different types of networks in use today are

- What the advantages and disadvantages are of the built-in networking that comes with Windows

Deciding What Your Network Does

The first step in any project is planning, and that certainly applies to the network project you are about to undertake. In order to make sure your network meets all of your needs, you need to first define what those needs are.

What Data Do I Need To Share?

Networks enable you to share your data. What kind of data do you want to share on your network? Do you have spreadsheets or other documents that you need to make available to everyone? Do you have a database to which everyone needs access?

Begin by identifying all of the documents and other data you want to share among the users on your network. If you have programs that you want to reside on one machine but be accessible for use by all machines on the network, then identify those also. Remember, a network does not entitle you to use the same software on more than one machine at a time. If you plan on using specific software on the network, and there is a chance that two users use that piece of software at the same time, you need to check into a *network license*. Basically, a network license is an agreement between you and the software developer that acknowledges that more than one user may be using the software at the same time.

For example, let's say you have a database application to which you want five different users on your network to have access. Instead of buying five copies of the software, you purchase only one. You then buy an additional four network licenses to use the software.

There are a couple of good reasons to do this. First, it's cheaper. The additional software licenses don't cost as much as the full packages do. Second, the software only has to be installed once. You can install it on one machine, and the rest of the machines that need to use the software simply connect to the computer that has the software and run it from there.

> **Note**
>
> A program running over the network is considerably slower than a program running locally off the hard disk. In many cases, you may want to go ahead and install the programs themselves on each of the individual workstations on the LAN and access just the data files over the network.

Should I Use E-Mail?

Another of the benefits of having a network that we have discussed is the ability to use e-mail. E-mail is an effective communication method because it is faster than writing a note and walking it to another office. It is also more convenient. The recipient does not have to be present at the time you send the message like they have to be if you were making a phone call, for example.

If you want to use e-mail on your network, then you need to have some software to take care of this function for you. E-mail is not a basic part of a network; it is an application that runs on a network. The best part is that Windows has e-mail built-in, in addition to its basic networking.

Will I Share Printers?

Printer sharing is almost synonymous with computer networking. In fact, many early networks were put in place for this function alone.

Because of the ever-decreasing cost of laser printers, printer sharing is not quite as important as it once was. Printer sharing can still help save you money, though. A good candidate for print sharing are the new color lasers. Prices for these are still in the $5,000 range. Rather than buy one printer for each workstation, you buy one or two printers for the entire network. How many printers you actually need depends on how much idle time the printer has at any given time.

Do I Want To Be Able To Use the Network When I Am Not at Work?

It is possible to set up your network to be used when you are not in the same location as the network. This is called Remote Access. If you plan to take advantage of this feature of your Windows network, you need to make sure you have the proper equipment. For more information on setting up remote access on your network, take a look at chapter 10, "Setting Up for Remote Access."

Weighing Your Networking Options

The two main types of networks in use with PCs today are Ethernet and to-ken ring. There are also a variety of other options to choose from, although none of the others are as popular, for a variety of reasons. Which one should you use? Let's take a look at some of the advantages of each.

Ethernet Networks

Ethernet is the most popular network in use today and has been around longer than the other networking technologies. Dropping prices and a relatively high data transmission speed have fueled Ethernet's wide acceptance.

Ethernet Won't Break the Bank

Ethernet is less expensive than token-ring networks. In fact, it is cheaper than most of the other network types. Why does it cost less? Well, two reasons, actually. First, Ethernet doesn't require much hardware to run. In its simplest configuration, all you need are the NICs for your machines and the cabling to connect the machines together. No supporting hardware is necessary. And second, the hardware you do need is inexpensive because of supply and demand. Since Ethernet is so popular, manufacturers of Ethernet equipment are very common, so competition is high and prices are low. That brings us to the next advantage of Ethernet.

Ethernet Is Everywhere

Ethernet networks are cheap, easy to set up, and a proven technology. This has made them the most popular network in use today. The very fact that they are so widely used is another benefit of using Ethernet. It is easy to find Ethernet parts, and it is also (relatively) easy to find expert help.

Token Ring Networks

The second most popular LAN technology is Token Ring. Token Ring was developed by IBM and came onto the scene in the mid-eighties. The internal workings of Token Ring are considerably more complex than those of Ethernet. This has led to fewer third-party vendors developing Token Ring products and kept costs for Token Ring equipment high. In addition, many of the vendors who do make Token Ring cards simply buy the controlling chip from IBM. This is not cheap, as you can imagine, further keeping the price high.

In spite of its higher price, Token Ring does have some advantages over Ethernet, including a higher data speed and better handling of heavy network traffic.

Higher Data Speed

A token-ring network, which is a generic type as well as the Token Ring developed by IBM, can operate at one of two data transmission speeds: 4 or 16 Megabits per second (Mbps). The network can only operate at the speed of the slowest card. Most of the token-ring adapters sold in the last couple of years operate at either speed with the flick of a dip switch. Many of the early adapters, though, were of the 4 Mbps-only variety, and this tended to limit your options a bit.

Assuming all of your adapters are the newer two-speed kind, token-ring networks are faster than Ethernet networks: 16 Mbps for token ring versus 10 Mbps for Ethernet. A little extra speed never hurts, unless you enjoy waiting, which we are willing to bet you don't.

Traffic? No Problem

Another advantage of token ring is that it performs very well in a heavily loaded environment. Heavily loaded means that a LAN has a lot of workstations that are trying to all transmit data at the same time.

As you learned in chapter 4, token-ring networks work in a round-robin sort of fashion. Every station is guaranteed to get a turn to transmit on the network. This is a distinct advantage over Ethernet. Let's say we have a network of 25 workstations, and they are all trying to transfer files over the network at the same time. On a token-ring network, each station gets its turn to transmit. The stations take turns transmitting bits of their respective files until all of the data has been sent to the receiving workstations.

With Ethernet, it is a different story. Here we have a first-come, first-served type of environment. Each workstation starts to transmit its data as soon as it is ready. But what happens if more than one workstation tries to transmit at the same time? As you recall from the previous chapter, we have what is called a collision. The data that was being transmitted has to be resent, and all the machines on the LAN wait some random amount of time before trying to send any data again. This is precisely the problem. On a heavily loaded network, the number of collisions becomes quite high. Instead of getting the data moved to where it needs to be, all of the computers are wasting time with collisions and the subsequent waiting period. Under extreme conditions, the throughput on the network can drop as low as 50% of the total of 10 Mbps. Token ring doesn't suffer from this problem, and even heavily loaded token rings have throughputs in the area of 90%.

Other Networking Options

Ethernet and token ring are by no means the only types of networks available. There are a number of other options, which are not as popular.

ARCnet

ARCnet is a precursor to Ethernet and Token Ring. Though slower, at around 2.5 Mbps, it has a reputation for being extremely reliable when it comes to making sure the data gets delivered. In the early days of computer networking, ARCnet was the most popular network, even though Ethernet came out first. Why? Because it was cheap.

These days, though, ARCnet has fallen out of favor. Its transmission speed is simply too slow for many of today's network applications. Even more important has been the dramatic price decrease for Ethernet adapters and hubs. There is simply no reason to buy ARCnet when you can run Ethernet at four times the data speed for about the same price.

FDDI

FDDI stands for fiber-data-distributed interface and is sometimes pronounced *fiddey*. FDDI operates at a much higher data speed than either token ring or Ethernet, 100 Mbps. FDDI usually uses fiber-optic cable, (thus the name) although it can also be made to work with copper cable. FDDI is not very widely implemented compared to Ethernet and token ring because it is a newer technology and more expensive.

Serial Connections

Actually, it is possible to set up a network using just the serial port on your computer. To accomplish this task, you use what is known as a null modem cable (you can purchase one at any computer store). This is similar to using remote access to connect to machines via a modem, except here the machines are local and directly connected. The serial network is definitely the least expensive of all the available options but with some severe drawbacks: an excruciatingly slow transmission speed and a limitation on the maximum number of stations on the network.

Fig. 5.1
You can use your serial port to create a quick LAN in times of emergency.

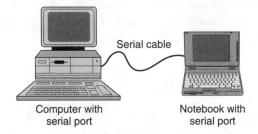

Serial cable

Computer with serial port

Notebook with serial port

The average data transmission speed of a serial-based network is far below the other technologies already mentioned, typically around 115 Kilobits per second. This is well below even 1 Mbps. The other major drawback is the maximum number of stations on the network: two. There are only two ends to a serial cable, and each end must plug into the back of one of the computers.

Serial networks are not good, all-purpose LANs, but they can be excellent quick-and-easy solutions, so they deserve mention here.

Which Network Type Should I Use?

If you are putting together a small network with fewer than 30 stations or so, Ethernet is a fine choice. Not only is it inexpensive and easy to set up, as already mentioned, but it is relatively fast. The disadvantages of Ethernet are that it does not handle high network traffic very well. However, the small number of workstations you will be attaching to your network probably aren't going to generate a large volume of traffic.

Ethernet Cabling

There are actually a couple of different types of Ethernet, and the difference is in the type of cable used to connect the computers. Ethernet can be run over two different types of cable: coaxial cable and unshielded twisted-pair (UTP) cable. Ethernet over coaxial cable is also known as 10Base2 Ethernet or *thinnet*. Ethernet over UTP cable is known as 10BaseT.

Ethernet over Coaxial Cable: Thinnet

Ethernet can actually be run over thin or thick coaxial cable. The thick kind is the original version of Ethernet but has gone out of fashion for a variety of reasons. The thicker cable is harder to manage, and the connections to the computer workstations can be unreliable due to the older style of connectors.

Thinnet, as the popular version of Ethernet over coaxial cable is called, uses a much thinner coaxial cable and has more reliable connectors. The thinnet topology is a bus configuration and is less expensive than 10BaseT Ethernet.

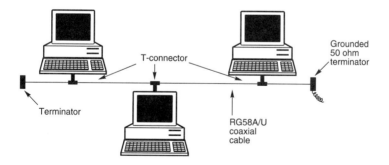

Fig. 5.2
With 10Base2 all workstations on the LAN are attached to the same coaxial cable in a bus configuration.

Thinnet is not trouble free. One of the disadvantages of thin Ethernet is what is known as the "single point of failure." Single point of failure means that there is a point on the network, which, if it goes bad, can bring the entire network down. With thinnet, that single point is the cable itself. Since every machine is attached to the same cable, if there is a problem anywhere on the cable, none of the machines will be able to communicate.

Ethernet over UTP: 10BaseT

10BaseT refers to Ethernet over UTP cable. This type of Ethernet LAN came about much later than the coaxial cable varieties. 10BaseT has a few key advantages over 10Base2:

■ UTP cable is cheaper and easier to work with than coaxial cable.

■ 10BaseT workstations are easier to connect than coaxial stations.

■ The cables in 10BaseT Ethernets are not single points of failure.

Fig. 5.3
10BaseT Ethernet uses a star configuration. Each cable is attached to a single workstation and the central hub.

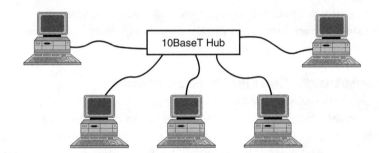

10BaseT Ethernet does not have a bus configuration like 10Base2. Instead, it uses a star configuration. Each workstation is wired back to one central location, the Ethernet hub. This device serves to connect all of the workstations together. The central concentrator is the reason that 10BaseT costs more than thinnet. These hubs can range in price from a couple hundred to several thousand dollars, depending on the features and manufacturer.

The star configuration of 10BaseT Ethernet removes the cable as a single point of failure for the network. Each cable segment contains only two devices: the workstation and the hub. If the cable goes bad for some reason, all of the workstations on the LAN will not be affected. Only the single workstation on that cable segment will lose services. This helps make 10BaseT more reliable.

Should I Use the Windows Built-In Networking?

If you do not currently use any type of network, Windows built-in networking is probably the networking option for you because

■ It is included with Windows; everything you need is right there. If you decide to set up some other network, there are going to be additional costs.

■ Windows networking is as easy to set up as most other networks. Just select from a few different options and you are ready to go.

> **Note**
>
> Windows comes with everything you need to connect to a variety of other networks in addition to the Windows network. You can actually be connected to more than one network at a time. The network systems supported include Microsoft Windows NT Server, Microsoft LAN Manager, Microsoft TCP/IP, Novell Netware, Banyan VINES, UNIX NFS, and Artisoft LANtastic. Windows may also work with other networks with software provided by the manufacturer.

Should I Replace My Existing Network with the Windows Network?

The built-in Windows peer-to-peer networking is ideal for small LANs. If you already have a LAN in place in your organization, should you move from your existing network? Yes and no. The built-in Windows networking is good for small LANs. It is not really suited to large networks with hundreds of workstations.

The nice feature of having the networking built right in to the operating system is that you don't have to worry about compatibility issues. You are guaranteed that it works with your operating system because it is part of your operating system.

From Here...

For more information on Ethernet, setting up your network, remote access, and using Windows with third-party networks:

■ Chapter 6, "The Pieces of a Network," talks about some of the things to watch out for when you begin picking up the pieces for your LAN and creating a "network-shopping list" so that you can go get the things you need to get started.

■ Chapter 7, "Setting Up a Windows Network," tells you how to put your new network together.

■ Chapter 10, "Setting Up for Remote Access," discusses how to set up your network so you can use it from home.

- Chapter 19, "Connecting to Other Networks," walks you through the necessary steps to get you up and running on networks such as Novell Netware, Microsoft LAN Manager, OS/2 LAN Server, and UNIX NFS.

- Appendix A, "Technical Specifications of Network Protocols," gets into the guts of the Ethernet protocols and you learn more about how they work.

Chapter 6

The Pieces of a Network

Putting in a network can be a tough job, particularly if you are installing more than just a few machines. At times, it may seem like you have a million things to take care of to get the network up and running. You have to pick out, buy, and configure network interface cards (NIC). Software drivers need to be configured. And on top of that, you've never even set up a network before.

Don't worry, that feeling happens to everyone and that is why this chapter is here. Everything you need to get ready to network is covered, and some things to look for to make sure you create the best network you can are pointed out.

In this chapter, you learn

- How to be sure your NIC works with the Windows network

- What quality equipment and a good manufacturer are

- Where to get your hardware for a good price

- What parts you need to get your network running

Avoiding the Pitfalls of Your New LAN

In any project, there are things you have no way of knowing about unless you have done one of those things before. This section contains some items to look out for so that your network installation goes as smoothly as possible. It also points out the potential problems to avoid.

Ensuring Compatibility

Compatibility is a simple idea: do all the pieces of your network work together the way they are supposed to? As you get your network ready to go, you need to make sure everything is going to work together. Not only must the hardware all work together but the software must be able to work together with both the hardware and the other software on your network.

Hardware Compatibility Issues

Hardware compatibility is definitely the more straightforward of the two types of compatibility. The first thing you need to make sure is that your NIC is going to work with your computer. Thankfully, all you need to do here is make sure you're buying an NIC that fits in your computer. To find out which types of NICs work in your system, check the manual that came with your computer.

You also want to buy an NIC that fits with the type of cable you are using. If you are using coaxial cable, you need to buy a NIC that has a connector for coaxial cable.

You also need to make sure that all the hardware you buy is appropriate for the type of network you will be running. If you decide on an Ethernet network, you want to make sure that all the NICs you purchase are Ethernet NICs, or the network isn't going to work.

Software Compatibility Issues

The second area of compatibility is software compatibility. This is much trickier than hardware compatibility. In most cases, you can just look at an NIC and tell if it is going to fit in your computer or attach to the type of cabling you have. But software isn't a physical object you can see.

In the past, you also wanted to make sure that your network software worked properly with your operating system software. But with Windows, Microsoft has taken care of that for you. The network software is built right into the operating system, so you can be sure they work together.

Fortunately, there is also a relatively easy way for you to tell if your hardware works with the Windows network software. Microsoft has a testing program for hardware vendors. Under this program, hardware manufacturers can send in their equipment to Microsoft for testing with the Windows operating system. If things check out all right, Microsoft gives the hardware the right to have the Windows logo on the box. So when you are looking for NICs, if you see the Windows logo, you can be sure that NIC will work.

Finding Quality Equipment

When you are buying your equipment, you want the highest quality products you can afford. But the problem with quality is that it is not a quantifiable thing. How do you measure quality?

The Price of the Equipment

One judgment of quality is price. For example, if you are looking at two NICs and one goes for $35 and the other goes for $100, that the manufacturer of the $35 NIC probably didn't get the NIC down to that low price by using only the very best component parts is a safe bet. The problem with using only price as a judgment of quality is that you don't know if the maker of the $100 NIC has artificially raised their prices to make a few extra bucks or if their product is actually more expensive because it uses more expensive and reliable components.

One other item for hardware that should be kept in mind, besides the hardware's manufacturing quality, component quality, and price, is the service issue. You want to buy from a company that stands behind their products. Whether a company stands behind their equipment is usually reflected by two things, warranty and support, which are discussed later.

Getting a Fair Price

Make sure you shop around when looking for network equipment. There are sometimes large discrepancies in prices from one vendor to another. Try checking mail order catalogues. There are many reliable mail order firms around, and they are almost always cheaper than local stores.

Good Ethernet NICs are very affordable. I have seen them as cheap as $35, but I hesitate to buy the rock bottom priced NICs. A good, middle-of-the-road NIC goes for around $90–$100. You should feel comfortable with the quality of a NIC in that price range. Make sure you shop around. It won't take you very long to figure out what the average price is for good equipment. Some quality manufacturers are 3COM, Intel, SMC, and Novell.

Warranties and Technical Support

Look for products with a warranty of at least one year—preferably longer. These days, in the highly competitive market of networking products, it is not uncommon to see warranties as long as five years. Perhaps the lifetime guarantee is just around the corner.

Good technical support can often mean the difference between getting your LAN working and a nervous breakdown. You should be able to call for help 7 days a week, 24 hours a day. There is nothing worse than calling for support on a Friday evening at 5:05 PM and finding out that you cannot get any help until the following Monday.

Another little "trick" that some companies are getting into is charging for support. Many of these vendors initially give free phone support but then begin charging after some time period has passed. After 30 to 90 days, depending on the company, it costs you every time you want to talk to someone about a problem you might be having. In other words, they expect that after 30 days (or however long the free support period is) you have the equipment installed and working. Granted, most of the problems you encounter occur when you are initially installing the product. However, things occasionally go wrong after the equipment has been working properly for some time, and you want to be prepared. Buy NICs with the longest technical support you can find, preferably support for its life.

Bulletin Board Support

Another thing to look for is a an electronic bulletin board system (BBS) for support. This should be available 24 hours a day. This can often be handy when you are looking for the latest version of a driver or are in need of a patch to get your NIC working properly. A BBS means you can get the solution in hand in a matter of minutes instead of days if they have to send you the files on floppy disk through good old snail mail.

Faulty Product Replacement

Harder to find—but a great bonus—is a company with *advance replacement* of faulty products. For example, if you have an Ethernet NIC that has gone bad, you call the manufacturer and report your defective hardware. Normally, you have to send the NIC back to the vendor, who might do one of two things. First, they can send you a replacement NIC as soon as they get your NIC, which gives you the fastest turnaround. Their second option is to test the NIC, determine what is wrong with it, and repair it. They then send you back the fixed NIC. This may take quite a bit longer. At a minimum, you are usually looking at three days in either case. One day each way, assuming both you and the manufacturer use overnight mail for the NIC, and one day to test, fix, and ship the NIC (either a new one or the repaired one).

Advance replacement speeds up the process. Also known as cross shipping, advance replacement means that as soon as the manufacturer discovers that you have a defective NIC they ship you a replacement. They don't even wait until your NIC arrives. If they use overnight mail for the NIC, you have it the next day instead of three days later.

Everything You Need To Start

There are some smaller details to putting a network together that might be easy to forget. That's where this section comes in. Think of it as sort of a networker's shopping list. Here you find out exactly what you need to buy to get your LAN up and running.

Your Network NICs

Your Ethernet NIC should be for the type of network you decided to put in. If you have decided to install a thinnet network, make sure you have a 10Base2 NIC. If you have decided on 10BaseT, your NIC should have an RJ45 jack. Many Ethernet NICs have both types of connectors. These NICs are some-times called combo NICs. You might want to think about getting these if you are putting in a thinnet in case you decide later to make the switch to twisted pair. If you are going straight to 10BaseT, though, don't mess with the combo NIC. Plenty of Ethernet networks progress from thinnet to twisted pair, but few ever change in the other direction.

Cabling and Hubs

When it comes to selecting the cabling for your Windows network, you have two options. You can either build the cables yourself (the cheaper of the two options) or buy them ready made (quicker, more convenient, and more reli-able).

Building the cables allows you to customize the cable lengths between work-stations. If you plan on taking this option, you need to purchase the cable and connectors separately. When the time comes to actually attach your workstations to the network, you cut the cable to the appropriate length and attach a connector to each end of the cable using a specialized device called a crimp tool, which you also have to purchase.

The difficulty with making the cables yourself is the possibility that you won't make them properly. That's why we recommend that you buy all your cables pre-made. These cables can usually be found off the shelf in lengths of 6, 10, 15, 25, 50, and 100 feet, and longer cables can be made to order for an

Tip

If you have a PCI local bus in your computer, you should definitely look into getting a PCI NIC.

II

Getting Started

additional fee. Pre-made cables have the advantage of being tested at the manufacturer's facility. Although they cost more than making the cables yourself, the peace of mind that a tested cable brings is worth the additional cost.

Thinnet

The cabling system for thinnet consists of three items:

- The coaxial cable itself, with male BNC connectors on each end

- One BNC T connector per workstation, which attaches the cable to the NIC

- Two BNC terminators, one at each end of the network

When you are ordering the cable for your thinnet, it is usually enough to say that you want "thin coaxial cable for Ethernet." Specifically, you want RG58 A/U thin coaxial cable with male BNC connectors on each end. Your cables must be of this type. If you decide to make these cables yourself, then you want to make sure the BNC connectors you buy are male.

> **Note**
>
> If you decide to make your own thinnet cables, you have some choices as to the type of connectors you can buy. The two types that you will probably come across are the crimp-on connector and the screw-on connector. We generally prefer the crimp-on type because you get a more solid connection with the crimp-ons. Don't forget, though, that you have to invest in a crimp tool if you go this route.

The T connector is the T-shaped device that connects the cables to the NICs in each of your workstations. You want to ask for BNC F-M-F T connectors. The F-M-F stands for female-male-female. The two female ends attach to the male BNC connectors on the ends of your cables. The male end is for connection to the female BNC connector found on the back of most 10Base2 Ethernet NICs.

The two BNC terminators form the two ends of your Ethernet cable. Usually, these devices are attached to one side of the T connector on the last workstation at either end of your LAN. When you buy your terminators, you want to make sure they are the 50-ohm variety. They should also have a male BNC connector so you can attach them to one of the female ends of a T connector.

10BaseT

The cabling system for a 10BaseT Ethernet is simpler than thinnet, consisting of only two parts:

- The twisted-pair cable

- The Ethernet hub

As mentioned in the previous chapter, in a 10BaseT Ethernet network all workstations are wired back to a central hub, or concentrator. With this in mind, you need cable lengths that stretch from each computer back to wherever you have the hub, instead of from computer to computer as you have in a 10Base2 thin Ethernet network. The cable for 10BaseT is the unshielded twisted-pair (UTP) variety, and you want both ends to have RJ45 connectors.

> **Caution**
>
> Be careful to specify that you need cables for Ethernet if you buy your cables ready-made. Some vendors do not attach all the pairs in the wire to the connector in an attempt to save money. Since token ring and Ethernet do not use the same pin-outs, you can run into a problem that you normally don't have if all pairs are connected. We recommend that you request your cables with all pairs connected. That way, you eliminate any chance of ending up with the wrong cable.

> **Note**
>
> The maximum allowable cable length between a workstation and a 10BaseT concentrator is 328 feet (100 meters).

Not all UTP cables are created equal. They differ in the network speeds they support. To help you determine what the capabilities of the different types of cable are, the Electronic Industries Association, or EIA, has developed a category system for UTP wire. The categories of wire range from 1 to 5. As you move from category 1 wire to category 5 wire, the transmission speed the cable supports increases. For 10BaseT Ethernet, you want to use category 3 cable or higher. Category 3 wire is rated for transmission speeds up to 10 Mbps.

II

Getting Started

> **Note**
>
> Category 3 UTP cable is for use in LANs up to 10 Mbps, which is the data transmission speed of Ethernet. If you are installing a 10BaseT Ethernet network today, but think that you may soon move to a higher-speed network such as 100BaseT, you cannot use category 3 cable. Instead, you want to go ahead and put in category 5. Ethernet runs just fine over this higher-grade cable, and since category 5 is rated up to 100 Mbps, it is acceptable when you upgrade your network.

Your Ethernet hub forms the heart of your network. In a 10BaseT network, it is the only single point of failure. If your hub goes down, everything stops working. Compare that to a cable run from the hub to a computer. If this cable somehow gets severed or quits transmitting data properly, only one workstation is affected, the one attached to that cable.

Since the hub is the heart of your 10BaseT network, it probably won't surprise you that it is the most expensive piece of your network. Ethernet hubs typically cost $30 per port. Usually you can find them wherever you buy your network adapters.

Your biggest decision when buying a hub, outside of the quality and price issues we have already discussed for all of your equipment, is how many ports to buy. Ethernet hubs come in 8-, 12-, 16-, and 24-port varieties. Don't forget to allow for growth.

From Here...

Tip
Many hubs have a single additional connector for attaching to a different cable type, such as thin coaxial. If you are planning to put in some UTP Ethernet and you have an existing thinnet, this port can be used to connect the two cabling systems into one LAN.

In this chapter, you learned how to make sure the equipment you buy is compatible with your computer hardware and software. You also learned what to look for with respect to pricing, warranties, and technical support to make sure you buy good networking equipment. Finally, this chapter discussed the types of Ethernet that are available and the pieces required to build an Ethernet network including NICs, cabling, and hubs.

To find out more about networks take a look at

- Chapter 7, "Setting Up a Windows Network," discusses how to build your peer-to-peer network.

- Chapter 21, "Using the Built-In Network Tools," tells you about the tools you use to manage your network once you have put it together.

- Appendix A, "Technical Specifications of Network Protocols," provides a more in-depth look at how networks work.

Chapter 7

Setting Up a Windows Network

Setting up a Windows 95 network can be easy and straightforward. Today's technology allows you to spend less time setting up and configuring your hardware so that you can be more productive and spend time on the tasks you really need to get done. With the advent of Plug and Play and Windows 95, you could be sharing resources with your co-workers in less than a day.

By this time, you probably have your computers, network interface cards (NIC), cables, hubs, connectors, and, of course, copies of Windows 95. It might look like a complicated mess right now. But this chapter walks you through each step of the way to put it all together into a working network.

What's in this chapter:

- A quickstart checklist of network pieces

- How to connect the cabling for 10BaseT and Ethernet networks

- Installation tips for Windows 95 networks

- Using the Network dialog box

- Configuring the adapters, protocols, and clients

- Setting up a computer to share its files and printers

For the Impatient: A Quickstart Checklist

If you just can't wait and want to get things going as soon as possible, you might want to use the following quick checklist:

- Install NICs in all computers.

- 10BaseT setup:

  - Set up Ethernet concentrator and turn on power.

  - Plug unshielded-twisted-pair (UTP) cables in hub.

  - Plug UTP cables in RJ45 jack on back of computer.

- Thinnet setup:

  - Connect BNC T connectors to the female BNC connector on the back of each NIC.

  - Chain one computer to the next by running a coaxial cable from the male BNC ends to the female ends of the T connectors.

  - Attach 50-ohm BNC terminators to the open female T connectors on the first and last computers.

- Install Windows 95 if you have not already done so. During the setup, Windows detects your NIC and installs the default network setup.

- If you have already installed Windows 95 and are adding NICs now, you need to run the Add New Hardware Wizard from Control Panel. The Wizard detects the new hardware and installs the default network setup.

- Give each computer a unique name and set up the workgroup name from the Network dialog box.

- Reboot the computer. You should be able to see the other computers on your network from the Network Neighborhood.

> **Note**
>
> The default network setup for a small LAN such as the one you are setting up includes the Client for Microsoft Networks, your NIC, NetBEUI, and IPX/SPX. File and Printer Sharing are not enabled. You have to enable them from the Network dialog box.

If this quickstart list seems complicated or incomplete, you should work through the following sections. Each one gives you step-by-step instructions to successfully install your Windows 95 network.

Install the Hardware First

Before you can configure Windows 95 for network support, you must have the physical pieces in place. In other words, you need to connect the computers together with cable and install the NICs. After you have the NICs installed, you can install Windows 95 and it detects the addition of the new hardware automatically.

Before you begin installing the hardware, you should try to obtain the following tools. These tools can usually be found in a small "PC toolkit" sold at most computer stores for about $30:

> Small Phillips screwdriver
> Small flat-blade screwdriver
> 3/16-inch hex-nut driver
> 1/4-inch hex-nut driver
> Needle-nosed pliers
> Tweezers
> Claw-type parts grabber

Additionally, you should obtain a volt-ohm meter if you're setting up a thinnet network. It doesn't have to be an expensive or fancy digital-readout model. A simple one can be obtained at your local electronics store for about $10.

The screwdrivers and hex-nut drivers are used to open the computer's case and install the NICs. The needle-nosed pliers come in handy to move jumpers around on your network card. No matter how hard you try when you install the NIC, you'll probably drop a screw or jumper inside the computer case. You'll use the tweezers and claw grabber to reach for them in places where your fingers don't fit. Lastly, you'll use the ohm-meter to test the connections between the computers.

Caution
You might be considering using a cordless hand drill instead of screwdrivers. You should *not* use one. It is very easy to strip a screw or mounting hole with a hand drill.

Once you've gathered up the necessary tools, you're ready to start installing your network.

Your NIC

You install your NIC just like you install any other adapter, such as a modem or sound card. This is a four-step process: identify hardware settings, remove the system-unit cover, install the adapter card, replace the system-unit cover. You'll want to use the following steps, which include important safety precautions to protect you and your investment in your computers.

Determining Hardware Settings

If your NIC is a Plug and Play-compliant card and the computer supports Plug and Play devices, your hardware settings are configured for you. Skip ahead to the next section, "Removing the System Unit Cover."

If your NIC isn't Plug and Play compliant or if you have a Plug and Play NIC but the computer doesn't support Plug and Play devices, you need to manually configure some settings in order for the computer to find it. You'll need to identify the base I/O address, Interrupt Request channel (IRQ), and base RAM address. While each computer may have different peripherals or cards installed, most computers usually have settings available.

If you've already installed Windows on the computer, use these steps to view what settings are already in use by other devices:

1. Right-click the My Computer icon and select Properties from the pop-up menu. This displays the Systems Properties sheet (see fig. 7.1).

Fig. 7.1
The Systems Porperties dialog box shows the various pieces of your system.

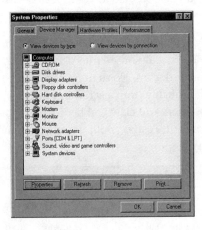

2. Select the Device Manager tab.

3. Since My Computer is already selected in the list of devices, choose the Properties button at the bottom of the page.

4. Review the resources used by other devices in each category by selecting the appropriate option: Interrupt Request (IRQ), Input/Output (I/O), and Memory (see fig. 7.2).

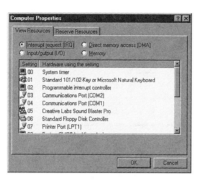

Fig. 7.2
Select Properties to view resources used by other devices.

5. Compare these to the settings that can be used by the NIC as identified in the manufacturer's documentation. Write down an available setting for each.

If you haven't yet installed Windows 95, use table 7.1 to determine an available base I/O address, table 7.2 for a free IRQ setting, and table 7.3 for an available base RAM address.

Table 7.1   Base I/O Addresses Commonly Taken by Other Devices

I/O Address Range	Standard Usage
000-0FF	Unavailable For Use by Devices
1F0-1F7	Hard Disk Controller
200-207	Gameport Joystick
220-22F	Sound Card
240-24F	Sound Card
2F8-2FF	Communications Port (COM2)

(continues)

Table 7.1 Continued

I/O Address Range	Standard Usage
330-33F	MIDI Adapter (Sometimes part of sound card)
376-376	Hard Disk Controller
378-37A	Printer Port (LPT1)
3B0-3DF	Display Adapter
3F0-3F7	Floppy Disk Controller
3F8-3FF	Communications Port (COM1)
4D0-4D1	PCI Bus
CF8-CFA	PCI Bus

Table 7.2 IRQ Lines Commonly Used by Other Devices in Your System

IRQ	Standard Usage
0	System Timer
1	Keyboard
2	Programmable Interrupt Controller
3	Communications Port (COM2)
4	Communications Port (COM1)
5	Printer Port (LPT2)
6	Floppy Disk Controller
7	Printer Port (LPT1)
8	Real-Time Clock
9	Used by IRQ2
10	Usually Available (Sometimes a Sound Card)
11	Usually Available

Table 7.2   Continued

IRQ	Standard Usage
12	PS/2 Port Mouse
13	Numeric Data Processor (Math Coprocessor)
14	Hard Disk Controller
15	Usually Available

Table 7.3   Common RAM Addresses in Use by Other Devices

RAM Address Range	Standard Usage
0A0000-0C7FFF	Video Adapter RAM
0E8000-0EBFFF	PCI Bus
0EC000-0FFFFF	Plug and Play BIOS

Lastly, you'll need to configure the NIC to use these settings. If your card is an older style, you may need to move jumpers on the card to specific settings. Consult your manufacturer's manual for these settings.

If your NIC requires the use of a SETUP program, you should run this from a command prompt after you install the NIC but before you run the Add New Hardware Wizard. Consult your manufacturer's manual on how to use the SETUP program.

Removing the System Unit Cover

Once you've determined the hardware settings for your new NIC, you're ready to open up the computer. This exposes the expansion slots where you'll install the NIC.

To remove the system unit cover, follow these steps:

1. Gather your tools and NIC at the computer and situate yourself in a comfortable position. Don't shuffle your feet around while you work because it causes static electricity.

Tip
To help remember which computer has which jumper settings, write down the values on a mailing label and apply it to the backside of the computer.

II

Getting Started

> ### Note
>
> Shuffling your feet causes static electricity, which is one of the leading causes of damage to electronic components. So once you begin working on the computer, try not to move around too much. Avoid plastic, vinyl, styrofoam, and fur in the work area. Consider buying a disposable grounding wrist strap for under $5 at your local electronics store.

Tip

If you purchased a disposable grounding wrist strap or have a reusable model, now is the time to properly ground yourself. Follow the manufacturer's instructions on how to apply it and attach it to a valid ground source.

2. Shut down the computer, turn off the power, and touch a metal part of the system unit case to discharge any static electricity you may have built up. Now, unplug the power cord from the back of the system unit.

3. Turn the system unit around so that you're facing the rear of the unit. Locate the five to seven screws around the border of the case that hold the system unit cover in place.

4. Use the 1/4-inch hex-nut driver to remove the cover screws.

5. Slide the cover off the system unit until it stops. Certain models slide forward, but others slide backward. Many models don't slide open all the way.

> ### Caution
>
> Don't pound or sharply strike the system unit cover. You may damage the hard drive inside the computer.

Tip

If the case won't move very easily, work your way around the back edge of the case using a flat-head screwdriver to gently pry it open. Once you've got the case moving a little bit, you should be able to slide it until it stops.

6. Lift up the front of the cover and remove it from the chassis.

You're now ready to install the NIC in an available expansion slot.

Installing the Network Interface Card

To install the NIC in the computer, you'll need to locate an available expansion slot on the motherboard. Most computers' motherboards are arranged in a similar manner. However, you'll need to know what type of slot your NIC requires.

Most NICs today require either an ISA or PCI expansion slot on the motherboard. The NIC's package should clearly state which type it is. However, if the packaging or documentation is unclear, here is an easy way to tell the difference. A PCI card has a two-part connector on its edge approximately 4 1/8-inches long. An ISA card has a two-part connector as well, but its connector is longer at 5 5/16-inches. The slot in which you'll insert the card matches these dimensions.

To install the NIC, follow these steps:

1. Using the appropriate screwdriver, remove the blank metal bracket from the back side of the system unit at the expansion slot you expect to use. Set the screw aside to be replaced in a few steps.

2. Carefully remove the NIC from its anti-static bag.

> **Caution**
>
> When you work with the NIC, handle it only by the metal bracket or edges. Try not to touch the connector that plugs into the expansion slot or any of the circuits or chips on the NIC.

3. Slowly press the NIC into the expansion slot (PCI or ISA).

4. To secure the NIC's metal bracket to the system case, replace the screw you removed in step 1 of this section.

> **Caution**
>
> Don't over-tighten the screw. If you strip the mounting hole threads, any other NIC you install won't be securely fastened. Once you feel resistance, give it only another half-turn.

Tip
You may need to press in on the bottom of the metal bracket so it doesn't get stuck on the case. You may also need to wiggle the card from front to back a little bit to make it go into the slot. However, don't tilt the card side-ways.

You're now ready to replace the system cover. If you had to rearrange jumpers on the NIC, this is your last chance to write down the resource settings for base I/O address, IRQ, and base RAM address. You'll need them if the Add New Hardware Wizard can't detect your NIC.

Replacing the System Unit Cover

Now that the NIC is installed, you're ready to close everything up. Replacing the cover is practically the reverse of removing it. To replace the system unit cover, use the following steps:

1. Gently set the cover on the chassis. Make sure the guide rails on the inside edges of the cover are properly seated.

2. Slide the cover back onto the system unit until it stops. Certain models slide forward, but others slide backward.

II

Getting Started

Tip

If you are using a grounding strap, you can safely remove it from the grounding source at this point. If you have to install network cards in other computers, don't remove the temporary grounding strap from your wrist. You won't be able to reuse it once it is removed.

> **Caution**
>
> Don't pound or sharply strike the system unit cover. You may damage the hard drive inside the computer.

If the cover doesn't seem to close all the way, don't force it closed. Open the cover slightly and check around all the edges. Make sure all the tabs line up with their intended slots and that no cable connectors from inside the computer are getting caught.

3. Use the 1/4-inch hex-nut driver to replace the cover screws.

4. Replace the power cord into the back of the system unit.

Repeat the above procedures for each computer that needs a NIC. Once this step is complete, you're ready to run the network cabling between all the computers.

Cabling

Once you have your NIC installed, it is time to connect the computers together with your network cables. The type of cable you use and how it is connected together depends on what kind of Ethernet you decided to set up. The two most common types are 10BaseT and thinnet. They both provide basic networking ability without costing a fortune. The next two sections discuss how to set up your cabling for each type.

Setting Up the Cables for 10BaseT

If you decide on a 10BaseT Ethernet network, you need to have two things: a UTP cable for each computer and an Ethernet concentrator.

Tip

The concentrator doesn't have to physically be at the center of all the computers just in a place where they can all reach with their network cables.

In a 10BaseT network, the individual computers are not directly connected by the cables. Instead, each computer is connected to the concentrator. When one computer wants to send data, the data travels to the concentrator and from it is simultaneously sent to all the other computers connected to the concentrator. If a cable breaks between a computer and the concentrator, everyone else can continue to use the network except for the one computer. In contrast, on thinnet, if the cable breaks, all data flow stops.

The first thing you need to do is unpack the concentrator and get it set up where you want it. Plug it in and turn it on. Check the documentation that comes with the concentrator to make sure that it is functioning properly.

Now, take the UTP cable and plug it in at both ends. One end goes into the RJ45 jack on the back of your Ethernet adapter on the computer. The other end is plugged into one of the RJ45 ports on the Ethernet concentrator. When connecting the cables, just snap them into place the way you would when you are plugging a phone cord into a wall jack. Push until you hear the click.

◀ See "Cabling and Hubs," p. 83

Note

It doesn't matter which ports on the Ethernet concentrator you use to plug in your devices. For example, if you have an eight-port concentrator and three computers, you could use ports 4, 6, and 8 to plug in the three devices. You don't have to start with port 1, and the ports you choose don't have to be consecutive. Although, some might argue that it is more aesthetically pleasing to do so.

Setting Up the Cables for Thinnet

If you decided on a thinnet network, you need to have three things: a segment of coaxial cable to run between each computer, a BNC T connector for each computer, and a pair of 50-ohm coaxial terminators. You don't need an Ethernet concentrator as used in a 10BaseT Ethernet network.

In a thinnet network, the individual computers are connected together by one long string of coaxial cable segments. When one computer wants to send data, the data travels onto the coaxial cable and passes through each T connector until it finds the destination. If any part of the coaxial cable breaks, none of the computers can communicate with each other. In contrast, in a 10BaseT network if a cable breaks, only the computer connected to the concentrator stops working. The other computers can continue to communicate and share data.

Start setting up your thinnet cabling by attaching the T connectors to the back of each of the computers. You can do this by pushing the T connector onto the round adapter socket. Line up the slots on the shank of the T connector with the slots on either side of the female BNC connector on the network adapter. With the connector pushed all the way down, twist the connector clockwise until you feel resistance and release. The two small pins on the adapter's connector hold the T connector in place. This push-and-turn method is similar to undoing a child-proof lid on an aspirin bottle. You use this same method to attach any BNC-type connectors, whether they be on a T connector, a cable end, or a terminator.

II

Getting Started

Once the T connectors are on the adapters, you can run the coaxial cables between the computers and connect them to the Ts. Simply push and turn, the way you did when attaching the T connectors until you have connected all of the computers.

After all of the computers have been attached, the two computers on the "ends" of the network will have an open space on their T connectors. Place one terminator on the empty socket of one of the T connectors. Go to the other computer and pull out your volt-ohm meter to verify that the network cabling is ready to go.

Set the volt-ohm meter so that it measures resistance (ohms) in a range from 0–100 ohms. Place the black lead from the volt-ohm meter on the center pin of the open socket of the T connector. Place the red lead on the metal casing of the T connector. Your volt-ohm meter should read somewhere between 49 and 51 ohms. If it is outside this range, either your cable segments are too long or there is a break in the cable. To find out the cause, work your way back down the line of cable, repeating the above test at each T connector.

Once you've verified that the network cabling is ready, attach the second terminator to the open socket of the last computer's T connector.

At this point, the hardware installation of your network is complete. Your next step is to install Windows and configure it to use your new NICs.

Install Windows 95

If you have not already installed Windows 95, now is the time to do so. During the installation, Windows detects your new network adapters and installs the proper drivers, network clients, and protocols for it.

Installing Windows can be a simple process. However, Windows offers lots of opportunity for customization. In fact, entire books have been written on how to install it. In this section, you learn how to begin the installation for your computers. If Windows came pre-installed on your computers, you can skip this section. If you are upgrading from DOS or Windows 3.x, follow through the corresponding section below to begin your installation process.

Upgrading from DOS

If you're upgrading from DOS and have never used any version of Windows, installing Windows will be a life-changing event. If you have used Windows before, you are still in for a significant boost in productivity when you use it. Upgrading from DOS can be fairly painless if you follow a few simple steps.

1. Boot the computer like you normally do, allowing all drivers and com-mands to execute from the CONFIG.SYS and AUTOEXEC.BAT files.

2. From a DOS prompt, change to the directory where the Windows 95 installation files reside and enter **SETUP**. For example, if you have the Windows on floppies, you'll insert the first floppy in the drive and enter **A:** (or B: if necessary) and then **SETUP**. If you're installing from the Windows CD-ROM, and if your CD-ROM drive is D:, then you'll enter **D:** and then **SETUP**.

3. Follow the on-screen prompts of the Windows 95 Setup Wizard.

4. When prompted by the Setup Wizard, select the Typical Setup option. Based on Microsoft's research of their product, this installs the most likely set of tools and accessories you'll need on a day-to-day basis.

5. Continue with the rest of the installation as the Setup Wizard guides you.

The Windows Setup Wizard installs drivers for your NIC, the Client for Microsoft Networks, and protocols to communicate with other network users. You should repeat the above process for each computer being upgraded from DOS, using a new copy of the Windows installation package each time.

Your next step is to tell Windows you want to share your hard drive so that other users on the network can share a common place to store files.

Upgrading from Windows 3.x

If you're upgrading from Windows 3.x, installing Windows 95 from floppy or CD-ROM is just like installing any other program from within Windows. And once you start using Windows 95, you'll see a significant increase in your productivity when you use it.

To upgrade from Windows 3.x, use the following steps:

1. Boot the computer like you normally do, allowing all drivers and com-mands to execute from the CONFIG.SYS and AUTOEXEC.BAT files.

2. Start the current version of Windows installed on the computer.

3. From the Program Manager, choose File, Run. The Run dialog box appears. In the Command Line text box, enter the drive letter that contains the Windows 95 installation files and the command **\SETUP** (see fig. 7.3). For example, if you have the Windows 95 on floppies, you'll insert the first floppy in the drive and enter **A:\SETUP** (or B: if

II

Getting Started

necessary). If you're installing from the Windows 95 CD-ROM, and if your CD-ROM drive is D:, you enter **D:\SETUP**.

Fig. 7.3
Enter **SETUP**
with the appropri-
ate drive letter.

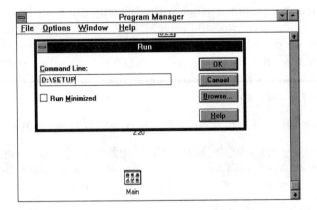

4. Follow the on-screen prompts of the Windows 95 Setup Wizard.

5. When prompted by the Setup Wizard, select the Typical Setup option. Based on Microsoft's research of their product, this installs the most likely set of tools and accessories you'll need on a day-to-day basis.

6. Continue with the rest of the installation as the Setup Wizard guides you.

The Windows 95 Setup Wizard installs drivers for your NIC, the Client for Microsoft Networks, and protocols to communicate with other network users. You should repeat the above process for each computer being upgraded from Windows 3.x, using a new copy of the Windows 95 installation package each time.

Your next step is to tell Windows 95 you want to share your hard drive so that other users on the network can share a common place to store files.

Configuring Network Support

If you already had Windows installed on the computers, the next step is to install the adapter and configure the protocols, clients, and services. To do this, you need to go to the command center for Windows 95 networking, the Network dialog box.

Follow these steps to open the Network dialog box:

1. Open the Start menu and choose Settings, Control Panel.

2. Double-click the Network icon in Contol Panel.

Using the Network Dialog Box

Figure 7.4 shows the Configuration page of the Network dialog box. This is the place that you come to make changes to the network settings. The Identification page of the Network dialog box allows you to identify the computer to the rest of the network. The Access Control page gives you the ability to decide how people can access the computer's resources.

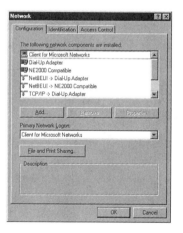

Fig. 7.4
The Network dialog box is the configuration center for networking.

II

Getting Started

Identifying Your Computer to the Rest of the Network

The Identification page of the Network dialog box contains three text boxes: Computer Name, Workgroup, and Computer Description (see fig. 7.5). During the Windows installation process, you were prompted to fill in this information. To change any of this information at a later time, simply enter it in here and choose OK.

Fig. 7.5
Identify your
computer from the
Network dialog
box.

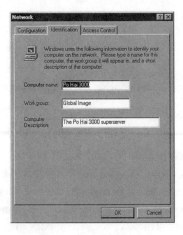

Then following is a summary of the information you can change in the
Identification page:

- Computer Name   This is the name that other users see for this
  computer when they are browsing the network using the Network
  Neighborhood or the Explorer.

- Workgroup   This specifies the workgroup in which this computer
  resides. This isn't as important on a network with a small number of
  users. However, it becomes very important when you have a larger
  number of users. To find out more about workgroups, see chapter 8,
  "Using the Network Neighborhood." For now, you should just make
  sure that you assign all of the computers to the same workgroup. In
  other words, type the same workgroup name for each one.

- Computer Description   This is an extra informational field that other
  users on the network can see when they get properties for the computer
  in the Network Neighborhood or Windows Explorer. For example, you
  might enter **Bob's PC in the Back Office**.

Setting Your Access Control

Windows 95 supports two levels of access control. The first is share-level
access control (see fig. 7.6). Under share-level access control, you control
access to your shared devices with a password. For example, if you have two
folders on your desktop, Applications and Utilities, and you want to share
them, you can assign a password to each and make them available. Anyone
who wants to access the folders and their contents just types in the password.
They have access.

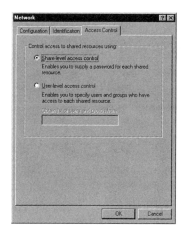

Fig. 7.6
Set the type of access control you will use.

Let's change the scenario slightly, though. Let's say you want to give access to some folders to some people and other folders to other people. Under share-level access control, you have to share each folder and give the appropriate passwords for each of the shared folders to the appropriate people. If you have six shared folders, some poor soul has to remember six passwords for the folders on your computer.

User-level access control addresses this issue. Under user-level access control, each user is assigned a single password. The user is then allowed access to certain resources. For example, you set up user Ken to have access to anything on your CD-ROM and two folders on your hard disk. Under share-level access control, you would have three passwords: one for the CD-ROM and another for each of the shared folders. Under user-level access control, Ken logs into your machine with his one password. He gets all of the appropriate access rights as assigned by you when you set up the shares for Ken.

The problem with user-level access control is that you have to have a Windows NT or Novell NetWare server to use it. Windows 95 has no facility for creating network user accounts with passwords. In order to do this, it must rely on a separate machine that is capable of verifying users: a dedicated server.

If you happen to have one of the above mentioned servers, you should probably use user-level access control. Otherwise, you are stuck with share-level.

II

Getting Started

Configuring Your Network Drivers

If you want to make changes to the network components you have installed, you can make these changes via the Network dialog box. Specifically, if you installed Windows before installing the hardware, you'll need to configure the new NIC along with a network client.

Network Adapters

Your adapter driver is the piece of software that Windows 95 uses to talk directly to your NIC. Think of your adapter driver as sort of a translator between your NIC and the other network components. Any time one of the other components wants to do something on the network, it has to go through the network component, who then passes on the message to the NIC.

Installing a Network Adapter

If you had your adapter installed when you installed Windows, there should be a driver installed for you, and if you added the adapter later, the Add Hardware Wizard adds the appropriate driver for the card it detects. Use these steps to add your network adapter:

1. Open the Start menu and choose Settings, Control Panel.

2. Double-click the Add New Hardware icon.

3. Choose Next in the Add New Hardware dialog box to continue.

4. When prompted, choose Yes to let Windows detect your hardware. Choose Next twice to have the Wizard begin detecting your new hardware.

5. To complete the installation, insert your Windows installation disks or CD-ROM as prompted.

6. Click Finish.

7. When prompted to restart the computer, select Continue.

Your network adapter is now installed.

If the Add New Hardware Wizard could not detect your NIC, then perform these additional steps:

1. Open the Start menu and choose Settings, Control Panel.

2. Double-click the Add New Hardware icon.

3. Choose Next in the Add New Hardware dialog box.

4. Answer <u>Y</u>es to manually specify your new hardware.

5. Select Network Adapter and then choose Next to proceed to the Select Network Adapters dialog box.

6. Select the card from the <u>M</u>anufacturers list box; then choose the card model from the Network Adapters list box (see fig. 7.7). Click OK.

If your Windows 95 driver for this NIC is not included with Windows 95 but came on a disk from the manufacturer, choose <u>H</u>ave Disk and provide the drive letter or path for the driver.

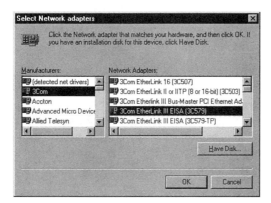

Fig. 7.7
Choose the manufacturer and the model of the NIC you're installing.

7. Windows displays the hardware settings for the NIC that will work with your computer (see fig. 7.8).

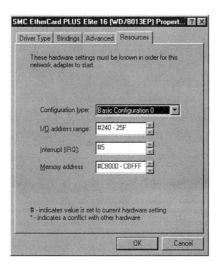

Fig. 7.8
You should review and write down the settings for your installed network adapter to save for future reference.

8. Configure the NIC to use these settings. Follow the NIC's manufacturer's user manual to change any settings.

9. Click Next.

10. Insert your Windows 95 installation disks or CD-ROM as prompted.

11. Click Finish.

12. When prompted to restart the computer, select Continue.

Configuring Your Adapter

Once you get your adapter installed, you will want to configure it. As a rule, Windows does all of the configuration necessary to make your network functional for you. Occasionally, though, you may want to make some changes yourself.

Figure 7.9 shows the Properties sheet for the network adapter component. To open this Properties sheet for your adapter, highlight the adapter name on the Configuration page of the Network dialog box, and click Properties. The first page of the Properties sheet for your network adapter is the driver type page. On this page, you can select the type of driver you use for your NIC. The default is to use the Enhanced Mode (32 Bit and 16 Bit) NDIS Driver. You should always use the enhanced-mode driver if it is available, as it is generally faster than the real-mode version.

Fig. 7.9

Choose the type of driver you want to use for your NIC by selecting one from the Properties sheet.

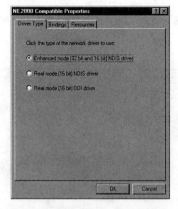

The second page of the Properties sheet is the Bindings page (see fig. 7.10). *Binding* a protocol simply means that you are enabling a given protocol for use on an adapter. Once you have bound the protocol to the adapter, it speaks to other machines on the network using the protocol you have selected.

Fig. 7.10
Select which
protocols you want
your adapter to use
from the Bindings
page.

To bind a protocol to your adapter, mark the box next to its name by clicking it. After you restart your computer, the protocol is enabled. If you don't have any protocols listed, the "Adding Protocols" section later in this chapter teaches you how.

Protocols

In chapter 4, "Understanding How Networks Work," you learned that protocols are what computers use as a sort of language to talk to each other. The Network dialog box is also where you select what protocols you install for your computer to use. If your computer is only going to talk to computers on a local Windows network, it probably only needs to know one protocol. But if you plan to have your computer connect with many different computers from around the world, it may need to know more than one protocol—in the same way that a person who was going to talk with many different people around the world might need to know several languages.

Adding Protocols

You add a network protocol in the same manner that you add a network adapter. For the purposes of a small Windows 95 network, you should have the NetBEUI protocol installed. This protocol should have been installed by Windows 95 by default, but if it wasn't, you can add it now.

In this example, you install the NetBEUI protocol for a small Windows 95 network. However, these steps work for installing any of the available protocols:

   1. Open the Network dialog box by right-clicking the Network Neighborhood icon and choosing Properties from the pop-up menu.

Tip
Windows defaults
to binding all
protocols you have
installed on the
computer. While it
won't hurt to have
them all bound,
you should unbind
all but the one you
have selected for
your network.

Getting Started

2. Add a new network component by clicking Add. The Select Network Component Type dialog box appears (see fig. 7.11).

3. Choose Protocol from the list of possible components types and then click Add to select the protocol. The Select Network Protocol dialog box appears.

Fig. 7.11

Choose Protocol from the list of network component types.

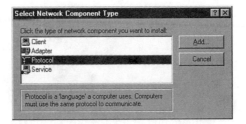

4. As shown in figure 7.12, select the appropriate network protocol from the Manufacturers list box and the Network Protocols list box. You can add only one new protocol at a time.

Fig. 7.12

Choose the manufacturer and then a protocol to install.

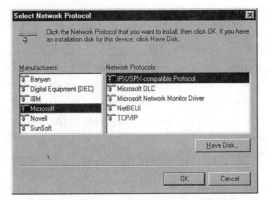

> **Note**
>
> If you are installing a small Windows network, you'll want to choose Microsoft and NetBEUI.

When ready, click OK to add the protocol to the Network Components list box.

5. Click OK on the Network dialog box to begin installing the software for the new protocol. You need the Windows 95 installation disks, CD-ROM, or a disk from the protocol manufacturer.

> **Note**
>
> If you've chosen to install TCP/IP, it's very important that you contact your network administrator. They will tell you the exact configuration you need to set. For example, your network could use a *Dynamic Host Configuration Protocol* (DHCP) server instead of using a specific TCP/IP address.

6. When prompted, choose Restart to make the change take effect. Until you reboot your computer, it does not know how to communicate using the new protocol.

From here, you'll want to install a network client and service. If you already have a network client or service installed, the following section explains how to make sure the link between the protocol and the client or service is established.

Binding Protocols to Clients and Services

Just as you must bind protocols to adapters, you must also bind the clients and services your computer uses to a protocol. You can do this by highlighting the protocol name and choosing Properties. This displays the Properties sheet for the protocol (see fig. 7.13).

Fig. 7.13
This is the NetBEUI Properties sheet.

The Bindings page contains a list of the names of the clients and services you have installed on your computer. To bind a service or client to the protocol, place a check in the box next to its name by clicking the service or client you want to use this protocol.

The default is to bind your protocol to every client and service you have installed. As recommended in the instructional text in the protocol Properties sheet, you should only bind the protocol to the clients and services that need to use it. The fewer bindings you have, the faster your computer is because it has less overhead associated with the network.

If you are setting up a completely new Windows network and you want to be able to share the resources on this computer, you should have the protocol (NetBEUI in the case of a Windows 95-only network) bound to the Client for Microsoft Networks and File and Printer Sharing for Microsoft Networks at a minimum. If the Client for Microsoft Networks or File and Printer Sharing for Microsoft Networks is not listed, read the later section "Clients for a Windows 95 Network."

Clients

A *client* is the piece of software that supervises the connection to another computer on the network. If a protocol is the language that your computer speaks to another computer, you can think of the client as the brain that understands the language and knows what to ask from the other computer.

Clients for a Windows 95 Network

In order to connect to other Windows 95 computers on the network, your computer needs to have the Client for Microsoft Networks installed. It is usually installed by default if you had a network card in the computer when you installed Windows 95. However, if you need to add it, you can do so using similar methods to add adapters and protocols.

To install the Client for Microsoft Networks, follow these steps:

1. Open the Start menu and choose Settings, Control Panel.

2. Double-click the Network icon. The Network dialog box appears (see fig. 7.14).

3. Click the Add button on the Configuration page.

4. Click Client in the Select Network Component Type dialog box.

Fig. 7.14
To install the Client for Microsoft Networks, click the Add button.

5. From the Select Network Client dialog box (see fig. 7.15), select Microsoft from the Manufacturers list box and Client for Microsoft Networks from the Network Clients list box.

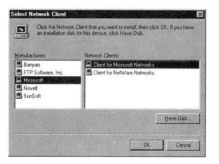

Fig. 7.15
Select Client for Microsoft Networks to install the software.

6. Click OK to install the client software. When prompted to restart your computer, click OK to complete the installation.

If this computer will be sharing its resources, read on.

Setting Client Options
Figure 7.16 shows the Client for Microsoft Networks Properties sheet. To get there, select the client on the Network dialog box and click Properties.

II

Getting Started

Fig. 7.16
Setting client
options from
the Client for
Microsoft
Networks
Properties sheet.

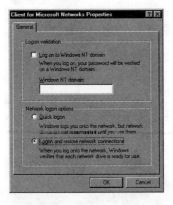

As you can see from the figure, there are two categories of options that you can set. The first is Logon Validation and applies to Windows NT networks. You can find out more about this option in chapter 19, "Connecting to Other Networks." The second category is Network Logon Options.

The Network Logon Options can be set to either Quick Logon or Log On and Restore Network Connections. If you choose to restore network connections, Windows automatically attaches you to any Windows NT resources you were using when you logged on the last time. If you select Quick Logon, you must re-connect to the other machine manually each time you log in. If you have resources you use frequently on another machine on the network, you should select restore network connections (the default).

Services

If you want to share the files and printers on this computer, you need to have File and Printer Sharing for Microsoft Networks installed. Once you have file and printer sharing installed, you can specify which folders and printers you want to share with others from this computer.

You can add this service now by using these steps:

1. Right-click the Network Neighborhood icon and select Properties from the pop-up menu. The Network dialog box appears.

2. As seen in figure 7.17, change the Primary Network Logon to Client for Microsoft Networks.

3. Select File and Print Sharing from the Network dialog box and choose I Want To Be Able To Give Others Access to My Files in the File and Print Sharing dialog box (see fig. 7.18). Click OK to accept your choice.

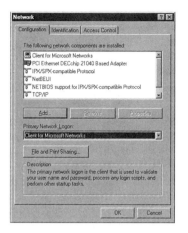

Fig. 7.17
Change the
Primary Network
Logon to Client for
Microsoft
Networks.

Fig. 7.18
To install File and
Print Sharing for
Microsoft Net-
works, choose I
Want To Be Able
To Give Others
Access to My File.

4. Click OK on the Network dialog box to save your changes. At this time,
Windows installs File and Printer Sharing for Microsoft Networks.

5. When prompted, choose Restart to complete the installation.

You've now installed all the required network components to enable sharing
your resources with other computers on a Windows network. However, turning on file and print sharing from the Network dialog box does not make
your hard disks and printers available on the network. It simply gives you the
ability to do so. If you want to share a disk or printer, you need to turn on
sharing for the item by going to the Sharing page of that item's Properties
sheet. For more information on setting up sharing for a device, see chapter 9,
"Sharing Network Hardware."

II

Getting Started

How Do I Know if the Network Is Working?

Once you have configured all of the machines on your network, checking to see if the network is working is simple. Simply double-click the Network Neighborhood icon on your desktop. If the network is functioning, you see the names of the other computers and their icons in the Network Neighborhood window.

If you only see a globe icon labeled Entire Network, your network may still be working, but your computer may not be in the same workgroup as the other computers on the network. Double-click the globe icon to see the workgroups on the network. If you see the names of some workgroups, your network is functioning. If instead you get an error message that the network is not accessible, you may have made an error in your setup. Check the following troubleshooting section for help.

Troubleshooting

Windows makes setting up a network easy, but things still go wrong. The following are some common network problems and possible solutions.

My network isn't working. What's wrong?

For thinnet, check to make sure that the cables, T connectors, and terminators are all connected. Make sure that both ends are terminated. Make sure you only have two terminators.

For 10BaseT, check that the cables are plugged in and firmly seated and that the concentrator is powered on.

Finally, check that the workstations have matching protocols loaded.

Windows 95 did not detect my NIC during the install. There is no record of it in the device manager, and nothing has been installed in the Network dialog box. Help!

Run the Add New Hardware Wizard and let it detect new devices. The Wizard will probably find it the second time. If it still doesn't, then you need to run the Wizard again and add the adapter manually, using the configuration settings you wrote down when you installed the NIC in the computer.

I don't see the driver for my network adapter in the adapters list in the Select Network Adapters dialog box when I am adding the driver for my network adapter.

If your adapter came with a disk that has a Windows driver on it, you should install the driver on the disk by selecting Have Disk in the Select Network Adapters dialog box.

If your adapter did not come with a Windows driver and is not in the list, chances are it is an adapter that is compatible with some other type of adapter. For example, many Ethernet adapters are NE2000 compatible. If this is the case, install the driver for an NE2000 Compatible card or the driver for the card that is compatible with your adapter.

When I try to bind my protocol to my clients and services, the client or service to which I want to bind the protocol is not in the list.

You probably don't have the client or service installed yet. Add it first by choosing Add from the Configuration page of the Network dialog box. Choose Client or Service, depending on what you want to add, and click OK. You have to reboot your computer for changes to take effect if you installed a service.

From Here...

In this chapter, you learned how to set up your network hardware, including installing your adapters and setting up the cabling system for both 10BaseT Ethernet and thinnet. You also learned how to configure Windows to use your network, using the Network dialog box to install and configure your adapter driver, protocol support, network clients, and network services.

Now that you have a working network, you probably want to find out more about actually using it:

- Chapter 8, "Using the Network Neighborhood," tells you more about finding and accessing other computers on your network.

- Chapter 9, "Sharing Network Hardware," teaches you how to configure your computer to share its files and printers with other computers on the network. It also explains how to access resources on other computers.

II

Getting Started

- Chapter 13, "Introduction to Electronic Mail," tells you how to communicate over your network using the e-mail capability that is built in to Windows 95.

- Chapter 19, "Connecting to Other Networks," shows how you can connect your Windows 95 network with other types of networks, such as Windows NT and Novell NetWare networks.

- Chapter 21, "Using the Built-In Network Tools," explains how to use the administration tools that come with Windows 95 to manage your network.

Part III

Using Your New Network

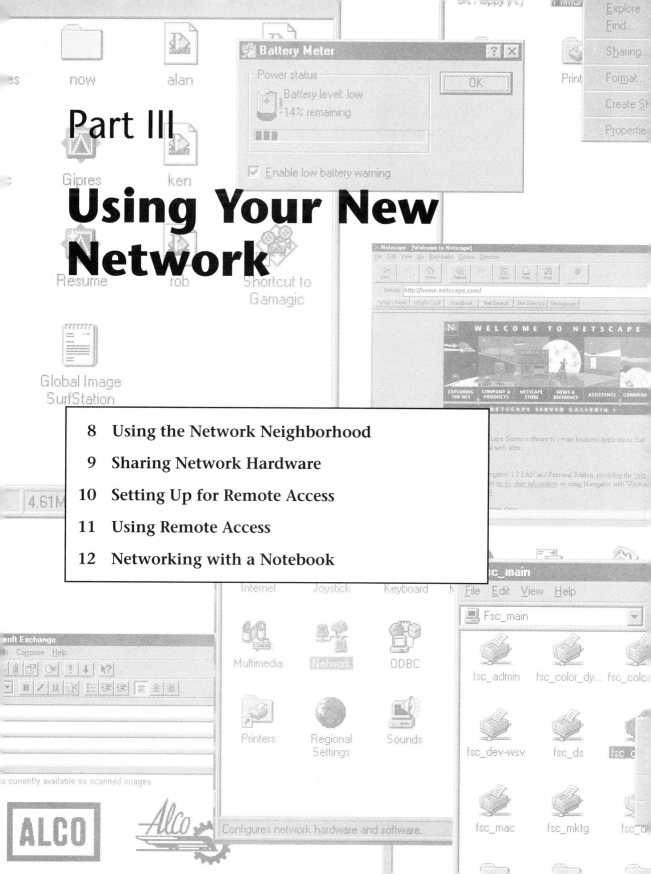

Chapter 8

Using the Network Neighborhood

Whether you're part of a very large corporate network or one of a handful participating in a departmental workgroup network, you'll appreciate the easy access to network resources through the Network Neighborhood. This chapter explains how to use the various functions of the Network Neighborhood and the Explorer to get the most out of your network.

Specifically, this chapter covers

- Finding network resources on your local and corporate network

- Attaching to servers, printers, and other network resources

- Discovering detailed information about the network servers and printers that you use

- Using Network Neighborhood functions through the Explorer

Viewing Network Resources

As a general rule, if you can't find something, you can't use it. With networks becoming larger and more interconnected, it is becoming difficult to find networked resources. Departments and divisions add servers and printers to corporate networks without much fanfare, yet the resources they hold may be crucial to the success of your business. This section will explain how to browse your network to find servers and printers on your local network as well as your corporate network.

Exploring Your Local Network

Your local network is made up of the servers and printers that you use most frequently. Typically, users will store the majority of their information on a single server that is used by their department or division. The department or division may also have several other servers that are used for database servers, print servers, or file servers.

Windows 95 displays the servers that are connected within your local area network in the Network Neighborhood. To see which servers are located there, double-click the Network Neighborhood icon on your desktop. Additionally, servers that are not located on your local area network or are connected through network hardware to other floors or buildings can be found by looking at the Entire Network, which is discussed in the next section, "Exploring the Entire Network." Figure 8.1 shows several servers that are part of a workstation's local network.

Fig. 8.1
The Network Neighborhood window shows servers that you frequently use.

Notice that the icons in the Network Neighborhood look the same. This is Windows' way of removing the mystery of one network server over another. For some time, it has been painfully obvious that one set of procedures was used to access one type of server, while a different set of procedures was used to access another. Windows now portrays all servers as equal network resources. For example, figure 8.1 shows a server named FSC_MAIN and one named SWELABNTS.

You can plainly see that these are network servers and if you had similar user privileges on each, you might not even know that these servers were vastly different in their capabilities. The FSC_MAIN server is a high-powered Novell NetWare server while the SWELABNTS server is a low-powered workstation running Windows for Workgroups. I will describe how you can obtain information on various network resources later in this chapter in the section titled "Exploring Network Resource Properties."

Exploring the Entire Network

Occasionally, you will need to access servers or printers that are located in other departments or divisions, new to your network, or local servers that you have not accessed before. In these cases you will not see servers within your local Network Neighborhood window. You will need to have the Network Neighborhood search for all of the other servers on your network.

Instructing the Network Neighborhood to search for other servers is easy. You may have noticed the globe icon, Entire Network, in the local Network Neighborhood window. Double-clicking the Entire Network icon will cause your computer to begin a network search for other servers. Figure 8.2 shows the animated icon that the Network Neighborhood displays for about ten seconds while your computer is searching the network.

Fig. 8.2
The Network Neighborhood displays an animated icon to let you know that it is searching your network for all servers.

Once the search is completed, you will see a new list of icons in your Network Neighborhood window. This list will include both the local server icons that you had seen before plus the additional servers that were found during the network search. Figure 8.3 shows an example of the Network Neighborhood window of the Entire Network.

Fig. 8.3
The Entire Network displays the servers found by searching your corporate network.

III

Using Your New Network

Again, you will notice that the servers are displayed as generic server icons, which have no preference for the network operating system or server capacity. This is especially helpful on a wide area network, which can span cities, states, or even countries where you may not know what kind of server you are accessing. With the Network Neighborhood, you won't need to know since it handles the connections to different servers without special commands.

> ## Note
>
> Remember that your system will only be able to see the servers for which you have loaded network clients. If you have not loaded a network client for XYZ network operating system, you will not see any of the XYZ servers on your network. Windows can handle all of the popular network operating systems, which include
>
> - Novell NetWare
> - IBM OS/2 LAN Server
> - Microsoft LAN Manager
> - Microsoft Windows NT Server
> - Banyan Vines
>
> See chapter 19, "Connecting to Other Networks," for more information about loading drivers for other network operating systems.

However, just because you can see the server does not mean that you will be able to access it. Most systems will not let you access their network resources unless you have the proper permissions. The next section, "Connecting to Network Resources," will cover the process used to access the network servers and printers you see in your Network Neighborhood.

Connecting to Network Resources

In the last section, you learned how to find network servers. This section will cover the procedures used to access the networked resources that the servers are offering.

Attaching to Network Servers

Once you have found a network server that you have been given permission to access, you will want to attach to that server so that you can begin using the shared drives and printers. To access a network server, simply double-click the server's icon in the Network Neighborhood window.

If your Windows user name and password are the same as the user name and password for the network server, you will see the shared folders for that server. If not, you will be prompted to enter the correct credentials to obtain access to the server. Figure 8.4 shows the dialog box that you will see when you attempt to log in to a server with an incorrect user name and password.

Fig. 8.4
You will be prompted to enter a new user name and password if your Windows credentials do not work with a network server.

Once you are attached to the server and are attempting to access a shared folder on a computer that does not support user-level credentials (such as Windows 95 peer-to-peer shared folders), you will be prompted to enter a password (see fig. 8.5).

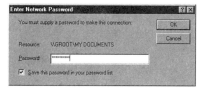

Fig. 8.5
You will be prompted for a password when you attempt to access a shared resource on a server that does not support user-level credentials.

Tip
Windows first tries the user name and password you entered when you started Windows. For faster access to network servers, you set your user name and password to match that of your network servers.

You may have noticed that on both dialog boxes shown in figures 8.4 and 8.5, a checkbox in the lower left corner indicates that you can save the credentials that you enter for this server in your local password file. This option allows you to build a user-name and password portfolio that gives you access to the various servers on your network. This is a very useful feature when your Windows user name and password do not match your server's credentials or when one or more servers requires different user names and passwords for access.

For example, if you have access to several servers on your network, but the password for each server is different, you could attach to each server, enter your valid credentials, and check the save option on the login dialog box. The next time you attached to these servers, you would not be asked to type in your password since Windows knows to use the saved user name and password in your local password file.

Since this option is so powerful, you may be concerned about having all of your credentials available on your hard drive. Don't worry, your local password file is encrypted to prevent someone from finding out your passwords. Of course, if you have logged in and step away from your computer, anyone who sits down at your machine can access any resources to which you have access.

Another way to log in to a network server is to right-click the server's icon in the Network Neighborhood. This displays a pop-up menu like the one shown in figure 8.6.

Fig. 8.6

The pop-up menu in the Network Neighborhood allows you to attach to a network server.

Selecting the Attach As option displays the Enter Network Password dialog box (refer to fig. 8.4). You may want to use this method of logging in to a server when your password has been changed or if you want to log in as a different user. Some users have different permissions on a server depending on their needs. If you are an administrator of a server, you may want to log in as a normal user for everyday tasks but attach as a supervisor to maintain the server at other times. This function will allow you to log in as a different user to perform these duties.

If you are already logged in to a server and you want to reattach as a different user or you simply need to log out of the server, you can use the Log Out option found on the pop-up menu (refer to fig. 8.6). Once you have issued this command, you will see the dialog box shown in figure 8.7 warning that you will not be able to use the resources on the server if you log out.

Fig. 8.7
Once you log out
of a server, you
can't access its
resources until you
log in again.

Mapping Network Drives

Network drive mapping is a function that Windows performs to simulate a
drive letter on your local machine that points to a network server. This is
typically done to maintain compatibility with older Windows and DOS programs, which cannot see the network drives without associated drive letters.
Windows can see network servers and shared resources without the need for
drive letters. Windows was built to be aware of the networking environment
and to fit into it without the need to trick the computer by assigning drive
letters to servers.

However, many older DOS and Windows applications need a drive letter
to work properly. For example, if your server named ACCOUNTING had a
shared folder named DATA that you needed to access from an older Windows
application, you could use the Network Neighborhood to map the drive letter
Q to that server's shared folder. If you would look at the directory of the Q
drive, you would see the contents of the DATA folder on the ACCOUNTING
server.

To map a drive letter from within the Network Neighborhood, follow these
steps:

1. Select the server that has the shared folder.

2. Right-click the shared folder to which you want to map a drive letter.

3. Select <u>M</u>ap Network Drive from the pop-up menu. This displays the
    Map Network Drive dialog box (see fig. 8.8).

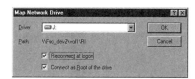

III

Fig. 8.8
The Network
Neighborhood
allows you to
assign a drive letter
to a server's shared
folder.

Using Your New Network

4. Select an unused drive letter to map to this folder.

5. If you want to always map this drive letter to the server's folder, mark
    the Reconnec<u>t</u> at Logon checkbox.

6. Choose the OK button to map the drive letter.

After you have completed the drive mapping, you will be able to see the mapped drive letter within the Explorer and My Computer. These drive letters will be marked using a network drive icon (see fig. 8.9).

Fig. 8.9
Your network drive letters will show up in the Explorer using a network drive icon.

Attaching to Network Printers

Network folders are associated with a server that shares them. Similarly, network printers are also hosted by servers. The server accepts print jobs from network workstations and places those documents into a queue that sends the printer the data to print out. The network printers may or may not be physically connected to a server on your network. Many network-ready printers come with built-in or add-on network adapter cards that can be used to connect to the server over the network rather than through a parallel port cable.

When a server sets up a queue to service a printer, that queue may be accessed by those who have been given permission to print on the printer. You may wonder why printing on the network needs to be restricted. One reason is that many companies charge back expenses for paper and toner to individual departments. By restricting access, printing costs are associated with the department that uses a particular printer. Additionally, some printers, such as color laser printers, plotters, slide printers, and some high-quality laser printers, may have special purposes on the network and high costs of operation.

To connect to a networked printer using the Network Neighborhood, you can follow these steps:

1. Select the server that is hosting the network printer that you want to print to.

2. Double-click the server's icon to display the available printers.

3. Right-click the network printer that you want to use. This displays a pop-up menu like the one shown in figure 8.10.

Fig. 8.10
The pop-up menu in the Network Neighborhood allows you to attach to a network printer.

4. Select the Install option from the pop-up menu. You will need to install the proper printer driver for the printer you are accessing. Make sure you know the manufacturer and exact model of your printer. In addition, find out any details, such as the amount of printer memory and which printer cartridges (if any) are installed in the printer.

5. The Add Printer Wizard will guide you through the process of installing the correct driver for your network printer.

6. The first decision you have to make is whether or not you will be printing using DOS programs. If you have DOS programs that will need to use this printer, Windows will have to capture a printer port to redirect the printing to the network. If you do not plan on printing to the network printer using DOS, select No, choose the Next button, and skip to step 10.

7. If you will be printing from DOS to the network printer, select Yes and choose the Next button. This displays a dialog box like the one shown in figure 8.11 that explains about DOS printing.

Fig. 8.11
DOS programs will
need to have a
printer port
assigned to a
network printer in
order to print.

Tip
If you have a local
printer, do not use
LTP1 for your
network printer
port.

8. Choose the Capture Printer Port button. This displays the Capture
Printer Port dialog box (see fig. 8.12). The Path contains the network
printer queue path that you have chosen through the Network Neighborhood. The Device box suggests a printer port to use. You may choose
any of the available printer ports on your computer by clicking on the
drop-down list box.

Fig. 8.12
Choose an
available printer
port to enable
DOS to print on
the selected
network printer.

9. Click the OK button. This returns you to the dialog box shown in figure
8.11. Click the Next button to continue the installation.

10. You are now prompted to select the manufacturer and the model of the
network printer (see fig. 8.13). Select the appropriate printer and click
the Next button.

Fig. 8.13
Choose the type of
printer that you
will be connecting
to over the
network.

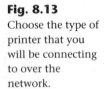
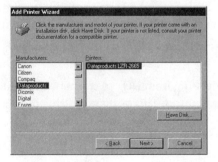

11. Choose a name for the network printer. Windows presents you with the default printer driver name, which you can change (see fig. 8.14). Try to pick a printer name that uniquely describes that network printer. For example, "Network Printer" is not very descriptive unless there is only one on your entire network.

Fig. 8.14
Choose a name for your network printer that uniquely identifies it.

12. If you want to select this network printer to be the default printer for your Windows applications, check the Yes option to this question and choose the Next button.

13. Windows now installs the printer driver you have selected and sets up a printer icon in your Printers list.

14. After installing the printer drivers, Windows asks you if you want to print a test page on the printer you have just installed. This is a good practice since it tests the communications between your Windows workstation and the network printer. You should always answer Yes to this question.

Note

Your network may contain several printers that are the same. If you have already installed the driver for one of the network printers, Windows asks if you want to keep the installed driver when adding another printer of the same type to your Windows installation. You should accept the default option, which does not replace your driver unless you have an updated driver disk from the manufacturer.

Additionally, some manufacturers may only have one driver for all of their printers, even though you can specify them individually. You may be surprised when you install printers to see that the driver has already been installed in your system.

III

Using Your New Network

Exploring Network Resource Properties

When using a network, there will be times when you will need to know some additional information about a server, shared folder, or network printer. This section explores how you can discover information about these network resources.

Viewing Server Information

Since the Network Neighborhood displays all servers with the same icon, you may not know what type of server you are accessing over the network. In some cases, it may be important that you know more information about a server so that you can work effectively.

For instance, it may be important to you to store your files with file names that are longer than older DOS programs allow. Therefore, you will want to store your data files on another Windows 95 or Windows NT Server instead of a Novell NetWare server since the Windows servers will always support your long file names.

In addition to finding out what type network operating system a server is using, you can also find out some more detailed information regarding your connection to a server. This kind of information may help you troubleshoot problems with your network connections.

To see the detailed information about a network server, follow these steps:

1. Right-click the server icon for which you want more information.

2. Choose the <u>P</u>roperties option. This displays a Properties sheet similar to the one shown in figure 8.15.

Fig. 8.15
The network server Properties sheet shows the type of operating system that your server is running.

If you want to see more information about your connection to a server, follow these steps:

1. Right-click the server icon for which you want more information.

2. Choose the <u>W</u>ho Am I option. This displays the WhoAmI Information dialog box (see fig. 8.16). Click OK to continue.

Fig. 8.16
The Who Am I option displays detailed information about your connection to the server.

3. Choose the <u>L</u>og Out option if you want to disconnect from the server and any shared resources that you may be using. This option is useful if your system administrator needs to perform maintenance on a server. You can log out of the server without affecting your connections to other servers on the network.

4. Choose the <u>A</u>ttach As option if you are not logged in to a server and you want to connect to that server using a user name and password that differs from your default Windows credentials. You will be prompted to enter your user name and password to gain access to the server.

> **Note**
>
> The Network Neighborhood may take a very long time to display a server's properties if that server is located at another location. Wide area networks between cities, states, or countries are often very slow. Be patient.

Viewing Network Folder Information

While you may know how much hard drive space is available to you on your local workstation, you may be unaware of how much network drive space is available. Additionally, you may need to copy a large amount of data from a network folder to your own hard drive. You will need to know how much drive space is needed to perform these operations.

You can determine the amount of drive space available on a network drive by using My Computer to graphically display the used and free space on a network drive. However, in order to perform this task, you will need to map a network drive letter to the server folder that you want to check. Follow the detailed mapping instructions that were presented earlier in this chapter in the "Mapping Network Drives" section.

Once you have mapped a network drive letter, follow these steps to display the amount of server space available:

1. Double-click the My Computer icon on your desktop.

2. Select the drive letter that you just mapped to the shared network folder on the server.

3. Right-click the drive letter icon. This displays a pop-up menu.

4. Select Properties from the pop-up menu. This displays a Properties sheet similar to the one shown in figure 8.17.

Fig. 8.17
Use My Computer to display the free space on a network drive.

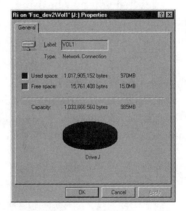

If you need to find out the size of a folder—in bytes—you can follow these steps:

1. Select the server from the Network Neighborhood.

2. Double-click the shared folders until you find the one you want.

3. Right-click the shared folder icon. This displays a pop-up menu.

4. Choose Properties. This displays a Properties sheet like the one shown in figure 8.18.

Fig. 8.18
The Apps Proper-
ties sheet shows
the number of files
and folders and
the amount of
drive space used by
a network folder—
in this case the
APPS folder.

Viewing Network Printer Information

Network printers can provide a wealth of information. For example, if you are
printing to a network printer, you can check the progress of your print job
from your workstation. Additionally, if your print job has not printed after a
long time, you may want to check the printer queue to see whose print jobs
are ahead of yours.

To check a network print queue, follow these steps:

1. Open the Start menu and choose Settings, Printers.

2. Double-click the printer that you want to check. This displays a window
like the one shown in figure 8.19. Notice that the user name and the
document name are displayed along with the print status for each print
job.

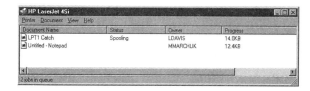

Fig. 8.19
You can check the
printer queue of a
network printer to
see whose print
job is ahead of
yours.

You can also check the printer's driver information by following these steps:

1. Open the Start menu and choose Settings, Printers.

2. Right-click the printer that you want to check. This displays a pop-up
menu.

3. Choose Properties to display the Properties sheet for your network
printer (see fig. 8.20).

Fig. 8.20
The network printer information can be viewed using the Properties sheet.

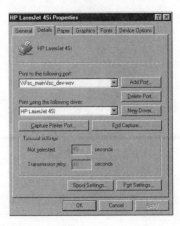

4. Select the Details tab to view the driver information related to your network printer.

Using the Network Neighborhood through the Explorer

The majority of this chapter has focused on using the Network Neighborhood, but its functions are also available through the Explorer interface. This section briefly shows how to access the Network Neighborhood functions through the Explorer.

Finding a Server on Your Network

The Explorer has a unique feature for searching the Network Neighborhood. If you have a large network or you cannot remember the entire name of a server, you can let the Explorer search the network for the computer that you want to connect to. To find a computer on the network, follow these steps:

1. Open the Start menu and choose Programs, Windows Explorer.

2. From within the Explorer, choose Tools, Find, Computer.

3. This displays a dialog box in which you can enter a server name or just part of a server name to search for. Enter as much of the server name as you know and choose Find Now.

4. The dialog box extends downward and displays all of the network servers it finds with names similar to the one you entered. Figure 8.21 shows the results of a search for a network computer.

Fig. 8.21
You can search for
a computer with
any portion of that
computer's name.

Viewing Network Drives within the Explorer

Like the Network Neighborhood, you can display the contents of a network
drive by clicking the Explorer's Network Neighborhood icon in the All Folders list and choosing the server you want to browse. In addition to these features, the Explorer provides the same folder and file display that shows the
hierarchy of the server's directories. You can obtain information about the
folders in the same way you did under the Network Neighborhood by right-
clicking the shared folders and choosing the Properties option. This procedure was explained in more detail earlier in this chapter in the section titled,
"Viewing Network Folder Information."

You will find that the Explorer window will work much the same way as the
Network Neighborhood window when it comes to showing network files and
folders. You may prefer one over the other, but you can choose the way you
want to browse your network.

Troubleshooting Your Network Neighborhood

You may encounter problems while using the Network Neighborhood. Often
these are the result of networking difficulties, but some may have other
causes. This section explores a few problems and suggests some possible rem-
edies.

I can't see any servers on the network. What's wrong?

Unfortunately, this symptom could indicate several different problems. First,
check to see if everyone is having this problem. If so, it could mean that your
network cable is damaged. If you are the only one with this problem, you
may want to check your computer's connection to the network. If this is the
first time that you have tried using the network, you may want to verify that

you have the Client for Microsoft Networks loaded within your component list in the Network dialog box.

I can see all of the Windows 95 workstations on the network, but I can't see our department's Novell NetWare server. Why not?

You should verify that your workstation has the Client for NetWare Networks loaded in your component list in the Network dialog box. You will only see servers for which you have loaded the appropriate clients.

I can see a server on the network, but I can only access one of the folders on that server. Why do I get an "Access is Denied" message on the other folders when I can see them in my Network Neighborhood?

Security access to a server's shared folders may be restricted to certain users. Just because you can see a folder does not mean that you can access that folder's contents.

From Here...

Now that you have learned about connecting to shared resources on the network, you may want to look into sharing your own resources with others on the network. Check out the following chapters for more information on the topics listed:

- Chapter 9, "Sharing Network Hardware," explains how to set up your workstation as a peer-to-peer server.

- Chapter 10, "Setting Up for Remote Access," explores how you can stay connected to the network even while you're on the road.

- Chapter 12, "Networking with a Notebook," describes the methods of connecting your notebook computer to the network.

- Chapter 19, "Connecting to Other Networks," explains the methods for connecting your workstation to other large servers on your network.

Chapter 9

Sharing Network Hardware

Whether your workstation is part of a multicontinental, enterprise-wide network or constitutes half of your network, you may want to share your resources with others on the network. The easiest way to do this is to use the built-in, peer-to-peer networking services that Windows 95 offers.

For example, if you were fortunate enough to get a workstation with a one gigabyte hard drive, you may need to make some of this space available to others in your department for document storage or archiving. Or your computer may be designated to be the department's server for the local laser printer. In either case, you can make use of the peer-to-peer networking in Windows to share your hardware on the network.

This chapter explores the issues that concern your contribution to your network. Specifically, the following topics are covered:

- Deciding what resources you'll share and with whom

- Setting up security for your shared resources

- Tuning your workstation for server duties

Deciding Who To Share With

If you have decided that your workstation will participate on the network as a peer-to-peer server, you must decide who you will share with. You will undoubtedly want to share with other Windows 95, Windows for Workgroups, or Windows NT workstations. But you may also want to share with non-Windows clients on the network, such as DOS workstations connected to a Novell network.

The main issue surrounding your decision to support Windows-only or Windows and DOS workstations is one of drivers. When you installed the networking functions of Windows 95, you probably also installed, by default, File and Printer Sharing for Microsoft Networks. This service allows you to share resources with other Windows workstations on the network, but not with NetWare users running DOS workstations. If you have no need to share with DOS workstations on a NetWare network, then you can skip ahead to the section, "Deciding What To Share."

Sharing Resources with NetWare Users

If you want to share your resources with both NetWare users and Windows users, you can install a different network service that replaces the File and Printer Sharing for Microsoft Networks. This other service requires a Novell NetWare server on your network to allow the user credentials to be validated. By installing the File and Printer Services for NetWare Networks, you can allow DOS workstations to access your shared resources as if you were another NetWare server.

If you decide that you want to share your resources with NetWare users as well as Windows users, you can replace your sharing service by following these steps:

1. Open the Start menu and choose Settings, Control Panel.

2. Double-click the Network icon. The Network dialog box appears (see fig. 9.1).

Fig. 9.1
The Network dialog box allows you to configure your workstation's sharing capabilities.

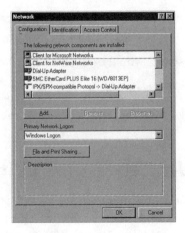

3. Choose the File and Printer Sharing for Microsoft Networks option from the components list.

4. Choose the <u>R</u>emove button.

5. Choose the <u>A</u>dd button. The Select Network Component Type dialog box appears (see fig. 9.2).

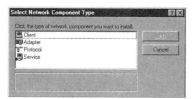

Fig. 9.2
Components can be added from one of four categories.

6. Choose Service from the list of components and choose the <u>A</u>dd button. This displays the Select Network Service dialog box (see fig. 9.3).

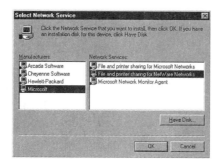

Fig. 9.3
Network services are chosen from the list of available drivers.

7. Choose Microsoft from the <u>M</u>anufacturers list box and File and Printer Sharing for NetWare Networks from the Network Services list box.

8. Choose the OK button.

9. When you have returned to the original Network dialog box, you see that the File and Printer Services for NetWare Networks option has been added to your components list. Choose the OK button to save your changes.

Windows loads the appropriate drivers from your Windows CD-ROM or disks and prompts you to reboot your computer. You now have the ability to share with both NetWare and Windows users installed on your workstation.

III

Deciding What To Share

When you have the correct drivers loaded into your system, you can begin thinking about what services you want your workstation to offer on the network. This section will describe the process of selecting resources to share and explain the steps to take to begin sharing them on the network.

Sharing Your Folders

Your hard drive may contain information that you want to make available to other users on the network, or your hard drive may be the largest one in the department, so your workstation is promoted to part-time server. In any case, if you have something to share on your workstation, you will want to learn how to make it available.

Let's assume a simple example that will illustrate the method of sharing folders on the network. Your workstation has a folder named DATA that contains some of your department's word processing documents and spreadsheets. Since your department is small, you do not have a dedicated server, so your workstation ends up as the departmental server.

You want to set up several folders that will contain information that can be accessed by various people in the department. So within the DATA folder, you also create a WP folder for all of the word processing documents, a BUD-GET folder that contains your department's budgeting information, and an OTHER folder that is used for miscellaneous files that are shared by users on the network.

To begin sharing these folders, follow these steps for each of the folders:

1. Double-click the My Computer icon on your desktop.

2. Select the drive on which the DATA folder resides.

3. Double-click the DATA folder to view the three folders that reside within it.

4. Right-click the WP folder. This displays a pop-up menu (see fig. 9.4).

5. Select the Sharing option. This displays a Properties sheet like the one shown in figure 9.5.

6. Select the Shared As option and fill in a short Share Name that will describe the contents. Windows will fill in the folder name, but you may change it. In this example, leave the share name as WP.

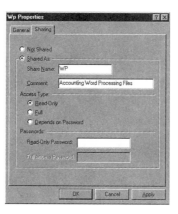

7. Fill in the Comment text box with a brief description of the folder.
In this example, the WP share will carry the comment **Accounting
Word Processing Files**.

8. Click the Full option under Access Type. This option gives your users
the ability to save or delete files within this folder. If you want to restrict access to certain folders for certain users, see the section, "Deciding How To Share," later in this chapter.

9. Click the OK button.

10. Repeat these steps for the other folders you want to share.

These steps provide the users on the network with access to three shared
folders. Figure 9.6 shows how the Explorer sees your shared folders from another workstation. Note that the left-hand column titled All Folders has the
Terminator server highlighted. On the right-hand column titled Contents of
'Terminator', the shared folders are shown. This is the same way that you see
and work with local folders through the Explorer.

III

Using Your New Network

Fig. 9.6
The Explorer shows the three shared folders from another user's perspective.

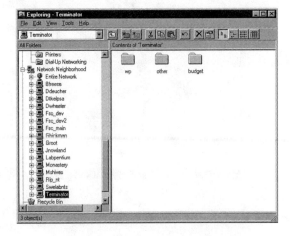

When you look at the icons shown in My Computer, you will notice that they have changed from plain folder icons to icons that show an arm holding the folder (see fig. 9.7). This icon indicates at a glance which of your folders are shared on the network.

Fig. 9.7
My Computer shows the shared folders as icons of an arm holding the folder.

CD-ROM Drives

Your computer may have a CD-ROM drive in it that you want to share with others on the network. Like many networks, some of the newer workstations will have local CD-ROM drives while many of the older workstations will not. Sharing your CD-ROM drive is similar to sharing a folder on your hard drive. The main difference is that you will be sharing the entire CD-ROM rather than a particular folder on that drive. As always, access to your CD-ROM drive can be password-protected to prevent unauthorized access. Security and passwords will be discussed later in this chapter in the "Deciding How To Share" section.

The steps for sharing a CD-ROM on the network are as follows:

1. Double-click the My Computer icon on your desktop.

2. Right-click the CD-ROM drive to display the pop-up menu.

3. Select the Sharing option from the pop-up menu to display the Properties sheet for the CD-ROM drive. This Properties sheet will look similar to the one in figure 9.5. Choose the Sharing tab.

4. Select the Shared As option.

5. Enter a short Share Name, such as **CD-ROM** in the Share Name text box.

6. Enter a longer description of the CD-ROM drive in the Comment text box. In this example, you may want to consider a description that indicates the speed of the CD-ROM drive. The comment **Double-speed CD-ROM drive** would be appropriate.

7. You can skip the Access Type section all together, assuming that sharing your CD-ROM drive raises no security issues. Since CD-ROMs are read-only, you will not need to assign full-access privileges to this shared drive. You may want to restrict access to your CD-ROM to certain users or lock out your shared CD-ROM altogether during a time when you need exclusive access to your CD-ROM. These security options are explained in more detail in the "Deciding How To Share" section later in this chapter.

8. Choose the OK button.

Users will see your CD-ROM drive as another shared folder in the Network Neighborhood and the Explorer.

Caution

Remember that a CD-ROM can be removed at any time. Unlike folders on your hard drive, you can only view one CD-ROM at a time. When your users need to share your drive with a different CD-ROM, make sure that no one is using the current CD-ROM before you pull it out of the drive.

III

Using Your New Network

Printers

Most networks will want to have a printer that is accessible to the workstations on the network. Windows provides the capability to share local printers in this fashion and to password-protect the access to these shared printers.

For example, many smaller networks or departmental workgroups only have one or two printers that are shared among the local network users. You may have been chosen to get the department's laser printer. Now you can share that printer with others in your department so they can take advantage of the laser's high-quality printing. Dot-matrix and bubble-jet printers can also be shared to allow your network users a choice when printing mailing labels or other documents in which your laser printer's quality and expense may not be best suited.

The steps involved in sharing a printer on the network are similar to those for sharing a hard drive. To share a locally installed printer, do the following:

1. Open the Start menu and choose Settings, Printers.

2. Right-click the printer that you want to share. You'll see a pop-up menu containing several options.

3. Select the Sharing option on the pop-up menu. This displays a Properties sheet (see fig. 9.8). Choose the Sharing tab.

Fig. 9.8
You can change the sharing options for your printer using this Properties sheet.

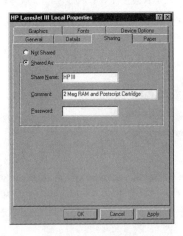

4. Select the Shared As option.

5. Enter a Share Name. This name should describe the printer that you are sharing. For example, the name **HP III** would be a good choice.

6. Enter a <u>C</u>omment. You should use the comment to describe any special features of your printer that others should know about. For example, you may want to add a comment like **2M RAM and Postscript Cartridge**.

7. Choose OK unless you need to restrict access to your printer. The next section, "Deciding How To Share," will explain the issues of security and your shared resources.

Once you have installed your shared printer, others on the network with the password can attach to it and print.

Caution

Remember that printers require the correct drivers to work properly. Others on your network will have to install the correct driver on their own workstations to print to your printer.

Deciding How To Share

This section describes how to restrict access to your shared resources. Since your workgroup network may be a part of a larger network, securing your resources is very important.

Since Windows allows you to manage security depending on which driver you have loaded, I explain how to administer your shared resources for both the Microsoft file and print services and the Novell file and print services.

Securing Access for Microsoft Resource Sharing

Sharing resources with other Microsoft Windows users is not as complex as sharing with Novell NetWare users. Windows implements the concepts of share-level security with the File and Printer Sharing for Microsoft Networks service. That means that each shared folder or printer can be assigned a password for one of two security modes: <u>R</u>ead-Only and <u>F</u>ull access.

■ The <u>R</u>ead-Only access security option allows users who have the correct password to browse folders, open files, and copy files from your shared folder. They cannot, however, make changes or delete the files or folders in your shared folder.

■ The Full access security option allows those with the correct password to use your workstation folder without restriction. This means that users can browse folders, open files, copy files, delete files and folders, or modify files in your shared folder.

Before you implement sharing security, make sure that you have read the section, "Deciding What To Share," earlier in this chapter. Follow these steps to change the security level of your shared folders:

1. Double-click My Computer.

2. Right-click the shared folder that you want to secure.

3. Select the Sharing option from the pop-up menu. You see a Properties sheet similar to the one in figure 9.9. Click the Sharing tab.

Fig. 9.9
This Properties sheet configures the security for your shared folders using share-level security.

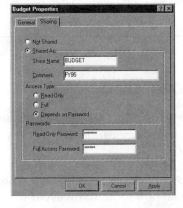

Tip
You may want to only secure Full access while allowing anyone to have Read-Only access. In that case, leave the Read-Only Password text box blank and fill in the Full Access Password text box.

4. Within the Access Type section of the Sharing page, you see three options: Read-Only, Full, and Depends on Password. Choose the Depends on Password option, which provides you with the most flexibility.

5. If you want to add a password for Read-Only access, enter one into the Read-Only Password text box. Similarly, enter a password into the Full Access Password text box if you want to secure read and write access to your folder.

6. Choose the OK button.

When users attach to your workstation now, they will be required to enter a password if you have set one up. If you secured both <u>R</u>ead-Only and <u>F</u>ull access, the user receives permissions to your folder depending on which password was used to gain access.

Securing Access for Novell NetWare Resource Sharing

If you have a Novell NetWare server on your network, you may choose to install the File and Printer Sharing for NetWare Networks as your network sharing service. This option gives you a great deal of flexibility when assigning permissions to folders on your workstation.

One of the biggest advantages of the NetWare sharing service is that you can allow DOS clients to access your workstation as if it was another NetWare server. The next section, "Catering to Your Clients," will discuss some of the implications of this type of sharing.

To set up NetWare security on your local shared folders, you must have already installed the File and Printer Services for NetWare networks. Once that network service is installed, follow these steps:

1. Double-click My Computer.

2. Right-click the shared folder that you want to secure.

3. Select the S<u>h</u>aring option from the pop-up menu. You see a Properties sheet similar to the one shown in figure 9.10. Click the Sharing tab.

Fig. 9.10
The Sharing page configures the security for your shared folders using user-level security.

4. Select the A<u>d</u>d button.

III

Using Your New Network

5. You will see an Add Users dialog box similar to the one shown in figure 9.11. From the list at the left, select the user or user group you want to grant access to, and choose the <u>R</u>ead-Only, <u>F</u>ull Access, or <u>C</u>ustom buttons. The <u>C</u>ustom access permissions are discussed later in this section.

Fig. 9.11

You can add users with different permissions to your shared folder.

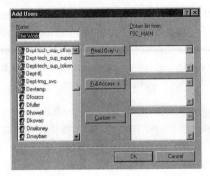

6. Choose the OK button.

Now the users that you have added to your folder security will be able to access the folder as you have specified. This method checks the users' security level against the server that you set up when you installed the File and Printer Services for NetWare.

The <u>C</u>ustom access button on the Add Users dialog box allows you to tailor access to a folder based on your needs. Figure 9.12 shows the Change Access Rights dialog box that lets you specify the custom options for restricting access to your shared folder. Most commonly, the custom access rights are assigned when straight Read-Only or Full access rights are insufficient. An example of this is when allowing users the ability to read and write to existing files but not to delete or create new ones. In this case, the [<u>R</u>]ead Files, [<u>W</u>]rite to Files, and List [<u>F</u>]iles options are selected. The List [<u>F</u>]iles option allows users to see the contents of the folder. The [<u>C</u>]reate Files and Folders, [<u>D</u>]elete Files, Change File A[<u>t</u>]tributes, and Change [<u>A</u>]ccess Control options would not be selected in this case.

Fig. 9.12
Custom options allow you to tailor specific permissions to a shared folder.

Catering to Your Clients

This section is primarily for users who want to set up the File and Print Services for NetWare users on DOS workstations. Remember, the DOS workstations are limited to the file name parameters of DOS. While this feature can be very powerful for your company, you should observe the following guidelines when setting up shared resources:

- Remember that DOS workstations will need to type in your server name and shared folder names, so keep them short.

- Avoid long file names when possible since DOS can only handle the eight-character name plus a three-character extension.

- Try to use only alphanumeric characters for your folders and files.

Exploring Performance Issues

After you have set up your workstation for sharing, you may notice some performance problems when others are using your resources. This section will briefly cover a few of the ways you can lessen the impact of the additional load of sharing your resources.

The Roles of Servers and Workstations

You should understand the two basic roles that your computer plays when it has to function as a peer-to-peer server on the network: your computer performs as a multiuser server and as a single-user workstation.

Your Computer as a Server

As a server, your computer must schedule time for network users to access the hard drive and printers along with the time that you need to run your

III

Using Your New Network

programs locally. Additionally, the network traffic and processor loads on your machine are much greater than if you were simply a single-user workstation.

If you plan on maintaining your computer as a peer-to-peer server, you should consider having extra RAM and hard drive space available for servicing network users. Also, a fast processor will help speed network requests while maintaining a good level of performance for your applications.

Your Computer as a Workstation

As a workstation, you normally have all of your computer's resources available for running applications. When you begin sharing these resources, you will diminish your ability to load applications and process data since you no longer are the only user on your machine. As a workstation that is sharing folders or printers, you should be aware of any heavy data processing that you will be performing. This will affect the network users who connect to your shared resources.

CD-ROM Sharing

When you are sharing a CD-ROM on the network, you should be aware that your actions, such as removing the CD-ROM from the drive, will affect anyone connected to your CD-ROM. But you should also be aware that some CD-ROM drives use a spin-down mode that, after a certain period of time, will stop the CD-ROM from rotating in the drive.

This is primarily a power-conservation tactic, but it will affect your CD-ROM sharing performance. Additionally, when your computer accepts a request for the CD-ROM that has spun down, your computer may hang for a second or two while the drive spins up again. This can affect your performance for your local applications and increase your frustration level.

DriveSpace Compression

DriveSpace compression is an excellent way to increase your available disk space. Unfortunately, that additional disk space comes with a performance penalty. Each time your computer reads or writes to its hard drive, DriveSpace decompresses or compresses the data that is being transferred. This is usually a small load on your computer when it is being used as a single-user workstation. However, under a moderate load from network users, you may experience significant performance degradation.

Use DriveSpace if you need to squeeze some extra space out of your hard drive, but you must also expect that performance will suffer.

Power-Saving Features

Power-saving features are found on most of today's computers. These features often include spinning down the hard drive and placing the CPU in a sleep state. Unfortunately for your network users, when your machine is in a sleep state, it must be awakened before any access can occur. This power-up time takes only a few seconds, but it will affect a network user's performance.

Troubleshooting Your Shared Resources

There are many things that can go wrong when sharing your folders or printers on the network. Here are a few common questions and their answers.

I have set up my workstation to share a folder, but no one can access my shared folder. What's wrong?

You may have set up a password within your sharing options. Make sure that your users know the password, or remove the password if it is unnecessary.

Some of the users who print to my printer get garbage printouts. Why?

Your users may be using the wrong printer driver for your printer. Make sure that they have set up the correct driver before they print.

My Novell DOS workstations cannot access my computer. Why not?

Make sure you have given your users appropriate permissions to access your folders. Also, make sure you have loaded the File and Printer Services for NetWare networks.

From Here...

Now that you are sharing your workstation's resources on the network, you'll want to take a look at some other networking topics that are covered in the following chapters:

- Chapter 10, "Setting Up for Remote Access," explains how to create a connection to a remote network through Windows.

- Chapter 12, "Networking with a Notebook," describes the various connectivity options that are available to use on your notebook computer on your network.

III

Using Your New Network

- Chapter 13, "Introduction to Electronic Mail," discusses Microsoft Exchange, which allows you to send and receive e-mail on your network.

- Chapter 17, "Connecting to the Internet," explores the methods of getting online with the world's largest network, the Internet.

Chapter 10

Setting Up for Remote Access

Connecting to a network from a remote location hasn't always been easy. If you were able to connect, it was usually with proprietary communications software providing the access point into the network. In other cases, you might have used a terminal emulation program to watch the output of a computer that you were controlling remotely. In most cases, you were able only to transfer files from the remote location to the network.

Windows 95, however, makes most connections considerably easier. You can remotely get at all your folders and files on your network with no problem. Windows has the ability to call into hosts like the Internet, Windows NT Servers, Shiva LanRovers, NetWare Connect servers, and many others. You'll be able to choose what type of connection to establish and how to dial the access numbers. Windows even gives you the ability to access printers, fax servers, and e-mail on the network. In some cases you'll be able to share your computer's resources with other users on the network.

Accessing a network from a remote location can be complex at times. Consequently, understanding what remote access is all about comes in handy.

In this chapter, you'll learn

- What remote access is
- What remote access lets you do
- How to set it up
- How to create a dial-up connection

What Is Remote Access?

To understand the ideas of remote access, let's briefly examine a traditional local area network (LAN). A network usually consists of two or more computers connected by some sort of cable. This cable allows the computers on the network to share information. Depending on your needs, this cable may be one of many types (see chapter 5, "Selecting the Right Network"). Adding a computer to a LAN is as simple as installing a network adapter into the computer and connecting the network cable. This can be done for as little as $200 in today's market.

> **Note**
>
> In some cases, computers have shed their umbilical cord to the network and gone wireless. These wireless networks transmit the information using radio waves. However, due to information security concerns, wireless networks are often implemented over distances no farther than the perimeter of a building.

Let's say you want to connect a home office, laptop, or notebook computer to the corporate network while away from the office. At the office, the network cable bandwidth is usually 10 megabits or greater. To reach the office network, you'll need to connect via a telephone company service. To match the office's 10 megabits, the telephone company can provide what is called a T3 line. A T3 line easily costs twice as much *per month* as the initial investment for a regular LAN connection.

T3 lines are designed to be a permanent link between two points. They frequently link many users between separate buildings or countries. Therefore, to dedicate a T3 line for a single workstation would be an inefficient use of financial and technical resources.

Let's also consider the typical amount of network traffic emanating from a single computer. Unless it's performing database work, only small pieces of information are occasionally sent to printers, file servers, fax servers, mail servers, and other networks. In the majority of the cases, a low-speed connection will usually do just fine. A low-speed connection (relatively speaking) is one made with a modem.

Therefore, remote access is the action of connecting with a modem and sharing information on a network that is not directly linked to the computer. In some cases, the home office, laptop, or notebook computer can even share its resources with computers on the remote network.

What Does Remote Access Let Me Do?

Remote access gives you many of the same capabilities as a network connection. Using remote access, you'll be able to access files from servers on the remote network, print documents on network printers, send faxes, and send and receive mail.

You'll also be able to connect to other public networks, such as the Internet. On the Internet, you'll have access to the World Wide Web, FTP servers, Internet Relay Chat (IRC) live discussion rooms, and newsgroups. You'll also be able to send electronic mail to any other person on the Internet. Once you've established the connection, read chapter 18, "Using Internet Services in Windows."

If you connect to a Windows NT 3.x Remote Access Server, you'll also be able to share the computer's resources with other computers on the remote network. For example, if you'd like to allow someone to print a document at your home for you to preview, you would share your printer. Or if you wanted your assistant to place some files on your computer while you checked your electronic mail, you would share your hard drive for others to access.

If you are charged with the responsibility of managing a network, you'll be able to monitor the activity on the server and change access privileges by using the NetWatcher application (provided with Windows). If you install the Remote Registry service on both computers, you'll be able to monitor the remote server performance using the System Monitor.

Now that you know a little about remote access, let's set up your computer to access the remote network.

How Do I Set It Up?

Setting up your computer to access a remote network can be very easy if you proceed thoughtfully. You need to add the optional Dial-Up Networking component of Windows. You'll also need to install a modem and the appropriate drivers from Windows. Finally, you'll add a dial-up account for each remote access server you plan to call.

III

Using Your New Network

Setting Up a Remote Connection

The first step towards accessing a remote network is to add the Dial-Up Networking component of Windows. Once installed, you'll be able to create dial-up accounts. If you chose the Portable configuration when you installed Windows, it's likely that Dial-Up Networking is already installed. You can quickly check by double-clicking My Computer on the desktop. If the Dial-Up Networking folder is displayed, as in figure 10.1, you're already ahead of the game. Your next step is to set up a modem.

Fig. 10.1

If the Dial-Up Networking folder is visible in My Computer, setting up a modem is the next step.

If Dial-Up Networking doesn't show up in My Computer, you'll need to install the component. Using your Windows installation disks or CD-ROM, perform the following steps:

1. Open the Start menu and choose Settings, Control Panel.

2. Double-click the Add/Remove Programs icon in Control Panel (see fig. 10.2).

3. Select the Windows Setup tab in the Add/Remove Programs Properties sheet. Select Communications from the Components list box. Select Details to view the optional Communications-related components of Windows (see fig. 10.3). The Communications dialog box appears.

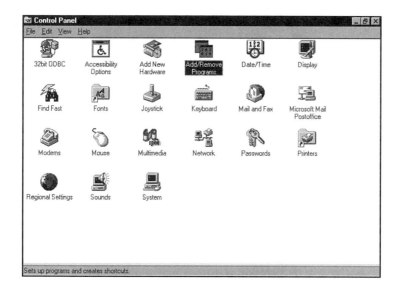

Fig. 10.2
Double-click the
Add/Remove
Programs icon to
access the Add/
Remove Programs
Properties sheet.

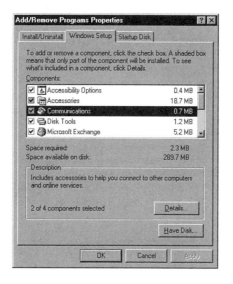

Fig. 10.3
Selecting Details
will display the
optional Commu-
nications compo-
nents of Windows.

4. By default, Windows installed only the HyperTerminal and Phone Dialer. You'll have to place a checkmark next to Dial-Up Networking in
the Communications Components list box (see fig. 10.4). Click OK to
continue. From the Add/Remove Program Properties sheet, click OK to
install the Dial-Up Networking component.

III

Using Your New Network

Fig. 10.4
Select Dial-Up
Networking
from the Compo-
nents box list to
install it.

You'll be prompted to insert disks from your Windows installation disks or CD-ROM. Once you do so, a dialog box appears letting you know the files are being copied to your system's hard drive.

> **Note**
>
> At the end of the installation process, you'll be prompted to restart your computer. You won't be able to access any dial-up connections until you do so.

5. Select OK to restart your computer. This prepares your system to use Dial-Up Networking. As your system restarts, one or more small dialog boxes will flash by too fast to see them. These are reporting that shortcuts are being added to the Start menu under Programs, Accessories.

> **Caution**
>
> If you've configured your computer to dual-boot, be sure you select the option to boot Windows 95. If you boot the previous version of DOS or Windows, the final adjustments won't be made until your computer restarts in Windows 95 mode.

Once your machine has restarted, you've completed the first step towards accessing a remote network. You'll need to tell Windows which modem you plan to use to connect to that remote network. The next section leads you through the process of identifying the modem and selecting the communications port.

Setting Up a Modem

To access the remote network, you'll need to define a modem as part of your Windows configuration. You can use an internal or external modem. If you aren't sure your modem has been configured to work with Windows 95, right-click My Computer on the desktop. Select Properties from the pop-up menu. Select the Device Manager tab in the System Properties sheet.

If your modem is not listed under the Modem device type or the Modem device type does not exist, you'll need to add your modem (see fig. 10.5).

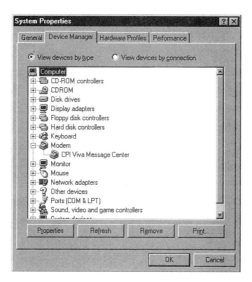

Fig. 10.5

If a modem is already installed, it is listed on the Device Manager tab of the System Properties sheet under the Modem device type.

By following these steps, you'll install a new modem:

1. If your modem is an internal model, follow the manufacturer's instructions to install it. If it's an external model, don't forget to plug in the power adapter. In either case, don't forget to run the phone cable from the wall jack to the modem.

2. Open the Start menu and choose Settings, Control Panel.

3. Double-click the Modems icon. If this is the first modem you're adding, go to step 6. If you already have a modem configured and you're adding another one, select Add (see fig. 10.6).

Fig. 10.6
If you're adding a
second modem,
select Add to
configure your
new hardware.

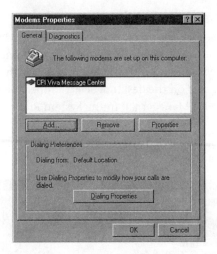

> **Note**
>
> You may be tempted at this point to use the Add New Hardware Wizard
> instead. While that's a logical choice, using the Install New Modem Wizard is
> faster. The Add New Hardware Wizard scans your entire system for new hard-
> ware. The Install New Modem Wizard goes by very quickly because it's only
> searching the communication ports.

4. The first dialog box of the Install New Modem Wizard appears (see fig.
   10.7). It's usually best to let Windows try to detect your new modem
   because the program is preconfigured with hundreds of models. Clicking Next causes Windows to scan your communication ports for modems. If you want to select the modem on your own, click Don't Detect
   My Modem; I Will Select It from a List.

Fig. 10.7
If you don't want
Windows to
detect your
modem, mark the
checkbox.

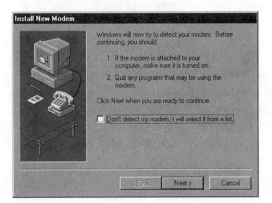

5. As shown in figure 10.8, if the Install New Modem Wizard found a modem on a COM port, it shows you what make and model it found and on which COM port.

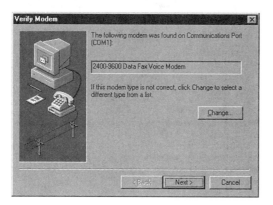

Fig. 10.8
If the Install New Modem Wizard found a modem on a COM port, it displays the result. If it's incorrect, select Change.

If the Install New Modem Wizard didn't select the right make and model for your modem, select Change to manually specify the new modem. From the Install New Modem dialog box, shown in figure 10.9, select from the available Manufacturers and Models. If you have a disk from the manufacturer with a Windows driver, insert the floppy in the drive and select Have Disk. Select OK in the Install New Modem dialog box to continue.

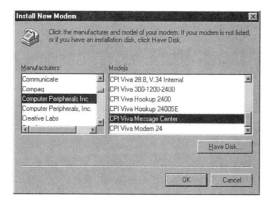

Fig. 10.9
Select the manu-facturer and model from the dialog box, or select Have Disk if the manu-facturer sent a Windows driver with the modem.

III

Using Your New Network

6. If this is the first modem you're adding to Windows 95, you'll be prompted for some information about your current location. The Loca-tion Information dialog box needs to know the country you're in; your area (or city) code; what number, if any, you have to dial to access an outside line; and whether the phone system at your location uses tone or pulse dialing (see fig. 10.10).

Fig. 10.10
Location information is required to complete the modem installation.

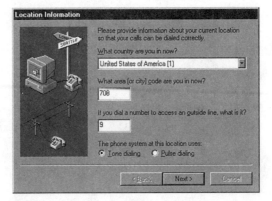

Click Next to display the last dialog box of the Install New Modem Wizard. When complete, select Finish to complete the installation.

7. The Modem Properties sheet is displayed at the end of the installation process. The default values for the modem properties should be acceptable. Click OK to close the Modem Properties sheet.

Your Windows 95 software components and hardware configuration are ready for you to create a dial-up account. Read the next section to learn how to create one.

Creating Dial-Up Connections

Defining a dial-up connection is the last step to establishing a connection with a remote network. Before you attempt to set up the link to the remote network, you should contact the administrator of the desired remote access server. You need to know the type of remote access server that your computer will be communicating with. The server should be one of the following:

■ PPP Server   One like Windows NT 3.5 Server or an Internet provider.

■ NRN Server   A NetWare Connect server is a good example of this type.

■ Windows for Workgroups or Windows NT 3.1 Server   A server that often uses NetBEUI to communicate.

■ SLIP Server   A server that uses the SLIP protocol to communicate by way of the TCP/IP protocol.

Once you've determined the server type, you'll need to determine if your
LAN has a network protocol that is compatible with the protocols supported
by Windows. Use table 10.1 to determine which protocols are required to
connect to the desired server.

Table 10.1 Supported Combinations of Server Types, Communication Protocols, and Network Protocols To Access a Remote Network

Host Type	Communication Protocol	Network Protocol(s)	Remote Computer Can Share Its Own Resources?
Internet, PPP server, Windows 95, Windows NT 3.x, Shiva LanRover, NetWare	PPP	IPX, NetBEUI, TCP/IP	Yes
Internet, UNIX, SLIP	SLIP, CSLIP	TCP/IP	No
Windows 95, Windows NT 3.x, Windows for Workgroups 3.11, LAN Manager	RAS	NetBEUI	Yes
NetWare Connect	NetWare Connect	IPX	No
Direct Cable Connection	Serial, Parallel	PPP	No

For example, let's say you have a Windows computer on the road and you
want to connect to your Novell NetWare server at work to access files. The
dial-up server at work is a Windows NT 3.5 Server running Remote Access
Services. Table 10.1 shows you'll need to use a PPP communication protocol
with an IPX network protocol to access the NetWare server.

You'll use these pieces of information to guide you through the following
steps to create a dial-up connection:

1. Verify that you have the required network protocol installed. You can
   do this by right-clicking the Network Neighborhood icon on your desktop and selecting Properties from the pop-up menu. In the Network
   Properties sheet, scroll through the installed network components to
   verify that the correct protocol is part of your current configuration.

III

Using Your New Network

> **Note**
>
> If the protocol doesn't appear in this list, you must install it. See chapter 7, "Setting Up a Windows Network."

Tip

If you haven't already installed the Dial-Up Networking component, see "How Do I Set It Up?" previously in this chapter.

2. Open the Start menu and choose Programs, Accessories, Dial-Up Networking. When the Dial-Up Networking folder opens, double-click the Make New Connection icon. This starts the Make New Connection Wizard.

3. In the Make New Connection Wizard dialog box, enter a name for the computer that you are dialing (see fig. 10.11). Then choose Select a Modem. Only those modems you've previously configured on this computer are listed. Select Configure to check or modify the properties of the selected modem. If you do select Configure, you'll see the same Modem Properties sheet that appeared when you installed the modem. When you're ready to move to the next step, select Next.

Fig. 10.11
Enter a descriptive name and select a modem when connecting to the access server.

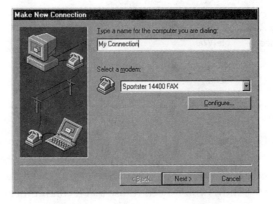

4. To identify where your host can be reached, enter the Area Code, Telephone Number, and Country Code (see fig. 10.12). Windows uses the area code and country code to create the correct dialing string. By clicking Next, the final dialog box for the Make New Connection Wizard appears. To complete the first phase of your configuration, click Finish.

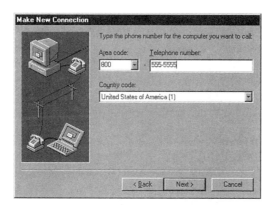

Fig. 10.12
Enter only the area code, telephone number, and country code of the Dial-Up Networking connection.

5. Once you have named the connection and specified a modem, you must specify the type of server that you're going to connect to. Open the Connection Properties sheet of the connection you want to configure. To do this, access the Dial-Up Networking folder by opening the Start menu and choosing Programs, Accessories, Dial-Up Networking. Then right-click the desired connection name and select Properties from the pop-up menu.

6. From the Connection Properties sheet, you'll want to select the Server Type to specify the specific server type for this connection. The Server Types dialog box appears (see fig. 10.13).

Tip
When you enter these values, don't try to take into account your location by entering long-distance and outside-line codes, credit card numbers, or area codes. You may define these local settings when installing the modem.

Fig. 10.13
Choose the type of server that you're going to connect to.

From the Server Types dialog box, choose the Type of Dial-Up Server to which you're going to connect by clicking and holding the scrollable arrow. You have the following options:

- NRN NetWare Connect

- PPP: Windows 95, Windows NT 3.5, Internet

- Windows for Workgroups and Windows NT 3.1

> **Note**
>
> Note that the options and allowed network protocols change with each server type. For example, using NRN NetWare Connect, the only advanced option is Log On to Network. The only network protocol allowed is IPX/SPX Compatible. For Advanced options, Windows allows certain activities for the selected connection.

- Log On to Network   When the connection is made to the remote access server, Windows attempts to log on to the network with the user name and password that you used when you started your computer.

- Enable Software Compression   If both sides of the connection support compression, the data is compressed before being sent over the connection to increase the transmission speed.

- Require Encrypted Password   If both sides of the connection support encryption, Windows encrypts the password you use for increased security against intrusion.

7. Windows also permits you to limit the network protocols transmitted over the connection. You can set the connection to use or restrict NetBEUI, IPX/SPX, or TCP/IP protocols. If the host supports TCP/IP, you can specify additional settings for dynamic or manual TCP/IP configuration. As shown in figure 10.14, you can manually configure or allow the remote access server to

- Assign an IP address

- Assign a name server address

- Use IP header compression to speed up the connection

- Use the default gateway on the remote network

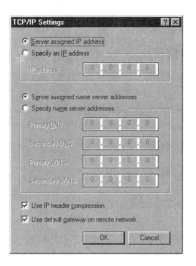

Fig. 10.14
If the remote
access server
supports TCP/IP,
additional
configuration
options can be
specified.

> **Note**
>
> Not all remote access servers support all the options. Unless these settings are correct, your connection may not work. Be sure to contact the administrator of the dial-up server for the correct values for all fields.

8. Once you've modified the settings to your liking, save your changes by selecting OK on each dialog box until you return to the Dial-Up Networking folder.

Now that you've defined the dial-up connection for remote access, you're ready to make the call. Chapter 11, "Using Remote Access," shows you how to initiate the connection and use Remote Access to its fullest.

Troubleshooting Your Remote Connection

If you're having problems installing the modem, try these suggestions:

- If it's an external modem, verify that the power adapter has been plugged into both the wall and the modem.

- On every modem, verify that the phone cable is strung between the wall jack and the line jack on the modem. Often, modems have two phone jacks: one for the phone line to the wall and another for a telephone. If the cables in these two jacks are reversed, the modem won't be able to access the outside line.

III

Using Your New Network

- From the Diagnostics page on the Modems Properties sheet, select the port from the list that you suspect is not working. Then select <u>M</u>ore Info to verify that you can communicate with the modem. Selecting this option begins a series of tests to check the responses of certain commands sent to the modem. If the Highest Speed shows No Response in the Port Information section of the More Info dialog box, the computer is not able to establish a connection with the modem. Check the IRQ, I/O port, and serial cable (if external) for conflicts or damage.

- Make sure that you attached the external modem to the right COM port.

- If you've chosen to use hardware flow control, verify that the serial cable for your external modem supports hardware flow control. If it doesn't, switch to software flow control instead.

From Here...

In this chapter, you've learned what remote access is, what you can do with it, how to set up a modem, and how to create a dial-up connection to establish the communication link. You're set to make the call to the remote access server. Chapter 11, "Using Remote Access," shows you how to make the connection. The following are some related topics you might want to review:

- Chapter 3, "Welcome to the World of Networks," tells you what a network is and what the different type of networks can do for you.

- Chapter 7, "Setting Up a Windows Network," shows you how to install network adapters and software network components such as clients, services, and protocols.

- Chapter 8, "Using the Network Neighborhood," tells you how to find network resources once you've made the connection to the remote network.

- Chapter 9, "Sharing Network Hardware," shows you how to share your resources with other computers on the remote network.

- Chapter 15, "Working with Microsoft Exchange," leads you through the steps to send and receive mail using Microsoft Exchange.

- Chapter 17, "Connecting to the Internet," teaches you the special circumstances to connect via a TCP/IP protocol.

Chapter 11

Using Remote Access

In chapter 10, "Setting Up for Remote Access," you learned how to install and set up a remote network connection using Windows Remote Access Service. Since getting connected is only part of the process, this chapter covers the effective usage of a remote network connection.

Remote networking involves many factors which are not apparent to locally connected computers, such as connection costs, extended transfer times, and network access security. By reviewing the topics in this chapter, you learn how to minimize your costs of connecting remotely and maximize your security, throughput, and functionality of your remote connection.

In this chapter, you learn how to

- Connect to remote disks and folders

- Connect to remote printers

- Manage your application and file access from remote servers

- Use Windows security and compression when connecting to a remote server

Connecting to a Remote Network

When connecting to a remote network, Windows uses the modem to act as a network adapter. This connection allows the networking functions within the Network Neighborhood and the Explorer to operate is if they were connected to the network locally. To Windows, your computer appears to be on the local area network even though you may be thousands of miles away.

Since the Network Neighborhood and the Explorer can't tell the difference, you may be tempted to use the network as if you were locally connected.

However, while the functionality may be the same, the speed and cost of the connection are much different and must be factored into the decisions you make while connecting remotely to your network.

Making the Connection

After creating a dial-up network connection, as discussed in the section "Creating Dial-Up Connections" in chapter 10, let's go through the steps to connect to a remote host. This chapter uses the example of a dial-up connection called Work (see fig. 11.1).

Fig. 11.1
The Work icon indicates a dial-up connection to your remote network.

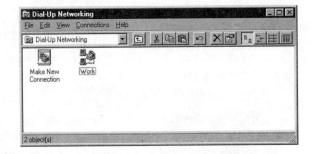

To initiate the connection to the remote network, follow these steps:

1. Open the Start menu and choose Programs, Accessories, Dial-Up Networking. When the Dial-Up Networking folder opens (refer to fig. 11.1), double-click the icon that represents your remote network connection. In this example, it is the Work icon.

2. The Connect To dialog box appears (see fig. 11.2). Verify that the phone number and user name is correct.

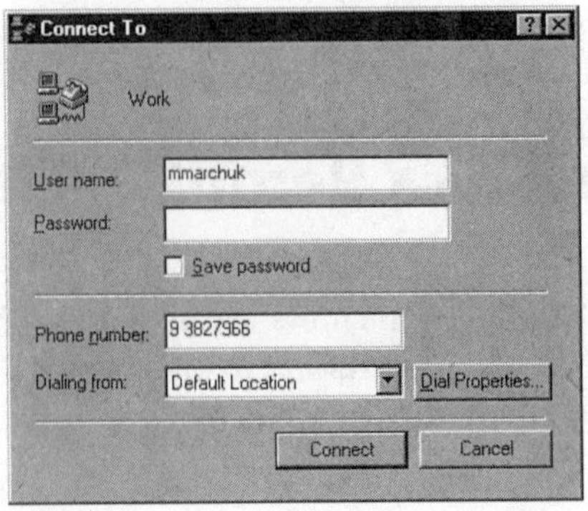

Fig. 11.2
Verify your information and enter your password to connect to a remote network.

3. Type in your password in the Password text box. This is the password that has been established for you on the remote access server. If you want to save this password and user name combination in your Windows password file, mark the Save Password checkbox.

4. Check the location in the Dialing From text box. If you are not dialing from the location indicated, you may need to set up special dialing codes that account for outside line access, long distance access, or credit-card numbers. See the next section, "Changing Your Location," which explains how to configure your dialing locations.

5. Choose the Connect button.

At this point, your modem initializes and dials the remote server that you have set up. The connection also validates your password and other security options that your server controls. Some of these security options are explained in the "Security" section found later in this chapter. Once you have connected, you see a dialog box like the one shown in figure 11.3.

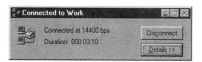

Looking at the dialog box, you'll notice a Details button. By choosing this button, your dialog box expands to look like the one shown in figure 11.4.

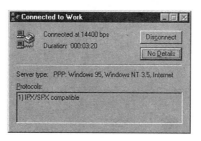

You may need to know about which protocols you are using to help trouble-shoot the connection to your network if something is not working. See the "Troubleshooting" section at the end of this chapter for more information. To remove this extra information from the dialog box, choose the No Details button.

Fig. 11.3
Your remote access connection indicates the connection speed and the duration of your call.

Fig. 11.4
The Details button shows which protocols your connection is using with the remote network.

III

Using Your New Network

Once you are connected, you may minimize the connection dialog box until you want to end your call by choosing the Dis_connect button on the connection dialog box.

Changing Your Location

Since you may be accessing a remote network using a notebook computer that travels with you between sales calls or meetings, you may need to reconfigure your location setup to work properly. This section explains the various options for configuring your locations to work with Dial-Up Networking.

To configure another location, follow steps 1–3 listed in the previous "Making the Connection" section. When you see the Connect To dialog box shown in figure 11.2, you'll be at the right starting point to configure a new location. Now follow these steps to create a new location called Hotel.

1. From the Connect To dialog box, choose the _Dial Properties button. This displays the Dialing Properties sheet (see fig. 11.5).

Fig. 11.5
The Dialing Properties sheet allows you to change the configurations for your location.

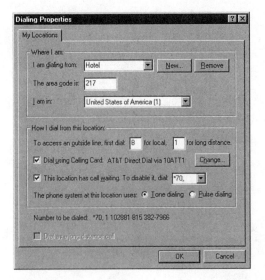

2. Choose the _New button found in the Where I Am section.

3. Select a name for your new location. For this example, the new location is called Hotel because many people may be accessing their networks from a hotel room while on a sales trip.

4. Enter the area code for your location.

5. If you are calling from outside of the United States, choose the country that you are calling from.

6. Most hotels have phone systems that require a special code to access an outside line or a long distance line. Check with your hotel clerk to see what these codes are and enter them in the How I Dial from This Location section.

7. If you are using a calling card, mark the Dial Using Calling Card checkbox and change or verify the card number by choosing the Change button.

8. If the location has call waiting, you want to disable this feature to prevent data loss or a disconnection if another call comes in while you are on the phone.

9. Verify which type of dialing mechanism the phone system uses to dial. Most phone systems use Tone Dialing; however, older phone systems and some foreign countries use Pulse Dialing. Pick up the phone and press a number to see which dialing mechanism you need to use.

10. If the call is long distance, mark the Dial as a Long Distance Call checkbox to allow Windows to include the long distance code you entered in step 6.

11. Choose OK to save this new location.

Now you can use this new location setup when dialing into your network; Windows handles the various dialing parameters to make sure your call gets connected.

Sharing Remote Disks and Folders

Using the Network Neighborhood, you can explore the servers available on a remote network in much the same way as you could if you were locally connected. The Work connection can be used to show how to see remote servers and their shared resources using the Remote Access Service.

The following steps show you how to connect to a remote server and copy a file from one of its folders to your local hard drive:

◄ See "Connecting to Network Resources," p. 122

1. Initiate a connection to the Work network by following the steps outlined in the section "Making the Connection."

2. Once you are connected, minimize the connection dialog box.

3. Double-click the Network Neighborhood icon located on your desktop. Windows starts searching for network servers, remote and local. Finding the remote servers may take a few minutes since the connection to you is much slower than a local area network.

4. The available servers are displayed in the Network Neighborhood window.

5. Double-click the particular server you are attaching to in the Network Neighborhood window. This displays the available server volumes.

Tip
Remember that larger files may take a very long time to copy to your hard drive. When Windows estimates the time to copy the file, you can always cancel the copy process if you don't want to wait.

6. Click this file and drag it onto your desktop. This initiates the file copy procedure from the server to your local machine.

Earlier in this section, it was mentioned that the Network Neighborhood and the Explorer react basically the same way they do on a machine that was attached to a local area network. The differences in the functionality of the network connectivity rest with the protocols and drivers that may be needed to connect to a remote server.

For example, any non-native network drivers such as Artisoft's LANtastic or IBM's LAN Server, may not work over the modem connection. This is because of the way that these network drivers are installed. Non-native network drivers sit external to Windows, although Windows can still access them. However, some of these non-native network drivers must be installed exclusively. That means that no other network drivers can be loaded. If you have an Artisoft LANtastic network, you cannot also load the Microsoft Client for NetWare networks.

◀ See "Configuring Network Support," p. 100

Servers that require these non-native drivers cannot use the Windows-native modem adapter for remote access since they are external to Windows. To ensure that you can connect to a remote network, use a Windows-native network driver.

> **Caution**
>
> NetWare users who use the NetWare 4.1 VLM drivers for access to NetWare Directory Services cannot access the network from a remote location because these drivers are not native to Windows. Obtain the native NetWare drivers from Novell to allow remote connectivity through Remote Access Service.

Sharing Remote Printers

Remote printers work similarly to printers connected over a local area net-work. When you are connected to your remote network, you can print to the network printers that you have access to as if you were locally connected. Keep in mind the printing process takes much longer than if you were locally connected. A one-page Word document with an embedded logo may only take up 50K on the hard drive but may require 500K to print the fonts and graphics on the page.

In addition to printing while you are connected to your remote network, there is a feature that allows you to print to a network printer even though you are disconnected. To use this deferred printing feature follow these steps:

1. Open the Start menu and choose <u>S</u>ettings, Printers.

2. Right-click the network printer that you want to print to while you are not connected. Figure 11.6 shows the pop-up menu that appears during this step.

Fig. 11.6
The pop-up menu allows you to configure the deferred printing option.

3. Select the <u>W</u>ork Offline option from the menu.

This instructs Windows to capture any print jobs that you send to this printer and hold them locally until Windows can attach to the printer. Then all pending print jobs will be sent to the remote network printer.

◀ See "Printers," p. 144

Caution

When Windows connects to the remote printer and begins sending the print jobs, your connection to the remote network may become very sluggish. If you know that you have pending print jobs, you may want to wait until after the print jobs have been sent before you begin any other remote network activity.

III

Using Your New Network

Using Fax Modems

You may want to send a fax from your remote location by using the fax server on your network. This can be done as easily as printing to a network printer, described in the previous section.

When sending a fax through a remote network fax server, remember that the transmission of the file or files to the fax server may take longer than if you had sent the fax from your location. Fax processing may be more efficient locally if you have the capabilities through your local modem.

Accessing E-Mail

You may use a remote E-Mail package such as cc:Mail Remote to call into your mail server and retrieve messages. With Windows Dial-Up Networking, you will be able to use the local area network version of cc:Mail to manage your messages.

If you are using other mail packages that do not specifically have remote access options, this may be the only method for retrieving mail remotely. In either case, the remote network connection opens up your remote connection to basically the same options you would have if you were locally connected. You can send and receive e-mail as if you were at the home office.

If you want to create e-mail to send when you get back to your office or send a fax using Microsoft Exchange, you'll need to read through this section to verify that all the options are set correctly for remote computing.

To install Microsoft Exchange as part of remote computing, follow these steps:

1. Connect your laptop to the network. The Microsoft Exchange client must be able to communicate directly with the postoffice to complete the installation.

2. Open the Start menu and choose Settings, Control Panel.

3. Once the Control Panel window appears, double-click the Add/Remove Programs icon. The Add/Remove Programs Properties sheet appears.

4. Click the Windows Setup tab to access the optional components of Windows 95.

5. In the Components list box, mark the checkbox next to Microsoft Exchange (see fig. 11.7). Click OK at the bottom of the dialog box to begin the installation.

During this time, Windows displays the progress of installation and updating of the shortcuts. Once complete, you will be returned to the Control Panel window.

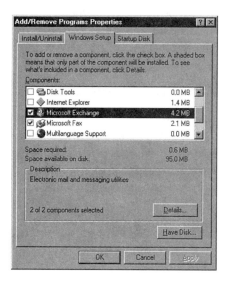

Fig. 11.7
Microsoft Exchange is added via the Windows Setup tab of the Add/Remove Programs Properties sheet.

6. Once the Exchange client is installed, you need to modify its properties for remote computing. To do this in Control Panel, double-click on the Mail and Fax icon. This displays the MS Exchange Settings Properties sheet.

7. From the Services tab, double-click the Microsoft Mail information service to be used for remote computing on your laptop. The Microsoft Mail dialog box appears (see fig. 11.8).

Fig. 11.8
The selected information service displays its Connection properties.

III

Using Your New Network

8. Enter the location of the postoffice in the text box at the top of the Connection page. If you aren't sure where it is, click the Browse button to search for it.

9. Choose Automatically Sense LAN or Remote. Since you'll probably set up this information service only once, choosing this option gives you the most flexibility in the long term. In any case, if Windows can't figure out which mode you're in, it will present you with a choice.

When you choose Automatically Sense LAN or Remote, Windows uses its capability to sense the correct choice of the three other options.

Selecting the Local Area Network (LAN) option causes Exchange to expect to find the postoffice using a network interface card or the Direct Cable Connection. It also includes the configuration choices you make on the LAN Configuration page in this dialog box.

Clicking Remote Using a Modem and Dial-Up Networking causes Exchange to look for the database over the dial-up connection. It also uses the configuration choices in Remote Configuration, Remote Session, and Dial-Up Networking pages.

However, if you know the laptop will never directly connect to a local area network, then choose Remote Using a Modem and Dial-Up Networking.

10. On the Remote Configuration page, make sure to select Use Remote Mail and Use Local Copy (see fig. 11.9). Use Remote Mail allows you to store your mail until you're ready to send it. Use Local Copy allows you to download a complete copy of the main Postoffice Address List to your computer. You'll need this list to address your messages while you're on the road.

11. Click OK to save your changes. Click OK in the MS Exchange Settings Properties sheet to finalize your settings.

12. From the Inbox dialog box, choose Tools, Microsoft Mail Tools, Download Address Lists. This places a copy of the main Postoffice Address list on your computer.

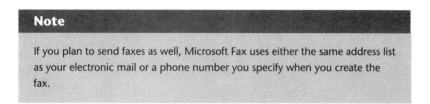

Note

If you plan to send faxes as well, Microsoft Fax uses either the same address list as your electronic mail or a phone number you specify when you create the fax.

13. Click OK to save your changes.

Fig. 11.9
Selecting Use Local Copy allows you to download a copy of the main Postoffice Address list.

As you can see, Exchange makes it easier to manage your mail from a remote location. For more information on Exchange, see chapter 15, "Working with Microsoft Exchange."

Remote Access Issues

While dialing up a remote network may open a new opportunity for connectivity, it also presents many potentially problematic issues. These issues are discussed in this section to apprise you of the pitfalls and options you have to make you remote connections smoother.

III

Using Your New Network

Security

Many small companies do not institute much security on their local area networks because a thief would have to physically break into the office to steal information or do damage to the systems. By using the dial-up capabilities, you also provide an open door to your systems for thieves and vandals. To protect against data loss or theft, you want to encourage the use of security measures both on the local area network as well as for the dial-up connections.

When using any of the dial-up servers that Windows Remote Access supports, there are many options for configuring security. These can range from simple user name and password challenges to encrypted packets, periodic system verification, and dial-back security.

To demonstrate two of the most common options, the Work connection used earlier is revisited. This time, the server that handles the dial-up connection requires user name and passwords as well as a dial-back option. Figure 11.10 shows the User Logon dialog box that appears when dialing into a Windows NT Remote Access Server.

Fig. 11.10

A Windows NT Remote Access Server that is configured for security prompts you for a user name and password if you do not enter one when dialing up a remote network.

The server is set up to manage dial-back numbers based on the authenticated user name provided. Once the server verifies that the password is correct for a particular user, the system will look up the dial-back number in its local table, hang up on the caller, and then dial the remote system at the phone number provided in the database. This ensures that the user who called is accessing the system from an acceptably secure workstation.

But you may be wondering about the hotel from which you called in another example provided in this chapter. What happens when the user may be on the road in different hotels or offices? Most systems also provide an option that lets the user specify the phone number at which their system can be reached for dial-back. While this may not be as secure as the pre-defined dial-back number, it allows system administrators the ability to audit their dial-up systems to catch possibly suspicious trends. Figure 11.11 shows the Convenience Callback dialog box that appears when dialing into a Windows NT Remote Access Server configured for dial-back security that allows the user to enter a phone number.

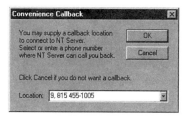

Fig. 11.11
A Windows NT Remote Access Server that is configured for dial-back security can prompt the user to enter the phone number where their system can be reached.

This mechanism of security is often an additional layer of security that prevents hackers from accessing data on the network. The network servers still maintain their own security, but now to even access the network you need a password.

Connect Time

Unlike local area networks, a remote connection has an additional cost for accessing the network. The phone charges from remote locations like a hotel may be very expensive. Some hotels may charge very high long-distance charges when dialing from the room. For example, accessing your e-mail from a hotel may cost a few dollars of connection time. Table 11.1 shows an average interaction by a user at a remote location.

Table 11.1 The Cost of an Average Remote Access Connection		
Activity	**Time To Complete (Minutes:Seconds)**	**Cost at 25 cents/ minute[1]**
Connect and log on to the network	1:00	$0.25
Connect to mail server	1:15	$0.31
Read two mail messages and respond	7:30	$1.88
Access customer data files	10:00	$2.50

(continues)

III

Using Your New Network

	Table 11.1 Continued	
Activity	**Time To Complete (Minutes:Seconds)**	**Cost at 25 cents/ minute[1]**
Send customer quote document to order entry	2:45	$0.69
Retrieve new daily-schedule document	1:30	$0.38
Total connection	24:00	$6.00

[1]*Costs are estimates and actual costs may vary. Connection speed is at 14.4Kb/s.*

By reviewing table 11.1, you'll see that if a company has many remote access users, it can be quite expensive. To offset this expense, it may be possible to implement the dial-back security option as a cost-savings device. Most companies have a volume discount calling plan for long-distance calls. The rate at which this call is charged may be significantly lower than the rates charged by a hotel. In order to use dial-back security for this, the hotel must also support direct-room dialing. This allows the remote access server to dial back to the user's computer properly. If the hotel requires a call to be processed through the front desk, you cannot use this option.

Transfer Speed

The transfer speed issue is very apparent when you try to do anything on the remote network. Browsing through the Network Neighborhood or the Explorer takes much longer and copying files may take from minutes to hours depending on the speed of your modem connection and the quality of the phone lines.

Consider the following scenarios shown in table 11.2 which involve a single file transfer between a remote network server and the local user's machine.

	Table 11.2 Modem Speeds Directly Affect Transfer Times and Costs	
Modem speed[1]	**Time To transfer a 200K Word file (Minutes:Seconds)**	**Cost at 25 cents/ minute[1]**
9.6Kb/s	3:10	$0.79
14.4Kb/s	2:07	$0.53
28.8Kb/s	1:03	$0.26

[1]*Costs are estimates and actual costs may vary. Modem speed using no compression options. Transfer time assumes 90% efficiency of transfer rate because of line conditions and transmission protocols.*

Based on table 11.2, faster modem speed translates to faster transfer times and less expensive transfer costs. Depending on the amount of data transferred, it may justify the expenditure for a faster modem to reduce the cost of copying the data across the modem.

Application Access

Many companies load applications on a server to accomplish several goals. First, loading applications onto a server allows the applications to be upgraded to newer versions quickly for all users. Additionally, the hard-disk space used by many applications is better taken up once by the server rather than used by every workstation. Also, many companies meter their application usage to avoid purchasing too many copies of software. When someone runs a program, the meter verifies that the company has enough licenses for all of the users currently running the program and then lets the new user start the application.

When connecting to a network from a remote location, you may want to have access to the same applications that are available to you when you are locally attached. If you try running software across the remote network link, you will find out why this is not a preferred option. For example, if you run Microsoft Word from a server, your local machine has to pull the executable from the server and any additional files required to load the program. In the case of Microsoft Word 6 for Windows, this means that around 3.4M must be transferred over the connection to start the program, which requires a 28.8Kb/s modem 18 minutes to accomplish. To add another element of frustration to this scenario, Windows does not provide you with an estimated time of completion dialog box like it did when you copied a file from a remote server. You just sit in front of the machine waiting for the program to start. Obviously, this is not a good choice for a remotely connected workstation.

It is recommended that any applications you use frequently should be installed locally on your machine. This reduces the loading time, the connection time, and your frustration time when working outside of the office—not to mention cutting costs. Many licenses permit you to have the software installed on more than one machine as long as you only use one of the machines at a time.

III

Using Your New Network

> **Caution**
>
> Before assuming anything about your software license, read it and make sure you understand its conditions. Each package may have different requirements to meet the multiple machine installation allowance. If you have questions about your software licensing agreements, call the manufacturer of your software.

Port Contention

Local area networks usually have network hardware called hubs that connect the workstations together. These network hubs have a number of ports on them into which the individual workstations are connected. When there are no more ports left on a network hub, no more workstations can be added without adding another hub.

With dial-up networking, the network hubs are really the dial-up servers that accept the phone calls through the attached modems. However, the number of dial-up ports is not made on a one-to-one basis. Dial-up workstations must share these dial-up ports since their are a limited number of phone lines. When a workstation is using a phone line, no other workstation can access the network through that port.

This contention for phone-line access into the network presents a difficult issue of capacity planning for most companies. If the company adds too many phone lines, many go unused—which results in an unnecessary expense. If the company does not provide adequate phone-line access, the users attempting to access the network get frustrated with the busy signals.

As a dial-up user, you should be considerate of others when dialing into your local area network. Unless you have a dedicated phone line for your personal access, you are most likely sharing that phone line port with several others. The time you spend connected to the network is time that these other users cannot access the network.

When connecting to a dial-up server you should

- Strive to make data transfers as short as possible by compressing data files locally with PKZIP or a similar compression program before you start the transfer.
- Access required data and store it locally if possible to reduce the need to re-access the same data.
- Use the fastest modem you can to reduce the transfer times.

■ Try not to read e-mail online if you have the capability to download it all at once.

■ Be considerate of other user's access needs.

If you follow these guidelines, your remote access times and your company's capacity needs and the remote access expenses will be greatly reduced.

Troubleshooting

These are some of the problems you may run into when using Dial-Up Networking and some suggested solutions.

When I try to connect to a remote computer, I get an error that says, Unexpected response from device *and a bunch of letters and numbers.*

This probably means your modem is returning connection information other than what Dial-Up Networking is expecting. Make sure you are using the right setup for your modem (for example, if you have a Supra FaxModem 288 and set it up as a Supra FaxModem v.32bis, you'll receive an error like this). Go back to the Modem Setup Wizard in Control Panel and have it detect your modem.

Note

When the Modem Setup Wizard can't identify a modem, it defaults to Standard Modem. While this sounds harmless, it may reduce your throughput or functionality. If this is the case, you'll need to specify your modem manually.

Tip
Don't try Dial-Up Networking with anything less than a 9.6Kb/s modem. You will be disappointed with the throughput.

After I establish a connection, I get an error that says, No domain server was available to validate your password. You were logged on without security validation. Some resources may not be available.

This means that Windows is expecting your computer to be connected to a Windows NT Server network, and it isn't. This is the default setting, so if you didn't explicitly turn it off, it's on. It won't affect your ability to use any shared resources on a NetWare or Windows 95 network. You can turn the option off in the Client for Microsoft Networks Properties sheet (see fig. 11.12).

I get connected okay, but when I open the Network Neighborhood, I get an `Unable to Browse Network` *error.*

This means that the computer you've dialed into isn't configured to support all the protocols you have specified in the Server Type dialog box in the Connection Properties sheet. Typically, you can access some resources (like the Internet or a NetWare server) but not others. You need to configure the host computer to support all the protocols you want to use. See the section "Creating Dial-Up Connections" in chapter 10 to determine which protocols you need.

Fig. 11.12
Deselect Log On to Windows NT Domain to prevent error messages when you connect using Dial-Up Networking.

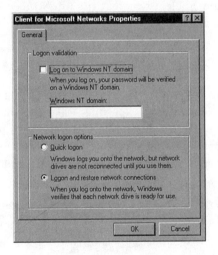

From Here...

This chapter has explored the usage of the remote access features of Windows, you have learned how to minimize your online time and expense while improving your overall throughput to your network.

You may want to explore these chapters to learn about other Windows networking features:

- Chapter 8, "Using the Network Neighborhood," tells you how to find network resources once you've made the connection to the remote network.

- Chapter 9, "Sharing Network Hardware," shows you how to share your resources with other computers on the remote network.

- Chapter 12, "Networking with a Notebook," guides you through the steps of using Windows' special notebook connectivity options.

■ Chapter 14, "Using Electronic Mail with Windows," helps you set up Microsoft Exchange to send and receive e-mail.

■ Chapter 15, "Working with Microsoft Exchange," leads you through the steps to send mail using Microsoft Exchange.

■ Chapter 17, "Connecting to the Internet," teaches you the special circumstances to connect via a TCP/IP protocol.

III

Using Your New Network

Chapter 12

Networking with a Notebook

As technology advances and prices drop, it is increasingly likely that you will have not one but two computers: a desktop computer that you use in your office, and a portable computer that you can take with you. Windows has made it much easier to use your portable computer with your network and has given you the ability to keep files synchronized between them.

In this chapter you learn

- Ways to extend your portable's battery life

- To install PCMCIA network adapters

- To use Dial-Up Networking from different locations

- To directly connect two computers

- To use files on more than one computer

Advanced Power Management (APM)

Keeping your laptop up and running while you're on the road is an important aspect of remote computing. Advanced Power Management (APM) lets you maximize the battery life of your laptop by suspending power usage of key components after a specified time period. As part of managing the remaining battery power, APM stops your hard drive from spinning when you aren't accessing it. By doing this, APM puts a major source of battery drain in a state of suspended animation. The same is true for your display: APM turns off the monitor after a period of inactivity to save battery time. On some laptops, APM can even slow down your CPU to save a large amount of battery life. When you need to perform calculations, access the hard drive, or use the display, APM quickly turns on the suspended devices for you.

Eventually, when your battery level does become too low, APM intervenes. For example, if applications are running, APM automatically saves open files.

Most laptop manufacturers provide a program or keyboard combination to change the setup of the time-outs. These changes must usually be made from DOS mode (see your laptop's manual for more details). By turning on APM, Windows uses the values you specified when you configured your laptop's BIOS for APM.

To use APM, do the following steps. If you aren't sure if your laptop supports APM, try this procedure anyway; you'll be able to tell in the first few steps.

1. Right-click the My Computer icon on your desktop and choose Properties at the bottom of the menu. This displays the System Properties sheet.

2. Click the Device Manager tab.

3. Click System Devices.

4. Double-click the Advanced Power Management Support system device.

5. Click the Settings tab in the Advanced Power Management Support Properties sheet (see fig. 12.1).

6. If it's not selected, mark the Enable Power Management Support checkbox.

Tip
If there is no listing for Advanced Power Management Support, your computer doesn't support it.

> **Note**
>
> If your computer does not come out of suspend mode, try selecting Disable Intel SL Support. This may allow your laptop to return from suspend mode without locking up.

7. Click OK to save your changes.

8. Click OK to close the System Properties sheet. When asked if you want to restart your computer, click Yes. If you want to wait until later to reboot your computer, click No. Be aware that APM won't become active until you restart.

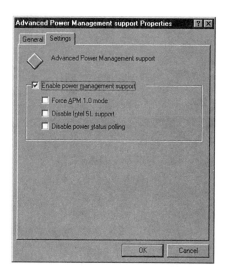

Fig. 12.1

You can enable Advanced Power Management by choosing Enable Power Manage-ment Support.

If your computer spontaneously shuts down without your interacting with it, this may be caused by Windows 95 communicating with APM much more frequently than Windows 3.x would. If you have this problem, select Disable Power Status Polling in the Advanced Power Management Support Properties sheet, which disables the battery meter on the taskbar.

If you want to force APM to use the mode compatible with Windows 3.1, mark the Force APM 1.0 Mode checkbox. Microsoft and Intel originally developed the power management interface into your computer's BIOS for use under Windows 3.1. Since that time, advances have been made in BIOS technology. However, not all BIOSs correctly handle the new features in APM 1.1. If you experience problems with your computer automatically moving into suspend mode, selecting this option may clear up those problems.

The next section teaches you how to add a status display that tells you how much battery power remains.

Showing the Battery Meter

When you use your computer away from an AC power source, battery life becomes an important factor in determining how much work you can accomplish. Windows can assist you by displaying a battery meter, which can be displayed on the taskbar, so you're always aware of the status of your battery.

To display the battery meter on the taskbar, do the following:

1. Open the Start menu and choose Settings, Control Panel.

2. Double-click the Power icon in the Control Panel window. The Power Properties sheet appears.

3. Click Enable Battery Meter on Taskbar if it's not already selected (see fig. 12.2).

4. Click OK at the bottom of the Power Properties sheet to save your change.

Fig. 12.2
You can choose to display the battery meter on the taskbar so that you're always aware of battery life.

Tip
If the battery meter shows that you're almost out of power, just plug in the AC adapter while the computer is running. The battery meter shows the plug icon to indicate that your battery is being recharged.

Fig. 12.3
The battery icon in the tray on the taskbar shows how much power remains when you move your mouse over it. If the battery is being charged, a power plug appears instead.

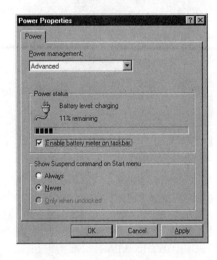

Now to check your battery supply, move the cursor over the battery symbol on the taskbar. As shown in figure 12.3, a box appears indicating the amount of power left. When the laptop is plugged into an AC adapter, a plug icon appears on the taskbar instead of the battery symbol (see the right side of fig. 12.3).

Finally, if you want to be notified that the battery is running out of power, you can turn on the low battery warning by following these steps:

1. Double-click the battery or power plug icon. The Battery Meter dialog box appears (see fig. 12.4).

2. Mark the Enable Low Battery Warning checkbox.

3. Click OK to save your change.

Fig. 12.4
The Battery Meter
dialog box allows
you to turn on a
warning that
notifies you when
the battery supply
is running low.

Enabling Suspend Mode

When using your laptop away from an AC power source, every minute of battery power is valuable. As discussed earlier, Advanced Power Management automatically suspends different functions of your computer based on your preferences. For example, you may have configured your laptop to go into complete suspend mode after 15 minutes. But if you know you're going to leave your laptop for a longer period, you can invoke suspend mode manually. This way, you won't have to shut all your programs down and then wait for Windows to restart again when you're ready to work.

When you manually activate the suspend mode, the current state of all your open programs and files is remembered, and your laptop is placed in a mode that uses much less power. When you want to use the computer again, all your files and programs are as you left them.

To immediately enable the suspend mode, do the following:

1. Open the Start menu and choose Settings, Control Panel.

2. Double-click the Power icon in the Control Panel window. The Power Properties sheet appears.

3. As shown in figure 12.5, choose Always under the Show Suspend Command on Start menu section to have the Suspend command show on your Start menu every time.

   Choose Only When Undocked to show the Suspend command on the Start menu when you've taken your laptop out of the docking station.

> **Note**
>
> If the Only When Undocked option is disabled, this means that your laptop is unable to dock. Your best option, in this case, is to always show the Suspend menu item.

Fig. 12.5
You have to
enable suspend
mode to be able to
access Suspend on
the Start menu.

4. Once you've made the appropriate choice, click OK to save your changes.

Now when you open the Start menu, depending on your choice, you'll have access to the Suspend command (see fig. 12.6).

Fig. 12.6
Opening the
Start menu and
choosing Suspend
immediately places
your laptop in a
state of low power
usage.

To restore your computer, turn the power on. (Check with your laptop's documentation if that doesn't work. You may have to do something else.) All programs and files are as they were before you initiated the suspend mode.

> **Note**
>
> Your network connections may not be restored when the laptop comes out of suspend mode. Therefore, it's a good idea to save any documents that you have open from the network before you choose to suspend the computer.

Connecting Your Portable to the Network

After you have set up your portable to maximize the amount of time that you will be able to run it, the next important step in productively using your portable computer is to connect it to your local area network. As with desktop computers, there are two ways to achieve this connectivity.

- Directly   Through a network adapter

- Remotely   Through a modem

Each of these options is examined in the following sections.

Using a PCMCIA Network Adapter

Today's portable computers are getting smaller and smaller, but users expect more and more functionality from them. Unfortunately, most portable computers no longer have room in them for a standard network adapter card. There is an answer though—a *PCMCIA network adapter.*

What Is a PCMCIA Network Adapter?

To solve the space problem in portable computers, the industry has developed a single standard for small insertable cards that can have a network adapter, a modem, or almost any device that you can find on a normal adapter card. This standard is PCMCIA, known as PC Cards under Windows.

How Do I Install a PC Card?

You insert a PC Card into an empty PCMCIA slot on your portable computer. There is an arrow on the card indicating how to insert the card correctly. There is also a connector cable that plugs into the end of the PC Card and connects to your networking wiring on the other end. Installing this card, as easy as that is, is the hardest part of installing a PC Card under Windows.

When you insert the PC Card, Windows automatically recognizes that it has a new card installed and installs the required drivers. When the automatic installation completes, you are almost ready to use the new card.

You must check to make sure that your PC Card is set up to use the proper type of connection. For Ethernet networks, this is either BNC coaxial cable or 10BaseT twisted-pair cable. Follow these steps to check that you have the proper medium specified:

1. Open the Start menu and choose Settings, Control Panel.

2. Double-click the Network icon. The Network dialog box appears.

3. Select your PC Card from the components list box and choose the Properties button (see fig. 12.7). A Properties sheet for that card appears.

Fig. 12.7
Choose the Properties button to change the settings of the PC Card.

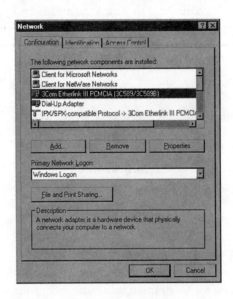

4. Choose the Advanced tab to display the Advanced page (see fig. 12.8).

Fig. 12.8
The Advanced page for a PCMCIA network adapter.

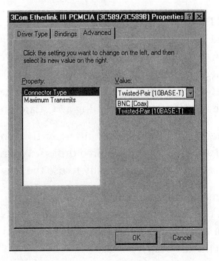

5. Select the Connector Type property, and see if the value matches your connection type. If not, use the drop-down list box to set it to the proper value.

6. Choose OK to close the Properties sheet.

7. If you changed the connection type, Windows prompts you to restart your computer. Choose Yes to restart so that you can use your PCMCIA network adapter.

When your computer restarts, or right away if you did not change your connector type, you can use Windows network services the same as you would from a desktop computer with a full-size network interface card.

Removing the PC Card

One nice thing about PC Cards is that you can take them out and put in a different type of card. Windows makes this very easy. These steps help you remove your PC Card.

1. Double-click the PC Card (PCMCIA) icon in Control Panel. The PC Card (PCMCIA) Properties sheet appears.

2. Select the card that you want to remove and choose the Stop button (see fig. 12.9).

Fig. 12.9
Choose Stop to shut down a PC Card.

III

Using Your New Network

3. Choose OK once the device has been shut down by the system (see fig. 12.10).

Fig. 12.10
The PC Card has
been shutdown;
click OK to
continue.

At this point, you can take the PC Card out of the computer. This is usually done using a small button next to the slot that ejects the card from the slot. A PCMCIA network adapter is not the only way to connect to your network.

Using Remote Access

In chapter 10, "Setting Up for Remote Access," you learned how to use Dial-Up Networking to connect to a remote network. Windows gives you a simple way to use Dial-Up Networking, even when you carry your notebook computer to a distant city. This feature, Dialing Locations, automatically adjusts the phone number dialed according to the specifications you set for a specific location. First, look at setting up different locations.

1. Open the Start menu and choose Settings, Control Panel.

2. Double-click the Modems icon. The Modems Properties sheet appears (see fig. 12.11).

Fig. 12.11
The Modems
Properties sheet.

3. Choose Dialing Properties. This displays the Dialing Properties sheet (fig. 12.12).

4. Choose New to start a new location. Enter the location name in the Create New Location dialog box. Choose OK to continue.

5. Mark the Dial Using Calling Card checkbox to use a calling card or credit card for calls from this location.

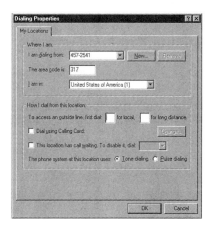

Fig. 12.12
The default
location displayed
on the Dialing
Properties sheet.

6. Enter the calling card information in the Change Calling Card dialog
box (see fig. 12.13). Choose OK to close this dialog box.

Fig. 12.13
Entering calling
card information
for this location.

7. Choose OK to save the new location (see fig. 12.14).

Fig. 12.14
Choosing the OK
button saves the
new location.

III

Now that you have multiple locations set up, when you use Dial-Up Networking to connect to a remote network, you can choose the location you are in from the Dialing From drop-down list box (see fig. 12.15). Note that when you are dialing from the default location, the number dialed is 3440698. When you change the location, as seen in figure 12.16, the number that is dialed changes automatically, to 8 102881 815 3440698. This change is the true power of Dialing Locations and is the main remote access feature that makes Dial-Up Networking useful from your notebook computer.

Fig. 12.15
Dialing 3440698 from the default location.

Fig. 12.16
Dialing 8 102881 815 3440698 from the Seattle office.

Connecting Your Notebook Directly to Your Desktop Computer

For those of you who have two computers but do not have a true network, Microsoft has provided a simple method of connecting two computers directly together to share files. Windows gives you Direct Cable Connection to do this. This is done by connecting your desktop and a notebook computer using either a serial (null modem) cable or a parallel cable. The two computers are connected by taking the cable and plugging it into both computers' serial or parallel ports.

To use Direct Cable Connection, one computer must be the *host computer* and the other the *guest computer*. The guest computer has access to the shared resources on the host computer, but the host computer does not have access to the guest computer.

Setting Up the Host Computer

Follow these steps to set up a computer to be the host computer of the Direct Cable Connection.

1. Open the Start menu and choose Programs, Accessories, Select Direct Cable Connection. This starts the Direct Cable Connection Wizard.

2. Select the Host option button and then choose the Next button (see fig. 12.17).

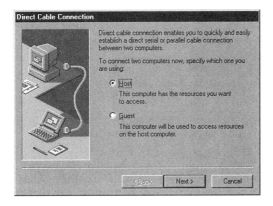

Fig. 12.17
Select Host on the Direct Cable Connection Wizard.

3. Select the port that the cable is connected to and choose Next (see fig. 12.18).

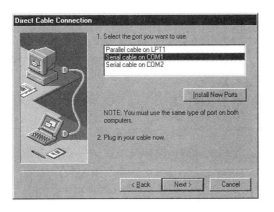

Fig. 12.18
Select the port that the direct cable is attached to.

III

Using Your New Network

4. Choose the Finish button to start the host side of the Direct Cable Connection.

The host side is now waiting for a connection from a guest. Now you can start the guest.

Setting Up the Guest Computer

Setting up the guest computer is very similar to setting up the host computer. The following steps show you how:

1. Open the Start menu and choose Programs, Accessories, Select Direct Cable Connection. This starts the Direct Cable Connection Wizard.

2. Select the Guest option button and then choose the Next button (see fig. 12.19).

Fig. 12.19
Select the Guest option button on the Direct Cable Connection Wizard.

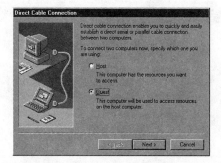

3. Select the port that the cable is connected to and choose Next.

4. Choose the Finish button to start the guest side of the Direct Cable Connection.

Once the connection is completed, a folder opens on the guest computer's desktop. This folder contains all the shared resources from the host computer. You can use these resources the same way you would any local resource.

Using Briefcase

When you work remotely, whether it's on a laptop away from home or on a desktop away from work, you often have to juggle multiple copies of the same file. With just a moment of carelessness, you can accidentally replace an updated file with an earlier version. Without a doubt, you're destined to print the wrong version at least once.

With the new Briefcase feature, you don't have to worry about any of that. Briefcase makes updating files a snap. If the program you used to create two versions of the same file supports merging file revisions (such as Microsoft Word for Windows), Briefcase tries to use the features provided by the program to merge the two versions together (however, not many applications provide this functionality yet). Briefcase then compares the dates of the files and keeps the newest one. You can use Briefcase with Dial-Up Networking and Direct Cable Connection or move it to a floppy.

Briefcase prompts you to update files that have been changed since you copied them into the Briefcase. That way, you won't forget to transfer the latest version.

The Briefcase icon resides on your desktop. If it's not there, you need to create it. To create the Briefcase icon, do the following:

1. On the desktop, click the right mouse button.

2. Click New from the pop-up menu.

3. Click Briefcase. The Briefcase icon appears.

To copy a file to Briefcase, do the following:

1. In the Explorer, locate and click the icon for the file you want to update. (The file has to be closed.) This file can be located on any drive, folder, or shared resource that your computer has access to.

2. Reduce the size of the Explorer window so that you can see the Briefcase icon.

3. Drag-and-drop the icon for the file you want to take with you onto the Briefcase icon.

The file is copied into Briefcase. When you double-click the Briefcase icon, you'll see a window showing the large icons of all items copied inside. To view file details, click View, Details. You'll get a screen similar to the one shown in figure 12.20.

Tip
If you share a Briefcase, you won't be able to synchronize any files that you drag-and-drop there while sharing is enabled. That means every document displays an *orphan status* and won't be updated.

Tip
If you know the name of the document but not the path, open the Start menu and choose Find, Files or Folders. Type in the name of the file you want to find. You can then drag-and-drop the icon right from Find window.

Fig. 12.20

A list view of Briefcase after two files have been copied into it.

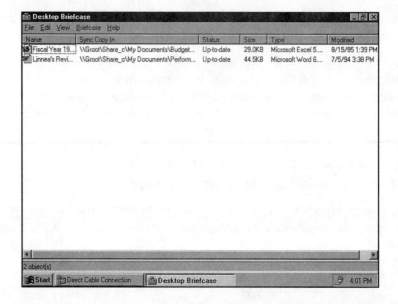

> ## Caution
>
> You can change the name of the file in Briefcase, but if you do, you'll sever the link to the original file. Then Briefcase won't keep track of which file has changed.

Another way to copy a file into Briefcase is to click the file's icon (the file has to be closed), and then click File, Send To, My Briefcase.

When you first copy a file into Briefcase, the status indicates that it's Up-to-date. Whenever you save changes to the original file, the status changes to Needs updating.

> ## Note
>
> If the Briefcase window is open when you save the original file, the status won't reflect the change until you close the window and open it again.

To update the Briefcase version of a file, do the following:

1. Double-click the Briefcase icon to open the window.

2. Click the icon of the file you want to update.

3. Click Briefcase, Update Selection. You'll get a dialog box similar to the one in figure 12.21.

Fig. 12.21
Briefcase shows you the location of each file and date and time each file was modified before it updates files.

The direction of the green arrow indicates which version of the file is replaced. In this case, the file on the right, the one located in \\GROOT\SHARE_C, replaces the file on the left, which is an earlier version located in Briefcase.

4. Click Update.

If you want the earlier version of the file to replace the later version, do the following.

Caution

Replacing the latest version with an earlier version this way backdates your original file. You lose all revisions made since the Briefcase version. Make absolutely certain this is what you want to do before you do it. It cannot be reversed.

1. In the Update My Briefcase window, select the file you want to update (see the preceding instructions).

2. Move the cursor to the word Replace and right-click. You'll get the screen in figure 12.22.

III

Using Your New Network

Fig. 12.22
You have the options to replace the latest version with the earlier version or to skip replacement altogether.

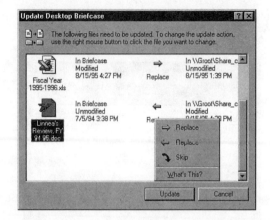

3. Click the green arrow to indicate the way you want the files updated.

4. Click Update.

If you aren't sure where the original file came from, Briefcase helps you find the original file. It also shows you all kinds of statistics about the versions.

To find the original file, do the following:

1. In the Briefcase window, click the icon for the file you want to find out about.

2. Click File, Properties. You'll see a Properties sheet (see fig. 12.23).

3. Click the Update Status tab (see fig. 12.24).

Fig. 12.23
The General tab in Briefcase indicates the date the file was created, modified, and accessed. The accessed date tells you when Briefcase was opened.

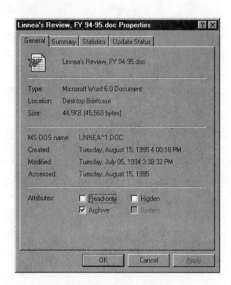

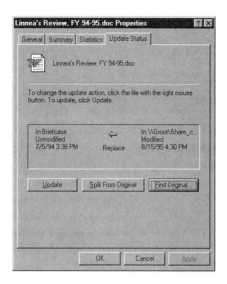

Fig. 12.24
Briefcase lets you
find and access the
original file.

4. Click Find Original to find the file. Briefcase opens the folder window.

5. Double-click the file if you want to open it.

The easiest way to use Briefcase to synchronize files from one computer to
another is to drag-and-drop the Briefcase to a floppy and take it with you.
Then when you get to your other computer, drag-and-drop the Briefcase onto
the desktop and follow the preceding instructions for updating files.

You can use Briefcase to synchronize files with Direct Cable Connection or
Dial-Up Networking, both described earlier in this chapter.

To use Briefcase to synchronize files on computers that are directly cabled or
connected via a Dial-Up Connection, do the following:

1. Share the Briefcase from the computer with the updated files. (Click the
   Briefcase icon, click the right mouse button, click Sharing from the pop-
   up menu, click the Sharing tab in the My Briefcase Properties sheet, and
   click Shared As.)

Caution

Remember to take sharing off the Briefcase icon after you've transferred it.
Otherwise, you won't be able to save linked files and all files will be orphaned.

---

2. Connect the computers with a Direct Cable Connection or Dial-Up Networking. You'll get a window similar to the one shown in figure 12.25.

Fig. 12.25

The remote computer displays all of the shared folders from the host computer.

3. Double-click on My Briefcase from the host computer. You'll get a screen showing you the files.

4. Drag-and-drop the file you want to update from the host to the remote. (Or you can right-click on the file you want to copy, and click File, Send To, My Briefcase.)

5. Click Yes.

To make sure you've copied the right file, double-click My Briefcase on the remote computer. Click View, Details. Notice that under Sync Copy In there is something similar to \\ROBIN\MY BRIEFCASE. That indicates the updated file came from a Briefcase folder on another computer.

If you don't want to bother connecting computers, you can simply copy the Briefcase to a floppy. Of course you can drag-and-drop the file, but there's an easier way to do it.

To copy a file from Briefcase to a floppy, do the following:

1. Open the Briefcase window and click on the file you want to copy.

2. Click File, Send To, 3 1/2" Floppy (A).

3. Make sure you put the Briefcase back on your other computer.

You can also send files this way to a fax recipient or a mail recipient.

Troubleshooting

There is no Advanced Power Management Support system device on the Device Manager tab. Where is it?

Your computer does not support APM.

Windows did not recognize that I put the PC Card in the PC slot. Why?

Make sure that the PC Card is fully seated in the slot, it might be loose. Also, check to make sure that Windows installed its PCMCIA Manager when you installed Windows—if not, then use Add/Remove Programs to install it now.

Direct Cable Connection is not on my Accessories menu. Where is it?

Direct Cable Connection was not installed when Windows was installed. Use the Add/Remove Programs Properties sheet to install the Direct Cable Connection option.

The port that I am using is not listed on the Direct Cable Connection ports list. Did I do something wrong?

You probably added a port after you had run Direct Cable Connection at least once. Use the Install New Ports button to let Direct Cable Connection find the new port.

Direct Cable Connection is very slow. What can I do about this?

You are probably using a serial cable for connecting. Switch to a parallel cable for additional speed.

I don't have Briefcase listed as an option under New. Why not?

Briefcase was not installed when Windows was installed. Use the Add/Remove Programs Properties sheet to install the Briefcase.

From Here...

Connecting your notebook computer to the network has never been easier. You can find out more information about Windows 95 networking in these chapters:

- Chapter 8, "Using the Network Neighborhood," explains how to find networked resources with the Network Neighborhood feature.

- Chapter 9, "Sharing Network Hardware," describes setting up your machine to share your hard drive and peripherals.

- Chapter 10, "Setting Up for Remote Access," discusses dialing into your network from home or on the road.

Part IV

Communicating by Computer

Chapter 13

Introduction to Electronic Mail

No networking product would really be complete without providing its users an effective means of communicating with others. Enter electronic mail or simply *e-mail*. The term applies specifically to the creation and distribution of messages, file attachments, and other documents and media via computer networks.

It wasn't so long ago that e-mail was generally limited to the transmission of simple text messages between people or groups of people connected to the same network. That's changed with the popularity and growth of online services and the public's rapid awakening to the Internet. E-mail has become a mature and powerful technology.

Whether you use it for business or pleasure, e-mail is your literal key to the global village. Take the case of The ALCo Collections, a worldwide organization of railroad historians and train buffs who have a common interest in the 121-year history of the now-defunct American Locomotive Company (ALCo). The power of e-mail allows widely distant members of this non-profit organization to collaborate on projects as easily as if they were right next door to one another.

One of the organization's recent book projects, for example, was developed and written by four people working together via e-mail from Australia, Canada, Germany, and India. Eighty percent of the photos in the heavily illustrated book came from contributors in these countries, as well as Peru and Iraq. Almost all of them were received by the book's U.S.-based editors as digitized images routinely attached to e-mail messages. The authors and contributors sent their material to The ALCo Collection's CompuServe (CIS) e-mail post office. Those who were CIS subscribers addressed their messages directly (**73410,1253**), while the others routed theirs via the Internet (**INTERNET:73410.1253@compuserve com**). The editors handled most of their replies in the same way. Best of all, the material moved in a matter of minutes, not days, between members of the editorial and production teams.

In this chapter, you learn about the following:

■ What e-mail is

■ What e-mail can do for you and your business

■ The different types of e-mail

What Is E-Mail?

There's nothing magical or mystical about e-mail. In its simplest form, it's the same as regular mail. You write a message, address it, and send it on its way. When the recipient gets it, it is opened and read.

Most e-mail programs share a common message format. As illustrated in the Microsoft Exchange message shown in figure 13.1, their respective finished products all have a To, From, Date, Subject, and a main message area. On-screen appearance and styles, however, can be subject to wide variation, even among different e-mail products from the same company.

Fig. 13.1

E-mail gives you a fast and efficient way of communicating with others.

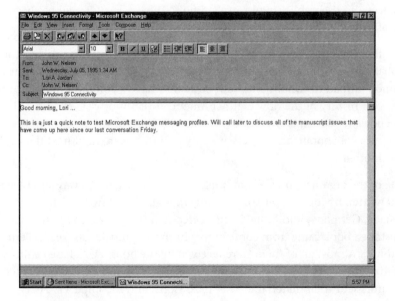

The only true difference between e-mail and regular mail these days is speed. People who are e-mail savvy frequently call regular mail "snail mail" because of its relative lack of swiftness. With regular mail, you're locked in to pick-up, transit, and delivery schedules set by the post office. Even with their respective overnight services, Airborne Express, Federal Express, United Parcel Service, and the Postal Service still make you live by their timetables. Not e-mail. You can work almost down to the wire on a deadline project, safe in the knowledge that, as an e-mail package, the finished product—perhaps a contract bid, a job proposal or detailed legal document—can reach its destination on time.

The Power of E-Mail

E-mail is more powerful than a regular mail message in many ways. Many of today's popular e-mail applications—including Microsoft Exchange for Windows—give you the ability to attach files to your messages (see fig. 13.2). Sending a spreadsheet or graphic with a covering letter to another person—or to a group of people at the same time—is a quick and easy task. So is sending your friends and relatives a picture of the baby's first step...or, better yet, the actual sound of its first real words.

Fig. 13.2

This brief Eudora e-mail message includes a graphic file as an attachment.

All in all, these and other advancements over the early days of limited, straight-text messaging, have taken e-mail's marriage of basic computer functions to a new plateau—to make your communications work easier and be more productive.

Forms

There are several third-party applications available that allow developers to build custom forms for e-mail packages. Forms work like a template, with a predefined set of on-screen fields for users to complete and act on.

Products like Microsoft's Electronic Forms Designer extend the power of Microsoft Mail by building high-capability mail applications in Microsoft Visual Basic. This means that an entire order-processing system, for example, can be built on the foundation of Microsoft Mail.

Workgroup Applications

Workgroup applications are extensions of the forms concept. They're based on the premise that a group of people working together on a common project can benefit from sharing the same documents and files. In almost every instance, these applications are designed to ensure that everyone receives updated copies on a common timetable.

Workgroup application technology varies in its implementation. It can be something as simple as an electronic routing slip, which is used to make certain everyone in a workgroup gets the latest revisions to a document. It can also take on the complexity of a complete document sharing/messaging/scheduling system like Lotus Notes.

An obvious question here is: How can two or more people work on one document at the same time, especially if they're miles apart? The answer, however, won't be found in your computer or any of its software. The answer is strictly human.

The success or failure of any team project rests within the team's organization. No matter how democratic the team may be in its approach to resolving the project's underlying issues and concerns, no matter how qualified each member is in the subject at hand, someone's got to take on the thankless role of the benevolent dictator. Right from the get-go, someone has to be tapped as the final arbiter of such things as document compilation and editing, distribution and routing, order of access, and reply and comment deadlines.

OLE Capability

Object Linking and Embedding (OLE) is one of the core technologies of Windows. As you'll investigate in chapter 15, "Working with Microsoft Exchange," OLE gives you the power to create compound documents from different pieces of information originating from different applications and programs.

With Microsoft Exchange, you can build an e-mail message that, like the one shown in figure 13.3, includes text prepared with Microsoft Word, a graphic from CorelDRAW!, and some statistical data from Microsoft Excel. Thanks, in part, to OLE, all three of these can be cut from their respective originating applications and pasted into a mail message.

Fig. 13.3
This Microsoft Exchange memo incorporates text from Microsoft Word, a graphic from CorelDRAW!, and a table from Microsoft Excel.

When you send the message to other users, they see all the data just as you did. If the recipient of this message double-clicks on any of the information, the creating application allows them to edit it. We'll get into the specifics of how this works in chapter 15, "Working with Microsoft Exchange."

Different E-Mail Networks

It's been said that there are as many variations in e-mail systems today as there are people on a typical rush-hour Tokyo commuter train. The capabilities of the systems' servers, mail-handling routines, and user interfaces range to the *nth* degree of sophistication, and the range of people they'll let you connect with is equally broad. Systems can be grouped in four broad categories:

- Local (interoffice) e-mail

- Online service e-mail

- Dedicated e-mail systems

- Internet e-mail

Each has different capabilities, best suited for specific types of user environments and all have a common limitation. Their reach—how far they send e-mail—is limited by the size of the network they're running on. A standalone interoffice network obviously can't reach the same number of potential destinations that a network gated to the Internet can.

Local E-Mail

This is the type of e-mail that most business users are accustomed to. Packages like Microsoft Mail, Lotus cc:Mail, DaVinci Mail, and Novell GroupWise are well-established examples of corporate LAN-based e-mail packages. Each is designed around a similar client/server model: a network server acts as a post office, maintaining a list of users and working as a clearinghouse for messages to and from these users. Each workstation connected to the server gains access to the post office through system-specific client software.

Most LAN-based e-mail systems provide such features as file attachments and extensibility through forms and workgroup applications. Gateways to other mail systems, a feature once limited to high-end packages, are also becoming commonplace.

E-Mail via Online Services

The phenomenal growth of online services like CompuServe, America Online, Prodigy, Delphi, and the new Microsoft Network has had an exponential effect on the popularity of e-mail. Each of these commercial systems gives its subscribers the ability to exchange messages within the system and, via the Internet, to other systems and services worldwide.

Online services are normally accessed through a modem that connects your computer to the system via a local telephone number. Once you're connected, you can download all the mail messages waiting for you and compose new ones to other users. It's a convenient way for you to stay in touch at a relatively low cost. Figure 13.4 shows a CompuServe message written with Microsoft Exchange running under Windows.

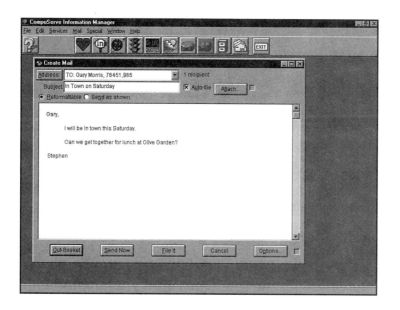

Fig. 13.4
Commercial online services like CompuServe, America Online, and Microsoft Network are valuable e-mail resources.

IV

Communicating

Dedicated E-Mail Systems

Dedicated systems such as AT&T EasyMail, MCI Mail and SprintMail are similar to online services, with one exception that's just now beginning to fade. These proprietary systems traditionally served only one purpose: to send and receive mail.

This limitation had been these systems' biggest shortfall. Their respective subscribers could only exchange mail with other users on the same system. In order to remain competitive, however, these systems have been adding gateway services that finally let their users correspond beyond old intrasystem boundaries.

Internet Mail

With some five million host computers serving more than 35 million users worldwide, the Internet offers vast possibilities for connectivity and communication between people. Most online services and a growing number of dedicated e-mail systems have gateways to the Internet, so users of these services and systems can go beyond the boundaries of their home networks in exchanging mail.

If you're a CompuServe (CIS) member, for example, you can exchange messages with anyone who uses America Online (AOL). All you have to do is use the Internet form of the person's AOL address. Replies would come back addressed to the Internet form of your CIS address.

Finding E-Mail Addresses

So how do you find your best friend's e-mail address? There's no true one-stop source for e-mail address information—at least, for the moment. But it isn't all that difficult to find someone's e-mail address. The easiest way is to ask for it, just as you'd ask for the person's physical mailing address or phone number. In fact, many people include their e-mail address(es) on their business cards and letterheads.

Another sure source of a person's address information can be found right in your own incoming e-mail. Electronic mail always has the sender's return address; the information is automatically attached to the message as it's being composed. Just look at the From line in the message header and you'll find it.

People you're trying to contact may also be listed in one of a growing number of e-mail address directories. They come in both white pages (residential) and yellow pages (business) form, just like the telephone book, and most bookstores and full-service computer outlets have them. You can also find them in the reference section of most larger libraries. If you belong to a trade association or professional organization, the odds are getting better that the home office has e-mail address information from its membership.

And then, there's the high-tech approach. You can use the Internet to search out specific names and addresses. We'll spend a lot more time on navigating and working with the Internet in part V, "Windows 95 on the Internet."

What Can E-Mail Do for Me?

E-mail can be a great tool if you're marketing a product or service. Being readily available to a customer or potential customer without playing phone tag gives you the opportunity of expanding your efforts without a lot of expense.

E-mail can make your office more productive, even if it's small enough that you and your colleagues can talk to each other without leaving your desks. Files can be exchanged, schedules can be kept up-to-date and phone messages can be delivered. These are just a few of the reasons why thousands of people just like you now consider e-mail to be an integral part of their day-to-day activities.

The benefits that you can draw from e-mail are limited only by how you choose to use it. One thing's certain, you'll likely find at least three of the following on any list you come up with after joining the fraternity of e-mail users.

- E-mail helps you meet last-minute deadlines

- E-mail can be permanent and portable

- E-mail is environmentally conscious

- E-mail is inexpensive

- E-mail beats walking to the mailbox on a rainy day

From Here...

E-mail can make you and your co-workers more productive and make it easier to communicate with each other. In this chapter, you saw an overview of the different kinds of e-mail available and some of the applications that can be built on an e-mail foundation.

- Chapter 14, "Using Electronic Mail with Windows," disusses how to set up your mail system.

- Chapter 15, "Working with Microsoft Exchange," discusses how to use this e-mail client that is an integral part of Windows.

- Chapter 17, "Connecting to the Internet," gives you the information you need to get started on the Internet.

Chapter 14

Using Electronic Mail with Windows

Windows brings more than a new user interface and expanded networking resources to your computer system. It also gives you a broad range of communications capabilities. They're all coordinated through a neat Windows feature that's officially known as the *Microsoft Exchange client* but usually just called *Exchange*.

In this chapter, you learn

- The Exchange concept

- The functions of Exchange

- How to configure supporting postoffices and Exchange profiles

- How to add CompuServe Mail to your Exchange resources

Introduction to Microsoft Exchange

Microsoft has long advocated the concept of giving its customers the capability of having fingertip access to a world of information resources. In the realm of Windows and e-mail, the concept is represented by Microsoft Exchange, which provides an effective basic platform for open communications between and among services.

Exchange is a universal information client designed to interact with any online or LAN-based mail system that supports *messaging application programming interface* (MAPI) services. However, CompuServe and the Microsoft Network were the only online systems to have the necessary driver software available to users when Windows 95 was first introduced to the public. System-specific drivers for America Online, Delphi, GEnie, and Prodigy were still in the works well after Windows August 1995 roll-out.

You can also use Exchange with Microsoft Fax to send and receive facsimile transmissions and as a vehicle for connecting with your organization's networked e-mail servers. As you'll soon see, Exchange uses the commonplace "inbox" metaphor in defining how it handles the entire range of electronic messaging products.

Thanks to its compliance with the latest specifications for *object linking and embedding (OLE)*, Exchange gives you the capability of creating and managing compound documents. Such a document might consist of text imported from a Word for Windows document, a graphic rendered in CorelDRAW!, and material from an Excel spreadsheet. Each element embedded in a compound Exchange document lives in harmony with its neighbors, and can be individually edited on-screen. The result is a virtually seamless combination of information from a variety of sources.

> **Note**
>
> Not all programs support embedding. If you want to incorporate material from such a program in a compound Exchange document, it must be copied from the source document and pasted into the new one.

Exchange also lets you incorporate web pages from the Internet in your electronic messaging, drawing on the resources of such World Wide Web browsers as Netscape Navigator and NCSA Mosaic. An adaptation of the latter serves as the foundation for the Internet add-on that comes as part of the optional Microsoft Plus! for Windows software package.

Another plus is that the operating functions of Exchange are *extensible*. Extensibility is an element of software design that allows third-party providers to develop so-called "plug-in" software for Windows-based customers. One example of this value-added approach, CompuServe Mail for Exchange (CIS Mail), is discussed later in this chapter.

The Windows Exchange client can also be strengthened through the addition of *functional agents*, another type of plug-in component that lets you automate one or more operating tasks. For example, you could tell an agent to connect to the Internet every day at a predetermined time and search through a number of UseNet newsgroups for messages about overweight

Norwegian Elkhounds, the latest problems with Intel processor chips, or what's new between Bill Gates and Janet Reno. The agent runs the search, marks and retrieves all such messages, and routes them to your Inbox.

The Exchange client is only a small part of a much bigger picture. Microsoft is also preparing a powerful Exchange server as part of its BackOffice package that has full extensibility just like the client.

What Does Exchange Do?

Exchange's primary job is to help you organize, access, and share information. It does this by performing the following tasks and functions:

- Transmitting and receiving e-mail to and from people on a common network

- Incorporating into your messages files and objects you've created in other applications

- Using its Address Book features to speed the addressing of your e-mail transmissions

- Creating and managing folders for the storage of related messages, files, and other items

- Managing and controlling the connections you use to access various in-house and online information providers

- Various file maintenance tasks such as moving, printing, and deleting messages

What's a Postoffice?

Clearly, Exchange is an extremely powerful communications tool. Before you can use it, however, you have to set up a *postoffice* file system for the delivery, storage and processing of e-mail, faxes, and other incoming transmissions. You also have to establish system files for such essentials as connection and routing parameters for outgoing material and the location of your Address Book. These files are known as your *Exchange profile*.

E-mail postoffices work a lot like regular snailmail postoffices. When someone sends you a paperbound letter, they drop it in a mailbox. From there, it's picked up and routed through the sender's local postoffice to yours. Your postoffice, in turn, completes the transmission and distribution cycle by delivering the letter to the designated address.

An e-mail postoffice system usually centers on a *dedicated network server*, which uses a set of directories to store mail for each of the system's users. When you send mail to another user, the e-mail client program on your workstation copies the message file to the server directory assigned to the intended recipient. The recipient's computer periodically polls that directory for new files. When it finds one or more, it copies the files and informs the recipient that there's mail waiting.

Windows Postoffices

The Windows postoffice feature is an effective vehicle for adding relatively hassle-free e-mail services to small networks of up to 20–25 users. The Windows postoffice does away with the need for a dedicated network server, replacing it with an easy-to-maintain, common-access directory hosted by one designated workstation within the network.

The ins and outs of e-mail system maintenance under Windows are very straightforward. Administration can be accomplished by anyone on the network once they've been set up in that role, and they can do it from any terminal on the network.

Microsoft Mail Postoffices

Microsoft Mail is one of the most popular e-mail packages available today. It has suitable client applications for DOS, Windows, Windows for Workgroups, Windows NT, and Macintosh. In addition, there are a number of gateways available that let users exchange mail with other e-mail systems, including other e-mail systems operating under Microsoft Mail and the Internet.

Microsoft Mail's postoffice is designed to run with Novell NetWare or Microsoft LAN Manager. It controls a set of directories on a network file server that all the client computers have access to. Network users simply connect to the shared directory periodically and check for new mail.

Using the Postoffice Setup Wizard

Windows' Postoffice Setup Wizard walks you through the process of creating an e-mail postoffice, setting up an administrator's account and maintaining a user's database. Once you and the Postoffice Setup Wizard take care of the preliminaries, the other folks on your network will be swapping all kinds of good stuff.

Tip
If you use Windows for e-mail services on a network with more than 20–25 users, the workstation that hosts the system's postoffice can become sluggish and bogged down. This can be a particularly vexing problem if you're using the host workstation for several other tasks simultaneously. It may be better to forego the Windows postoffice system and work with a larger system like Microsoft Mail.

> **Caution**
>
> Although Windows will let you structure more than one postoffice on a computer and use them for separate mail systems on the same network, the computer's overall performance level will diminish with each additional postoffice. Hold your system to a single office structure whenever possible.

Initial Setup

To set up a Windows postoffice, follow these steps:

1. Open the Start menu and choose Settings, Control Panel.

2. Click the Microsoft Mail Postoffice icon.

3. A Microsoft Workgroup Postoffice Admin dialog box appears (see fig. 14.1). The Create a New Workgroup Postoffice option will be marked unless your system already has an established postoffice facility. Click Next.

Fig. 14.1

You have a couple of options in the Microsoft Workgroup Postoffice Admin dialog box.

4. Now, tell the Postoffice Setup Wizard where you want your new postoffice. A directory on the root of a shared drive is the preferred location, but pick another spot if you want. The only requirements are that the location must be a pre-existing directory and it must be accessible to other users in your workgroup. Enter the path name in the Postoffice Location text box (see fig. 14.2) or click Browse to set the appropriate name from the Browse for Postoffice dialog box. When you're done, click Next.

Fig. 14.2
Pick a location for
the postoffice.

5. The Postoffice Setup Wizard then displays the dialog box shown in
   figure 14.3 and asks for the name of your postoffice. There's no need to
   change the default name that the Postoffice Setup Wizard appends to
   the postoffice's directory, **[d]:\...\wgpo000**, but you can if you'd like.
   Click Next to confirm use of the default name or <u>B</u>ack to enter a new
   name in the appropriate data field.

Fig. 14.3
This dialog box
provides a default
name for the
postoffice.

6. Next, the Enter Your Administrator Account Details dialog box asks you
   for information about your e-mail administrator (see fig. 14.4). By default, the Postoffice Setup Wizard lists your Windows login name, and
   the default password, PASSWORD. You can change either of these
   required items by clicking the entry field and typing the new information. Entries in the other data fields are optional. These fields are

intended to help you fine-tune individual user records. Your Windows postal system doesn't need the requested information as a condition of operation. Click OK.

IV

Communicating

Fig. 14.4
Use this dialog box for entering your administrator's information.

7. You're done! A message box like the one in figure 14.5 confirms the creation and location of your new Windows postoffice.

Fig. 14.5
A successful postoffice has been created.

Adding Users to a Postoffice

Once you've established a basic postal system, your next job will be to create a *user account* for each person who'll be using it. The Postoffice Setup Wizard comes into play here, too, as it will whenever you want to add, remove, or change individual users.

1. Open the Start menu and choose Settings, Control Panel.

2. Click the Microsoft Mail Postoffice icon.

3. The Microsoft Workgroup Postoffice Admin dialog box appears (refer to fig. 14.1), but the Administer an Existing Workgroup Postoffice is the marked user option. Click Next.

4. The Postoffice Setup Wizard displays another Microsoft Workgroup Postoffice Admin dialog box (refer to fig. 14.2), which asks you to confirm the location of your workgroup's postoffice files. Enter the path name in the Postoffice Location text box or click Browse to select the appropriate directory. When you're done, click Next.

5. The Postoffice Setup Wizard knows that too many cooks will spoil the broth, so it won't let just anyone into your system's e-mail administrator files. It'll show the e-mail administrator's name on a dialog box like the one in figure 14.6, but you've got to give the Wizard the right password to go any farther. Enter it and click Next.

Fig. 14.6
You need the correct password here.

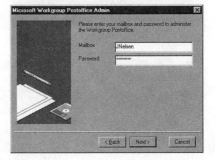

6. If your e-mail system is active, the Postoffice Setup Wizard displays the Postoffice Manager dialog box (see fig. 14.7) and its list box shows all the people in your workgroup who have e-mail accounts. If your e-mail system is inactive, the list box is empty. Click Add User to add a new user on to the system. To remove someone or to update their account, click their name and then, as appropriate, Remove User or Details.

Fig. 14.7
The Postoffice Setup Wizard dialog box shows who is in your workgroup.

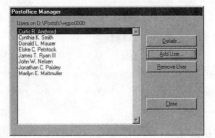

7. Adding a new user is just a matter of completing the Add User dialog box (see fig. 14.8). The Postoffice Setup Wizard always shows the default password, PASSWORD, when opening a new Add User dialog box. It can, of course, be changed by you or the individual user. Enter the user's name in the Name text box and the user's mailbox ID (eight characters, maximum) in the Mailbox text box. Entries in the other data fields are optional; Windows doesn't need the requested information as a condition of operation. Click OK.

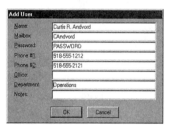

Fig. 14.8
When you add a user to your workgroup, just add their information here.

8. Repeat steps 6 and 7 for each new user you want to add to the system. When you finish, click Close in the Postoffice Manager dialog box.

The Microsoft Exchange Profile Wizard

The Microsoft Exchange Profile Wizard prompts you for basic system setup information the first time you start Exchange. Exchange uses this information to build an operational instruction base—or profile—that determines how particular information will be sent and received, how that information will be processed, and what service providers will be used. Profile data can also include user mailbox addresses, passwords, and hardware-specific setup information for your office, home, and travelling computers.

An *active profile* is the information or data set that defines your current messaging session. Depending on your particular requirements, you can create a single default profile for all messaging sessions or set up multiple special-purpose profiles that can be activated on an as-needed basis. Either way, the setup process involves the same basic steps:

1. Open the Start menu and choose Settings, Control Panel.

2. Click the Mail and Fax icon.

3. Windows displays the MS Exchange Settings Properties sheet (see fig. 14.9). This Properties sheet opens on its Services page. The page displays a list of all *information services* (that is, Microsoft Mail, Microsoft Fax, CompuServe Mail) in the active profile. To select a listed service, click its name and skip to step 5. The folder also includes five buttons: A<u>d</u>d, <u>R</u>emove, P<u>r</u>operties, Cop<u>y</u>, and A<u>b</u>out. If the information service you want to work with isn't listed or if the list box is blank, click A<u>d</u>d.

Fig. 14.9
The Services page shows all the services that are currently in this profile.

4. The Microsoft Exchange Profile Wizard displays an Add Service to Profile dialog box. The display on your screen includes a list of all the information services that are installed and available for use on your computer. If the service you want is listed, click its name and then click OK to start the setup procedure for that service. If the service isn't listed but you have the necessary setup files on floppy disk, CD-ROM, or your hard drive, click the Have <u>D</u>isk button.

> **Note**
>
> An *information service* is a user-installed or user-activated utility that enables messaging applications to do one or more of the following: send and receive items, store items in folders, and obtain user addresses and directory information. The standard information services provided in Windows are Microsoft Fax, Microsoft Mail, Personal Address Book, and Personal Folders.

5. Follow the Microsoft Exchange Profile Wizard's setup prompts as each appears on-screen. The particular service(s) you are installing will dictate the specific setup procedure and configuration information that's needed.

Microsoft Mail

The Microsoft Exchange Profile Wizard dialog box for Microsoft Mail is divided into eight tabbed sections:

> Connection
>
> Logon
>
> Delivery
>
> Log
>
> Remote Configuration
>
> Remote Session
>
> Dial-Up Networking
>
> LAN Configuration

The Microsoft Exchange Profile Wizard opens to the Connection page (see fig. 14.10). This page lets you specify how your computer is connected to your postoffice:

Fig. 14.10
Tell Microsoft Mail how to connect your computer to the postoffice.

- The Enter the Path to Your Postoffice text box should show the full path to the network location of your postoffice. The sample path in figure 14.10 is D:\Postofc\wgpo0000.

- The Select How This Service Should Connect at Startup options give you a choice of the type of postoffice connection Microsoft Mail uses: automatic detection of a LAN or remote (modem) configuration, LAN only, remote only, and offline. Because of its flexibility, most people opt for Automatically Sense LAN or Remote. If your postoffice can't detect a specific connection type when you start a mail session, Microsoft Mail will prompt you for one.

> **Note**
>
> To use Microsoft Mail remotely, you must first have Dial-Up Networking set up on your Windows system. See chapter 10, "Setting Up for Remote Access," for more information.

The Logon page lets you specify access information for your postoffice (see fig. 14.11). For security purposes, asterisks are shown on-screen in place of a user's actual password. Mark the When Logging On, Automatically Enter Password checkbox if you don't want to have to enter your password each time you start Exchange.

Fig. 14.11
Do you want to enter the password every time you logon? If not, mark the checkbox on this page.

Tip
You can save valuable system resources by setting longer intervals between mail deliveries and using the Immediate Notification option to alert users that they have mail waiting. This option requires the use of NetBIOS.

How will your mail be collected and transferred between your Inbox and your postoffice? Click the Delivery tab to set available delivery options (see fig. 14.12). Both the Enable Incoming Mail Delivery and Enable Outgoing Mail Delivery checkboxes are normally marked, allowing inbound mail to be routed from your postoffice to your Inbox and outward mail to go to your postoffice. You can block delivery of certain types of mail by clicking Address Types and making the appropriate selections. You can also set a standard time interval between mail deliveries.

> **Note**
>
> The information services in most active Microsoft Exchange profiles usually provide you with access to at least two address lists: your Personal Address Book list and a Global System List. Marking the Display Global Address List Only checkbox reduces the number of individual lists you'll have to scroll through when addressing messages.

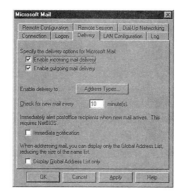

Fig. 14.12
You can have Microsoft Mail check for new mail automatically; just tell it how often.

The LAN Configuration page is of no concern to you unless your computer has a *local area network* (LAN) connection. If that's the case, the LAN Configuration page is where you specify whether the mail you receive is selected by mail headers and whether you want to use a local copy of the Exchange address book (see fig. 14.13).

Fig. 14.13
In the LAN Configuration page, you can choose to use a local copy of the Exchange address book.

■ Use Remote Mail   This option lets you preview new messages by their header information before they're downloaded. You can see who sent the messages, the subject of each message, its file size and an estimate of how long it will take to download. After you retrieve headers, you can mark each message for downloading or deletion.

■ Use Local Copy   This option allows you to use a local file copy of your Personal Address Book (a copy stored on your computer) rather than the copy in your Microsoft Mail Postoffice on the system server.

■ Use External Delivery Agent   This option allows for mail delivery with a minimum amount of overhead or use of system resources. However, it requires that EXTERNAL.EXE always be running on your system's server. See chapter 7, "Setting Up a Windows Network," for more information.

Want to keep tabs on your e-mail activity? Click the Log tab and complete the information requested on the Log page (see fig. 14.14). Click the Maintain a Log of Session Events checkbox to have your system track events such as error messages and logging on and off. The log of session events is an ASCII text file and is stored on the system wherever you want it and under whatever name you want.

Fig. 14.14
Track error messages and logging on and off with this page.

You can ignore the Remote Configuration page in figure 14.15 if your system doesn't have a remote-access connection through Dial-Up Networking and a modem. If it does, the options on this page are the remote-access equivalent of those for LAN connections. They let you specify whether the mail you receive is selected by mail headers and whether you want to use a local copy of the Exchange address book.

Fig. 14.15
This page is for remote-access connections only.

The options available on the Remote Session page shown in figure 14.16 can also be ignored if you're not set up for remote access connection via Windows Dial-up Networking feature. If you are, your choices here are in effect only when the computer is operating in a remote-access mode.

Fig. 14.16
If you want to automatically start up Dial-Up Networking, mark the When This Service Is Started checkbox.

IV

Communicating

> **Note**
>
> For specific information on remote access operations, refer to chapters 10, "Setting Up for Remote Access," 11, "Using Remote Access," and 12, "Networking with a Notebook."

Microsoft Fax

The Microsoft Fax Properties sheet is divided into four tabbed sections:

Message

Dialing

Modem

User

The Microsoft Fax Properties sheet starts you off with the Message page (see fig. 14.17). This is where you set specific default options for all your fax messages. The choices you make here should be based on your normal, day-to-day fax requirements; they can be changed at any time, either permanently or to meet the needs of a particular situation.

Fig. 14.17
Use the Microsoft
Fax Properties
sheet to set default
options for your
faxes.

- The Time To Send section gives you the choice of having Windows normally send your faxes at a specific fixed time, within a specific time range (that is, 11 PM to 6 AM) or as soon as possible.

- The Message Format section allows you to set editing options and printer paper formats.

- The Default Cover Page section lets you choose a default format for the cover sheet that's normally sent with your faxes. You can use one of the standard formats that Windows provides or create one or more of your own using the Fax Cover Sheet Editor that appears when you click the New button.

Click the Dialing tab to see the Dialing page and establish how Microsoft Fax interacts with your local and long-distance telephone carriers (see fig. 14.18).

Fig. 14.18
Use this sheet to
set up how your
fax dials.

- Do you have to dial 9 for an outside line? Do you have Call Waiting? Will you be billing your fax transmissions to a phone company calling card? Click the Dialing Properties button to set or change this kind of information about the phone system you're working with.

- Some fax numbers in your own telephone area code must be dialed with a 1 toll-call or long-distance prefix. Click the Toll Prefixes button to access a list that lets you set these numbers individually by their first three digits (known in phone company parlance either as "central office" or "exchange" numbers).

- The Retries section lets you set how many times Microsoft Fax will attempt to connect with a destination number that's busy and how long it will wait between each attempt. If you want to change either or both default elements of the 3 tries at 2 minute intervals, enter the appropriate number(s) in the Number of Retries or Time Between Retries text boxes.

Next, use the Modem page to select and set up the modem and (see fig. 14.19). The Available Fax Modems list box is empty if no fax modem is installed on your computer and fully configured for Windows-based fax service. If any fax modems are installed and configured, they'll each be listed by name. The Active Fax Modem section header above the list box will also show the name of whichever listed modem is currently set as your system's active fax modem.

> **Tip**
>
> The Toll Prefixes feature is a neat little tool, but you may no longer need it. Check the user information section of your phone book to find out whether the 1 prefix is still required when dialing numbers that are in your area code but are outside your local (non-toll) calling area. If it isn't needed, you can pass on this setup option.

> **Fig. 14.19**
> The Modem page lets you see which modems are installed.

■ To add a modem, click the Add button to activate the Install New Modem Wizard. See chapter 10, "Setting Up for Remote Access," for more information about the Install New Modem Wizard.

■ To change the operating parameters of a currently installed fax modem, click the Properties button and enter the appropriate information.

■ To delete a listed fax modem, highlight its name, and click the Remove button.

■ If your system has two or more available fax modems, you can set any one of them as the system's normal default. Just highlight its name and click the Set as Active Fax Modem button.

The User page is your last stop in the process of setting up a modem for Microsoft Fax service. Enter the appropriate information in this page (see fig. 14.20).

Fig. 14.20
The final page in setting up your computer for faxing.

Personal Address Book

You can't send mail without addresses, and computers don't do too well with that kind of information when it's scribbled on napkins, the backs of envelopes, and sundry other bits and pieces of paper. You need an online *Personal Address Book* (PAB) to store and organize contact information on all the people you send e-mail messages and faxes to. The Microsoft Exchange Profile Wizard helps you set up the necessary PAB files in just a few easy steps:

1. Open the Start menu and choose Settings, Control Panel.

2. Click the Mail and Fax icon.

3. Click Add to open the Add Service to Profile dialog box. Choose Personal Address Book and click OK.

4. The Wizard opens the Personal Address Book dialog box (see fig. 14.21). The Path text box shows a default path in your main WINDOWS directory for the location of the data file (named MAILBOX.PAB by default) where entries in your Personal Address Book are stored. By default, the Wizard sets the Show Names by option to display PAB entries in first-name order.

5. Click OK.

Fig. 14.21
Where do you want your PAB entries stored? Choose the place in this dialog box.

Personal Folders

The last bit of work in setting up your initial Exchange Profile is to specify the location of your Personal Folders File (PST). The Microsoft Exchange Profiles Wizard also makes this job easy:

1. Open the Start menu and choose Settings, Control Panel.

2. Click the Mail and Fax icon.

3. Click Add to open the Add Service to Profile dialog box. Choose Personal Folders and click OK.

4. The Microsoft Exchange Profile Wizard opens a Create/Open Personal Folders File dialog box. Highlight the file labeled MAILBOX.PST and then click Open.

5. When the Microsoft Personal Folders dialog box opens, you'll have the opportunity of setting an optional password for your new PST file (see fig. 14.22). Click OK to close the dialog box.

Fig. 14.22
The Microsoft
Personal Folders
dialog box lets you
set a password.

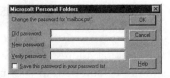

From here, it's just a matter of telling the Microsoft Exchange Profile Wizard how you'd like Exchange to open the next time you start Windows. Complete the entry field and click Next. The Microsoft Exchange Profile Wizard responds by displaying an updated MS Exchange Settings Properties sheet that includes the names of the various Exchange services you've set up. Click Finish and you're done.

Exchanging Mail with Other Systems

Okay, you've gotten the hang of how to set up Windows' basic e-mail capabilities. What's next? Cyberspace!

There are thousands of other e-mail systems out there, each loaded with users you can correspond with if you have reason or need to. Being able to send an e-mail message to a business associate in another place makes the communications process easier and more convenient. And it's great to be available to people all over the world right from your desktop.

CompuServe Mail for Exchange

Your ability to communicate with Microsoft Mail postoffices and Microsoft Exchange servers can also be extended through add-on applications from other vendors. CompuServe Mail for Microsoft Exchange, or CSMail, was the first of these third-party components to enter general distribution.

If you're a CompuServe (CIS) subscriber, you can use CSMail to

- Exchange messages with other CIS subscribers and with users of LAN-based e-mail systems, X.400 systems and the Internet.

- Send faxes and telexes.

- Log on to CIS and interactively process your incoming and outgoing mail.

- Schedule the automatic transmission and receipt of mail at regular times.

The initial general-release version of CSMail is included in the first-run version of Windows 95 that was introduced in August 1995. The program's installation, setup, and operational files are located under \DRIVERS\ OTHER\EXCHANGE\COMPUSERVE. The most-current version of the program will always be available for download from the CompuServe Software forum (GO CISSOFT). The software is free, but downloading will be subject to normal connect-time charges from your local or long-distance telephone carrier.

CIS Mail Exchange Profile

Adding a profile for CompuServe Mail for Exchange to your computer is a relatively painless procedure if you know what to expect. There are nine steps involved, and each has extensive on-screen help available:

1. Open the Start menu and choose Settings, Control Panel.

2. Click the Mail and Fax icon.

3. Windows responds by displaying an MS Exchange Settings Properties sheet. If CompuServe Mail is listed among your computers's current information service setups, highlight the list entry, click Properties, and skip to step 5. If it isn't listed, click Add.

4. An Add Service to Profile dialog box appears listing all of the information services that are available on your computer. If CompuServe Mail is among those listed, highlight the entry and click OK. If it isn't listed, click Have Disk and follow the on-screen prompts.

5. A new CompuServe Mail Settings dialog box opens (see fig. 14.23). Your name should appear in the Name text box; if not, click the text box and enter your name. Next, click the CompuServe Id text box and enter your account ID number (use the standard CIS number-comma-number format, not the number-dot-number Internet style). Then click the Password text box and enter your CIS password.

Fig. 14.23
Make sure your name is right and enter your CIS ID and password.

> **Note**
>
> If you omit your password, you'll be prompted for it whenever you start a CompuServe Mail session in Exchange.

6. Go to the Connection page (see fig. 14.24). Enter the appropriate information in the Phone Number, Preferred Tapi Line and Network text boxes.

Fig. 14.24
Use the Connection page to enter your phone number.

Phone number entries should be in the following format: +c (aaa) xxx-yyyy. The +c is the country code preceded by the plus sign. The area code, aaa, requires the parentheses; the rest of the phone number is standard.

> **Note**
>
> TAPI is the acronym for *Telephony Application Programming Interface*, a communications exchange standard highly promoted by Microsoft. The acronym doesn't enjoy widespread name recognition among consumers yet. For our purposes here, it's the same as a modem connection.

7. Click the Default Send Options tab to see the Default Send Options page (see fig. 14.25). Don't activate the Send Using Microsoft Exchange Rich-Text Format option unless you are absolutely certain that all of the people to whom you send e-mail via CIS use Microsoft Exchange. Recipients who don't use Exchange won't be able to read your messages. You should also leave the Release Date and Expiration Date text boxes blank. And, unless you want to send your e-mail as postage due (recipients pay all transmission fees) or split costs 50–50, there's no need to change the Payment Method default setting.

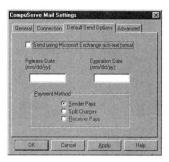

Fig. 14.25
If you want other people to pay your fees, mark the Sender Pays checkbox.

8. Click the Advanced tab to set currently available options relating to bulk e-mail operations (see fig. 14.26). Click Create Event Log to have Exchange generate an Inbox log of the messages sent and received during a CIS mail run. Click Delete Retrieved Messages to have CIS clear your online mailbox after Exchange collects any waiting e-mail. Click Accept Surcharges to let Exchange accept mail arriving as postage due. The Advanced page also has a subroutine that lets you set specific times for Exchange to contact CIS and process all pending incoming and outgoing mail. Click Schedule Connect Times to do so.

Fig. 14.26
To accept postage due e-mail, mark the Accept Surcharges checkbox.

9. Click Apply and then OK to complete the addition of CompuServe Mail to your computer's active Exchange Profile.

Microsoft Exchange is now set up to send and receive mail through CompuServe.

Note

If you run into unresolvable problems with the CompuServe Mail add-on for Windows, don't call Microsoft for help. Contact CompuServe instead.

From Here...

In this chapter, you've discovered how Windows uses e-mail to let you talk with other users on your local network and with folks all around the world. You've learned how to set up Microsoft Mail postoffices and Microsoft Exchange profiles—the two keys to effective Windows communications. And, you've seen how to add the resources of CompuServe Mail to your Windows world.

- Chapter 13, "Introduction to Electronic Mail," gives you the basics about e-mail.

- Chapter 15, "Working with Microsoft Exchange," discusses working with your e-mail in Microsoft Exchange.

Chapter 15

Working with Microsoft Exchange

If you've had any exposure to Microsoft Word, you'll find it's a snap to compose messages with Microsoft Exchange. No experience with Word, you say? No sweat. As with learning to ride a bike, you'll wobble a bit at first, but you'll get the hang of it. There are many e-mail applications available, but—as discussed in chapter 14, "Using Electronic Mail with Windows"—Microsoft Exchange is your built-in e-mail application made for Windows.

Once you understand how Exchange treats mail messages, you'll quickly pick up on the procedures for forwarding messages to individuals and groups, embedding objects, and attaching files.

In this chapter, you learn the nuts and bolts of working with your mail in Exchange:

- The Exchange Viewer
- Composing and sending messages
- Attaching files to messages
- Using OLE to create compound messages
- Reading, replying, and forwarding messages
- Printing your messages
- Keyboard and command-line shortcuts

The Exchange Viewer

All of your work with Exchange will involve using the resources of the Exchange Viewer (see fig. 15.1). To open the Viewer and start a work session, open the Start menu and choose Programs and Microsoft Exchange. You can also double-click the Inbox icon on your Windows desktop.

> **Note**
>
> When you begin an Exchange session by using Microsoft Mail, you can work *offline* by choosing the Offline button that appears when you first log on to Exchange. Offline creates no connection to your postoffice, but lets you write messages and hold them in your Outbox for later transmission.

Fig. 15.1

In double-pane view, the Microsoft Exchange Viewer window displays folders on the left and the contents of each folder on the right.

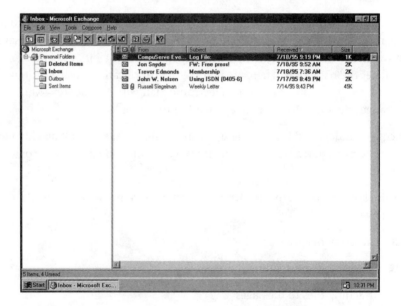

The Viewer works much like the Windows Explorer. The left side of your screen displays your Personal Folder files. These folders may contain e-mail messages, facsimiles, and files created in other applications. Being able to keep all kinds of data in a folder allows you to store related documents, spreadsheets, and messages in a common location. The right side of your screen will list the contents of a particular folder when you highlight and click the folder's name.

Personal Folder Files

New messages are automatically delivered to your Inbox folder whenever Exchange makes a mail run. The new material appears in **boldface** on the Viewer window, sorted in ascending order by date and time of receipt.

Information on the sender, subject, date and time received, and size of each message is provided. Additionally, mail messages are represented by an envelope icon. An exclamation point will appear to the left of the envelope if the message was sent marked high priority. A paper clip appears if there are any files attached to the message.

You can open an Inbox message for reading either by double-clicking the envelope icon to the left of its sender's name (shown in the From column) or by highlighting the message entry and then selecting the File menu and choosing Open. Exchange will display the message in a new window. When you're done reading, close the window just like you would any other.

Other default Personal File folders in Exchange include:

- Outbox, which temporarily holds messages marked for send until they're delivered.

- Sent Items, which holds file copies of messages that have been sent.

- Deleted Items, which holds items that have been deleted but not purged.

As you read the items in your Personal Folder files, you can write replies, forward the items to other people, delete them, or file them in other folders.

Creating New Personal Folder Files

You're not limited to the four Personal Folder files (Inbox, Outbox, Deleted Items, and Sent Items) that Exchange sets up by default. It's a simple process to add as many files as you need (within the limits of available hard drive space):

1. Choose Tools, Services.

2. Exchange will display a Name dialog box listing all information services currently active in your Exchange profile. Click Add.

3. When the Add Service to Profile dialog box appears (see fig. 15.2), double-click the Personal Folders listing in the Available information services display.

Tip

The Exchange Viewer gives you a choice of two display modes: single pane (Folders Off) and double pane (Folders On). Double pane is used in all Viewer graphics in this chapter. Single pane is the default mode that's set when Exchange is first installed, but most users quickly come to prefer the expanded double-pane display. Give it a try: choose View and click Folders. That's all it takes.

IV

Communicating

Fig. 15.2
Exchange allows
you to add your
own personal
folders.

4. Enter a name for your new Personal Folders group in the File name field
   of the Create/Open Personal Folders File (see fig. 15.3). Click Open.

Fig. 15.3
Create your own
personal e-mail
files like any other
type of file.

5. Enter the Name you want displayed on-screen for the new folder group.
   Next, pick a file encryption option (compressible encryption is the
   default; most small-network and standalone computer users opt for no
   encryption). Then if you want to use it, set the optional password protection mode by typing the appropriate information in the Password
   and Verify Password entry fields. Click the Save this password check-off
   box and then click OK (see fig. 15.4).

Fig. 15.4
Your personal
folders can be
password pro-
tected and
encrypted.

6. When the Add Service to Profile dialog box reappears, click OK to complete the addition process and return to the Viewer.

Individual items—and entire folders—can be transferred or copied between old and new folder files on the same system. They can also be moved to another location, such as a laptop or notebook computer.

Creating Individual Folders

Do you need more folders in a particular Personal Folders file? No problem! Creating them is as easy as one, two, three:

1. Click the Personal Folder that you want to add the new file to.

2. Following the sequence shown in figure 15.5: choose File, New Folder.

Fig. 15.5
This will add a new file to an existing folder you have selected.

3. When the New Folder dialog box appears, type the appropriate information in the Folder name entry field. Click OK. Exchange will return to the Viewer where, as shown in the Folders On mode in figure 15.6, you'll get immediate on-screen confirmation that your new folder exists.

Fig. 15.6
This confirms that your new folder exists.

Tip
To rename a folder, right-click on the current name. Choose Rename in the pop-up menu that appears and then type the new folder name in place of the old one. Press Enter to complete the process.

Arranging Folder Contents

Under the Exchange Viewer's default settings, the contents of your Personal Folders will be identified on-screen by date and time, name of recipient or sender, message subject, and total file size (rounded up to nearest full kilobyte). These defaults are established when Exchange is first set up on your system, but the program gives you full freedom to reorganize information displays any way you want.

1. Double-click the name to open the folder that you want to change.

2. Choose View, Columns.

3. Use the Available Columns and the Show the Following Columns sections of the Columns dialog box, as shown in figure 15.7, to make additions, deletions, or adjustments to the Viewer's on-screen display.

Fig. 15.7
The Exchange Viewer allows you to organize and display folder content in many ways.

You can rearrange the left-to-right order of your columns by highlighting a particular column name and clicking the Move Up and Move Down buttons The default settings and their respective column widths are as follows:

Column Heading	Column Width
Importance	10 pixels
Item Type	20 pixels
Attachment	13 pixels
From	23 pixels
Subject	39 pixels
Received	29 pixels
Size	9 pixels

Exchange offers an additional 37 column headings in the Available Columns for use in customizing your Viewer's organization and arrangement:

Application Name	Last Author	No. of Slides
Author	Last Printed Time	No. of Words
Category	Last Saved Time	Presentation Format
Comments	Links Dirty	Revision No.
Company	Manager	Scale
Conversation Topic	No. of Bytes	Security
Creation Time	No. of Characters	Sensitivity
Document Parts	No. of Hidden Slides	Sent
Document Subject	No. of Lines	Template
Edit Time	No. of Multimedia Clips	Title
In Folder	No. of Notes	To
Item Text	No. of Pages	
Keywords	No. of Paragraphs	

Tip

You can change column widths in a folder directly on-screen by placing your cursor on the separator bar between the headers of the columns you want to adjust. A split bar cursor will appear; use it to enlarge or reduce the column size.

Finding Messages and Other Items

It is easy to accumulate a lot of e-mail and fax messages in your personal folders, even if you're an absolute stickler about pruning dead wood from your files and directories. Thanks to its Find feature, Exchange helps you cut through the digital jungle and track things down when you need them. The feature is similar to the Find feature in most word processors when you are trying to find a particular word or name.

1. Choose Tools, Find, or use the Ctrl+Shift+F keyboard shortcut.

2. Enter the appropriate information in the From, Sent To, and Subject fields of the Find page shown in figure 15.8.

Fig. 15.8
The Find feature helps you locate a particular e-mail file much like the Find feature in a word processor helps you locate a word or phrase.

3. Click the Folder button to access the Find Items In Folder browser (see fig. 15.9), and use your mouse to highlight the folder you want to search. To search a group of folders, highlight the *next highest level* of files on the inverse tree displayed in the browser, and click the Include all subfolders checkbox. Click OK to return to the Find page.

Fig. 15.9
You can tell Find to search a specific file and all of its subdirectories.

4. Click Advanced to access the dialog box shown in figure 15.10 and fine-tune various key search parameters. For example, you can have the finder limit its search to file items you haven't read yet or items that are within a certain range of dates and/or file sizes.

Fig. 15.10
Find also lets you run searches based on message dates, file sizes and other special parameters.

5. Click Find Now. Exchange will scan all preselected files and folders, post the results in standard Viewer format, and, as shown on the right-hand side of the status bar in figure 15.11, remind you that it is continuing to monitor for new items that meet your search criteria.

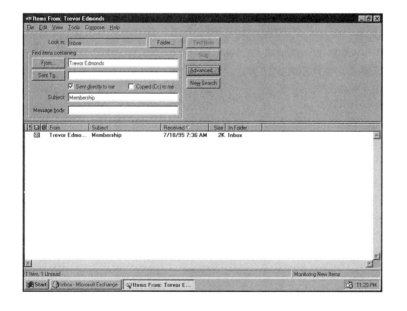

Fig. 15.11
The results of a Find search are displayed in detail.

Tip
You can minimize a Find window (click the "_" box in the upper-right corner of your screen) and have it update automatically as new mail with matching parameters arrives.

Sorting Messages and Other Items

When you first use Exchange, your messages will be filed and sorted by date and time received, sender's name, message subject, and total file size (rounded up to nearest full kilobyte). You're not limited to these defaults, though. Exchange gives you a wide range of file organization and sorting options.

1. Use your mouse to highlight the name of the folder whose contents you want to sort.

2. Choose <u>V</u>iew, <u>S</u>ort.

3. Use the Sort dialog box shown in figure 15.12 to set which column you want to <u>S</u>ort by and whether you want the sort in <u>A</u>scending (A–Z) or <u>D</u>escending (Z–A) order. Your selections will remain active for that folder until you change them.

Fig. 15.12
Exchange folder content and Viewer file displays can be sorted and arranged in a variety of user-specified schemes.

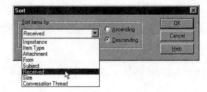

Moving and Copying Messages

With the exception of their results, the procedures for moving and copying files in Exchange are basically the same:

1. If the item you want to move or copy is already open, move to Step 2. If it is closed, highlight its name on the Viewer log screen.

2. Choose <u>F</u>ile, Mo<u>v</u>e or Cop<u>y</u>, as appropriate.

3. In the <u>M</u>ove to or <u>C</u>opy to section of the Move or Copy dialog box (see fig. 15.13), highlight the name of the folder you want to move or copy the item to. Click OK.

Fig. 15.13
Use this dialog box to move or copy a folder.

Composing E-Mail Messages

Now that you know how Exchange organizes and arranges your folders and messages—and how these factory defaults can be changed—let's cover the real bread-and-butter: writing, sending, and receiving the messages that wind up in these folders.

As we said coming into this chapter, Exchange makes it easy to write or compose messages. If you have any experience working with Microsoft Word, the job's a snap. Even if you're totally new to computers, it's an easy, intuitive learning curve.

To write a message, follow these steps:

1. Choose Co**m**pose, **N**ew Message (see fig. 15.14), or press the Ctrl+N shortcut combination on your keyboard.

Tip
A closed file item can also be moved to the Exchange Viewer by dragging it to a new folder in the same way that you move items between directories and subdirectories in Windows Explorer.

IV

Communicating

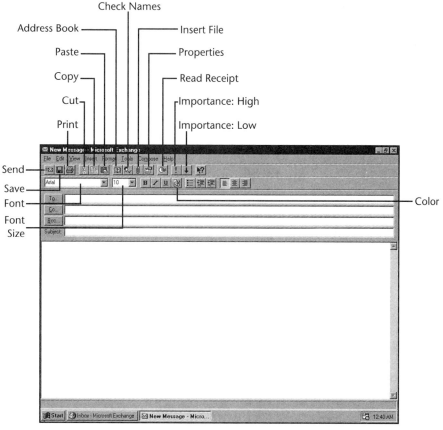

Fig. 15.14
The New Message screen.

2. In the appropriate entry fields, type the names of the people who'll be getting your message. Use semicolons to separate multiple names in the same field (i.e., **Marcia Rodney; Elske Petstock**).

Tip

Limit the name entries in the To: field of your e-mail messages to the people from whom direct action or response is expected. Use the Cc: (carbon copy) and Bcc: fields (blind carbon copy) to list those who'll be getting informational copies of the message. Cc: addressees are openly identified to all message recipients, while Bcc: addressees are identified only within that group and on your original.

Tip

If you're running Microsoft Office 95 or another 32-bit Microsoft application on your Windows system, you can check spelling in messages before you send, save, or print them. Just choose Tools, Spelling, or press F7 on your keyboard.

If you need help with e-mail or fax addresses, press the Ctrl+Shift+B shortcut combo, click the Address Book toolbar icon, or click the To:, Cc: or Bcc: buttons in the message header to open your Address Book files.

3. Type an appropriate message title or header in the Subject entry field.

4. Type the body of your message. To format a specific letter or block of message text, highlight the text in question. Then choose Format, Font for font type, style, size, and spacing, or Paragraph for indentation, line spacing, and tab settings. Or click the appropriate icon on the formatting toolbar.

5. The finished message is ready for sending, saving, or printing.

Using Your Personal Address Book

The Personal Address Book portion of your computer's Exchange messaging system holds the names and addresses of the people and organizations you send e-mail and fax messages to. But it's not just another one of those catch-all electronic card files that most computer users come to hate. It's a well-organized system that puts you in command of your contact information.

With the Personal Address Book in Exchange, you can:

■ Add and modify names and addresses in different address books

■ Find and select names within different address books

■ Create custom e-mail and fax distribution lists

■ Exchange name and address information between different address books.

Here's how you do it all, step-by-step:

To add a name and address to your address book, follow these steps:

1. Choose Tools, Address Book, or press the Ctrl+Shift+B shortcut combination on your keyboard.

2. In the Show Names From section of the Address Book dialog box, click Personal Address Book (see fig. 15.15).

3. Choose File, New Entry.

4. In the New Entry dialog box, click the type of address you want to add and enter the requested recipient or addressee information (see fig. 15.16).

IV

Communicating

Fig. 15.15
Choose which addresses you want to see.

Fig. 15.16
Each messaging service you use has an address dialog box that requires service-specific set-up information.

Need to find a name or address? Follow these steps:

1. Choose Tools, Address Book, or press the Ctrl+Shift+B shortcut combination on your keyboard.

2. In the Show Names From section of the Address Book dialog box, click the book you want to work with. The names in that book will appear on the left-hand side of the list box (see fig. 15.17).

3. Enter the last name of the person you're looking for in the Type Name or Select from List box or the last word in an organization's name. If the name is on file, your cursor will automatically move to it. If the name isn't on file, you can add it by following steps 3 and 4 in "Adding New Names," above.

Fig. 15.17
Names are on the
left-hand side.

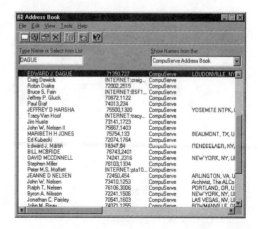

To modify names or addresses follow these steps:

1. Choose Tools, Address Book, or press the Ctrl+Shift+B shortcut combination on your keyboard.

2. In the Show Names from section of the Address Book dialog box, click the name of the address book you want to work with.

3. Double-click the name entry you want to modify to reveal its current Properties sheet (see fig. 15.18). Type in the necessary changes, then click OK.

Fig. 15.18
Edward J. Martin's
Properties sheet
lets you change
his information.

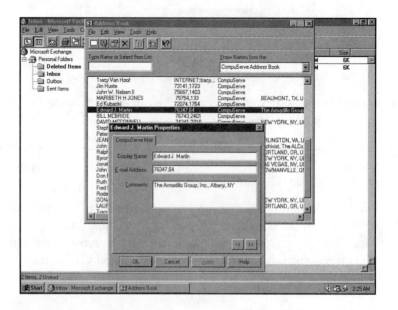

To import names and addresses, follow these steps:

1. Choose Tools, Address Book, or press the Ctrl+Shift+B shortcut combination on your keyboard.

2. In the Show Names from section of the Address Book dialog box, click the name of the address book you want to copy information from (source book).

3. In the source book's list of names, highlight the name you want to copy. Then choose File and click Add to Personal Address Book.

To make special distribution lists, follow these steps:

1. Choose Tools, Address Book, or press the Ctrl+Shift+B shortcut combination on your keyboard.

2. In the Address Book dialog box, choose File, New Entry.

3. When the New Entry dialog box shown in figure 15.19 appears, scroll down the Select the Entry Type list to the Personal Distribution List entry and double-click to open the New Personal Distribution List Properties sheet.

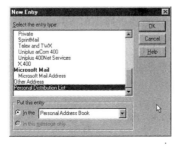

Fig. 15.19
Use the New Entry dialog box to select the type of entry.

4. Click the Add/Remove Members button.

5. In the Edit Personal Distribution List Members box, enter a name or highlight it on the displayed address box list. Click Members to add it to the distribution list. You can add as many names to the list as you want, and you can annotate the list by clicking on the Notes tab. Click OK when you're done to return to the New Personal Distribution List Properties sheet.

6. Click OK to complete adding the new distribution list to your personal address book.

Attaching Files to E-Mail Messages

One of the handiest uses of e-mail is to send files and cover notes to other people. The overnight express services offered by FedEx, UPS, and the Postal Service, among others, are pretty good. But they're no substitute for the speed and simplicity of e-mail file attachments.

Attachments show up as icons in the body of an e-mail message. The recipient can right-click the icon and choose Save to save it to his or her local hard disk.

To attach a file to an e-mail message, follow these steps:

1. Choose Insert, File.

2. The Insert File dialog box appears (see fig. 15.20). Double-click the name of the file you want attached to your message. Use the Look In drop-down list box to access different directories.

Fig. 15.20
Use this dialog box to insert a file.

Click the Text Only option button if you want the file displayed in your message as unformatted ANSI text. Click An attachment to send a copy of the actual file with the message. You can also link the attachment to your original file if the person you're writing to has access to the same file server that you work from.

3. Click OK to complete the attachment process. The message shown in figure 15.21 will give you an idea of the result. The attach file appears as an icon.

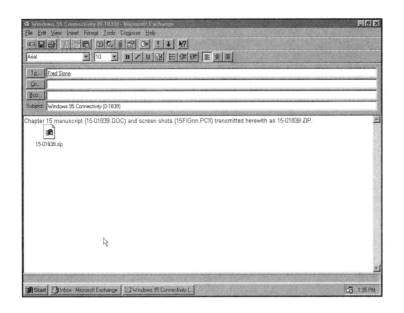

Fig. 15.21
An e-mail message
with an attached
ZIP file.

Note

You may be asking whether there's anything to this attached file stuff—anything that
you can benefit from. Well, take a closer look at figure 15.21. That illustration and
this text are part of 15-01839.ZIP, the attached file referenced in that one-line
message. The manuscript for the chapter was written in Albany, NY, and it was
transmitted, with attached graphics files, to Que's editorial offices in Indianapolis...in
an e-mail package prepared and dispatched with Microsoft Exchange.

Using OLE To Create Compound Messages

The power of Exchange's *object linking and embedding* (*OLE*) capabilities takes
the file attachment concept one step further. With it, you can fashion a message with multiple elements drawing on a broad spectrum of data types, including graphics, databases, spreadsheets, and multimedia.

Recipients can view all of this embedded data right in the document. They
can also edit the data if they have a copy of the source application you used
to create the data. For example, you can send colleagues an e-mail message
that includes an embedded spreadsheet you prepared with Microsoft Excel
and, with their own copies of Excel, they'll have full working access to the
file. This occurs automatically when they double-click the item or choose the
appropriate edit command while the item is highlighted.

To embed data into an e-mail message, follow these steps:

1. Choose Insert, Object.

2. The Insert Object dialog box in figure 15.22 will give you the option of inserting the contents of a file into your message or creating a new object. The new object may be any one of the following:

Bit-map Image	MIDI Sequence
Media Clip	Package
Microsoft Equation 2.0	Paintbrush Picture
Microsoft Graph	Video Clip
Microsoft Word 6.0 Document	Wave Sound
Microsoft Word 6.0 Picture	WordPad Document
Microsoft WordArt 2.0	

Make the appropriate choice(s) and click OK.

Fig. 15.22
You can inset the contents of a file or create a new object with the Insert Object dialog box.

3. The chosen application will start, taking over the Exchange menus and toolbar to allow you to complete your message creation work in the activated program.

4. The insertion process can be repeated within the same e-mail document, as the sample in figure 15.23 demonstrates.

As you can imagine, the embedding capabilities in Exchange are a great resource. They also have limitations. Embedding makes for easier integration and sharing of applications, but it doesn't allow you and your e-mail recipients to work from a single, instantly updated data source. An embedded object incorporates the actual object data, a picture of the data, and the name of the applications that created it.

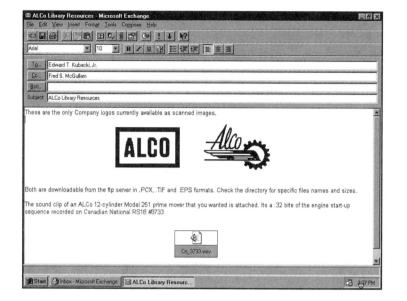

Fig. 15.23
A compound
e-mail message
including text, two
scanned images,
and a sound clip.

Sending Messages

Once you have a message ready to go, you can start it down the information superhighway immediately or hold it for later transmission.

Most people use the hold option when they have a lot of messages to send or when sending a particular message isn't time critical. This type of message traffic is stored in your Outbox folder, ready for transmission when you start a mail run. To use this option, click the toolbar Send icon, and then choose Send from the File menu.

To send a message immediately, choose Tools, Deliver Now. Exchange will ask you which messaging service(s) you want to use (that is, CompuServe, the Internet, The Microsoft Network). Click the appropriate service name(s) and Exchange starts your message on its way.

Replying to Messages

You can respond to a message right after you read it or do it later, as the situation warrants. Immediate replies can be written directly from the Viewer window that's displaying the message in question. If the message isn't open, you can call it up for reply from the main Viewer window by double-clicking its Folder file entry. Either way you do it, Exchange makes easy work of answering your e-mail:

1. To respond only to the sender, click the Reply to Sender toolbar icon or the Reply to Sender selection on the Compose menu. None of the other original recipients of the sender's message will be copied on your reply. To include copies for the full original distribution list, click the corresponding Reply to All options.

2. Type your reply.

3. When you're done, click the toolbar Send icon or choose File, Send. This will pass the message to your Outbox where it'll be held until you tell Exchange to send it on its way. For immediate transmission, press the Ctrl+M keyboard combination or choose Tools, Deliver Now.

Occasionally you'll get mail that you want to *forward* or pass on to someone else. Exchange's forwarding feature lets you easily send copies of a message to as many people as you want. The message shown in figure 15.24 illustrates a neat twist to forwarding: combining a reply to your original correspondent with forwarded copies of the original message.

Fig. 15.24

You can reply on a forward message.

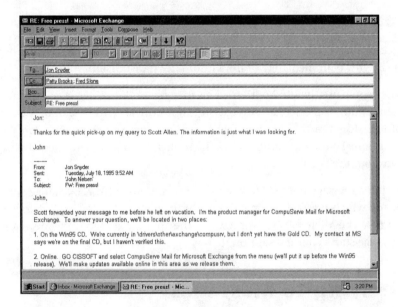

You can forward a message by double-clicking the toolbar Envelope icon. You can also highlight the message's Viewer entry and then either enter the Ctrl+F keyboard shortcut or choose Compose, Forward. You can then address the message by either typing in names in the To field or choosing them from your Address Book. Click the send button in the toolbar to send the message.

Printing Messages

Printed copies of the messages you send and receive are literally just a couple of clicks away.

1. If the item you want to print is already open, skip to Step 2. If it is closed, highlight its name on the Viewer log screen.

2. To print the item on your computer's default printer, just click the toolbar Print icon. If you want to specify a different printer or set certain options for the job, choose File, Print, or use the Ctrl+P keyboard shortcut. Either action will open the familiar Windows Print dialog box (see fig. 15.25). Click OK to complete the printing job.

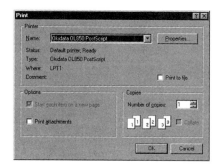

Fig. 15.25
When you initiate print commands from the File menu or via the Ctrl+P keyboard shortcut, Exchange prompts for options before sending messages and files to your printer.

Deleting Messages

Whenever you delete an item from your Viewer, Exchange actually moves it to your Deleted Items folder. This gives you a chance to recover things that you may have accidentally deleted. Once you strike them from the Deleted Items folder, however, they're gone for good.

To delete an item, highlight its Viewer entry and then either enter the Ctrl+D keyboard shortcut or choose File, Delete.

Shortcut Keys

As shown in table 15.1, Microsoft Exchange offers a broad range of keyboard shortcuts that can help you make the most of your time.

Table 15.1 MS Exchange Shortcut Keys

If You Want To...	...Try This Shortcut
Address Book (Open)	Ctrl+Shift+B
Align Text Left	Ctrl+L
Align Text Right	Ctrl+G
Bold Text	Ctrl+B
Bullets (On/Off)	Ctrl+Shift+L
Cancel	Esc
Center Text	Ctrl+E
Check Names	Ctrl+K
Close Active Window	Alt+F4
Collapse Selected Folder	Left Arrow
Copy an Item	Ctrl+Shift+C
Copy Text or Graphics	Ctrl+C
Cut Text or Graphics	Ctrl+X
Delete an Item	Ctrl+D
Delete Character to Left of Cursor	Backspace
Delete Character to Right of Cursor	Delete
Delete Word to Left of Cursor	Ctrl+Backspace
Delete Word to Right of Cursor	Ctrl+Delete
Deliver Mail	Ctrl+M
Expand Selected Folder	Right Arrow
Find Text	Ctrl+F
Forward a Message	Ctrl+Shift+F
Inbox (Open)	Ctrl+Shift+I
Indent Text Less	Ctrl+T
Indent Text More	Ctrl+Shift+T
Italicize Text	Ctrl+I
Message (Open Existing)	Ctrl+O

If You Want To...	...Try This Shortcut
Message (Start New)	Ctrl+N
Move an Item	Ctrl+Shift+M
Move Insertion Point One Word to Left	Ctrl+Left Arrow
Move Insertion Point One Word to Right	Ctrl+Right Arrow
Move Insertion Point to Bottom of Screen	Ctrl+Page Down
Move Insertion Point to End of Message	Ctrl+End
Move Insertion Point to End of Paragraph	Ctrl+Down Arrow
Move Insertion Point to Start of Message	Ctrl+Home
Move Insertion Point to Start of Paragraph	Ctrl+Up Arrow
Move Insertion Point to Top of Screen	Ctrl+Page Up
Next Item (Open)	Ctrl+>
Outbox (Open)	Ctrl+Shift+O
Paste Text or Graphics	Ctrl+V
Previous Item (Open)	Ctrl+<
Print Item	Ctrl+P
Properties (Display/Modify)	Alt+Enter
Remove Text Formatting	Ctrl+Spacebar
Repeat Last Find	Shift+F4
Replace Text	Ctrl+H
Reply to All Item Recipients	Ctrl+Shift+R
Reply to Item Sender Only	Ctrl+R
Save an Item	Ctrl+S
Save Item As	F12
Select All	Ctrl+A
Send a Message	Alt+S
Spell-Check	F7
Underline Text	Ctrl+U
Undo Last Action	Ctrl+Z

IV

Communicating

Tip
If you ever need an extra or replacement copy of the shortcuts list for Microsoft Exchange, click the Exchange Help icon and, using the Index option, load and print the Keyboard Shortcuts file.

Command-Line Options

Windows 95 also helps you build a shortcut that allows you to change what Exchange displays when you open the application. The four-step shortcut setup process is straightforward:

1. Create a shortcut to Windows 95's Exchng32 program.

2. Using your right mouse button, click the Microsoft Exchange shortcut and then click Properties.

3. Click the Shortcut tab and then type a space after the text that appears in the Target box.

4. Type one of the following command-line options:

If You Want To...	...Type
Open a New Message	**/n**
Open a New Message and Attach a File	*file-name*
Open a File as a Message	**/f** *file-name*
Open the Find Window	**/s**
Open the Address Book	**/a**
Open the Inbox without a Folder List display	**/i**

From Here...

In this chapter, you learned the ins and outs of sending, receiving, and managing your mail with Microsoft Exchange. For more information on using e-mail:

■ Chapter 13, "Introduction to Electronic Mail," introduces you to e-mail in general and its many functions.

■ Chapter 14, "Using Electronic Mail with Windows," tells you more about the features of Microsoft Exchange.

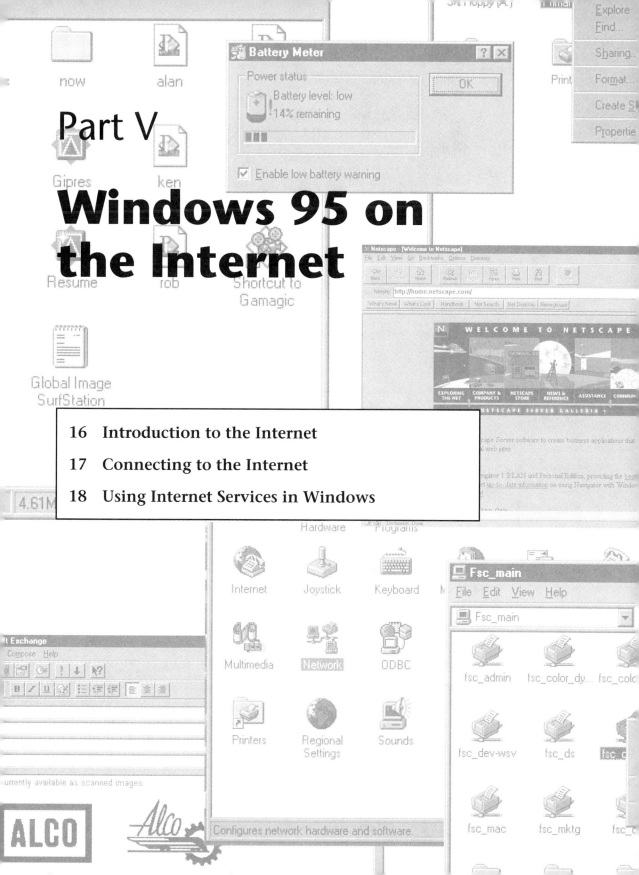

Part V

Windows 95 on the Internet

Files now alan

ıgic Gipres ken

ent Resume rob

Shortcut to
Gamagic

Global Image
SurfStation

Battery Meter ? X

Power status
Battery level: low
14% remaining

▮▮▮

OK

☑ Enable low battery warning

4.61MB

Netscape - [Welcome to Netscape]
File Edit View Go Bookmarks Options Directory

Back | Forward | Home | Reload | Images | Open | Print | Find | Stop

Netsite: http://home.netscape.com/

What's New! | What's Cool | Handbook | Net Search | Net Directory | Newsgroups

WELCOME TO NETSCA

EXPLORING | COMPANY & | NETSCAPE | NEWS & | ASSISTANCE
THE NET | PRODUCTS | STORE | REFERENCE

• NETSCAPE SERVER GALLERIA •

NETSCAPE AT WORK
See how companies are using Netscape Server software to create business applica
employees to information on internal web sites.

OPEN WINDOWS TO THE INTERNET
Netscape announces Netscape Navigator 1.2 LAN and Personal Edition, providin
and features for Windows users. Get up-to-date information on using Navigator wi
Download 1.2 with Netscape Now!

ew
Hardware

Programs

Internet Joystick Keyboard

Multimedia Network ODBC

Printers Regional Sounds
Settings

Configures network hardware and software.

Microsoft Exchange
Tools Compose Help

B / U ≣ ≣ ≣ ≣

logos currently available as scanned images.

Fsc_main

File Edit View Help

Fsc_main

fsc_admin fsc_color_dy... fsc

fsc_dev-wsv fsc_ds

fsc_mac fsc_mktg

ALCO

Alco

Chapter 16

Introduction to the Internet

The Internet or Net is the big business news in the 1990s. Reading the ads, watching the news, and listening to other business people talk, you might think there's no way your business can survive if you aren't on the Net.

The Internet is not a mandatory piece of your network—yet. However, when you are ready to connect to the Internet, Windows makes this easy to do.

In this chapter, you learn

- What the Internet is
- Who can use the Internet
- What business resources are on the Internet
- How to access the Internet

What Is the Internet?

The actual definition of *internet* is, "a network of networks." In reality, there can be any number of internets. All that's required is two or more networks (say, the one in Sales and the one in Accounting) to be connected.

When the word is capitalized, that is when things get interesting. The *Internet* is a network made up of around 53,000 networks all connected together. The networks can consist of a single computer to thousands of computers, and the networks can be located anywhere in the world. (Although connecting a single computer to the Internet is an expensive proposition; instead, single computers usually connect via a *service provider* or another online service that already offers an Internet connection.)

Any of the 4.9 million computers that make up these networks may communicate with any of the others. They can send e-mail, transfer files, even print on network-connected printers on the other side of the world. This kind of global connectivity is a necessity for some businesses. It can also be a convenience that businesses quickly learn to take advantage of. Imagine having e-mail, file transfer, and networking capabilities, such as remote printing, available between different divisions of a company (whether or not those divisions are in the same city, state, or country is irrelevent) for almost no additional cost. With the right software, this kind of network access is also almost completely transparent to users. As far as they are concerned, they could be communicating with someone in the same office.

How Are All the Networks Organized?

The Internet began as an experiment by the U.S. government. Simply put, it was designed and created so that the networks of the government could function no matter where network traffic was disrupted. In other words, the Internet was designed to have no central point, no central clearing house, and no central network neighborhood that had to exist for the whole system to function. This, in part, explains why the Internet can be so complicated. It was designed to operate, essentially, under chaotic conditions.

Computers that are connected to each other on a network communicate with each other via *protocols*. A protocol is nothing more than a prearranged method of communicating information over network cabling (even if that cabling is a phone line), with both sides of a connection using the same language. Communication over the Internet uses a protocol known as *Transmission Control Protocol/Internet Protocol* (TCP/IP). While the specifics of how TCP/IP work are not necessary to understanding how the Internet works (just like you don't have to understand how an engine works to drive a car), you do need to know some basics about TCP/IP in order to use the Internet effectively.

In any network, there needs to be a way to individually identify each machine. While it's easy for people to assign names to machines, computers don't work well with names; they do much better with numbers. Each machine on the Internet has a number assigned to it, and this number is called an *IP address*. An IP address is simply a 32-bit number that is unique to each machine. For example, Que has a machine on the Internet that has an assigned IP address of 198.70.148.9. Why is it written in this fashion? An IP address is broken down into four eight-bit parts, with each part separated by periods. The four parts are like a mailing address in that each part as you move along the IP number narrows down the specific location of the machine, just like an address on a letter focuses you on a specific geographical location (although the location of a machine on the Internet has more to do with where in the network it is, as opposed to a physical location). Internally, it's stored as a single number, but significance is placed on the individual parts. In order to connect or talk to any machine on the Internet, all you need is the machine's IP number. By the way, the value of each eight-bit part can range from 0 to 255, with certain values being reserved for special purposes.

Okay, so if you know the IP address of a computer on the Internet, you can connect to it (or send data to it). However, it's no fun trying to memorize numbers. Instead of making people memorize a bunch of addresses, the Internet uses a system called the *Domain Name Service* (DNS). DNS groups computers on the Internet into *domains*, which are nothing more than "clubs" that a system can belong to. However, "clubs" doesn't do the idea of a domain justice. You can think of a domain as serving the same purpose as the parts of an IP address, in that they tell you, essentially, where a system is located. DNS, however, allows English-like names to be used instead of hard-to-memorize 32-bit numbers. For example, go back to the example used earlier in this chapter. If you wanted to talk to Que's machine on the Internet, you have to know the IP address, which is **198.70.148.9**. Memorizing that number is no fun, so DNS allows you to reference this machine via a name that is easier to memorize. In this case, it's **www.mcp.com**.

So what does **www.mcp.com** actually stand for? You can figure out more from a machine's domain name by reading the name in parts, starting at the end with the primary domain. **com** means that this machine is part of the com, or commercial domain; hence, this machine belongs to a commercial organization. Other possible ending domain names are **mil** (military), **gov** (government), **edu** (educational institution), **org** (non-commercial organization), **net** (gateways and other administrative hosts), and **uucp** (sites that previously had no domain but do now).

Unfortunately, the rest of the name can be just about anything, depending on who set up the network that a particular machine is on. In the case of this example, **mcp** means Macmillan Computer Publishing and **www** means that this machine is used for the World Wide Web (a service of the Internet that allows users to view data in a hierarchical and graphical manner).

At this point, you're probably thinking "Great! How the names get assigned, with the exception of the primary domain, is completely arbitrary." You're right. However, companies and organizations tend to pick names that "make sense," so that they are easily identified. If you want your customers to be able to locate you on the Internet, it doesn't make much sense to pick some obscure, hard-to-remember name, does it? Some companies use abbreviations (like Macmillan Computer Publishing). Others, like Microsoft, spell out their name (in Microsoft's case, it's **microsoft.com**). The White House uses **whitehouse.gov**. When you go further down the hierarchy, companies stick to the same rules. **www.mcp.com** makes perfect sense when you know that www refers to the World Wide Web. Similarly, Macmillan has an *FTP site* (file transfer protocol, which is a protocol for transferring files across the Internet) for people to retrieve information from, and it has the easily remembered name of ftp.mcp.com. Macmillan could have called their FTP site **plotz**, but that wouldn't make much sense.

> **Note**
>
> By the way, each piece of the name can be referred to as either a domain or a *subdomain*, but don't let that confuse you.

The Purpose of the Abbreviations

As mentioned previously, the naming scheme is based on a hierarchy, read from right to left. The rightmost portion of an address refers to the type of the domain.

Let's look at a more complete Internet address to see how this works. You had a friend call you and tell you that they've started a new job and have an Internet connection. So, if you want to send them e-mail, you can address it to **mpl@wimail.us.denix.com**. What can you figure out from this?

Since names like this are read right to left, you start at the end. From the previous discussion, you know that **com** means a commercial organization. Moving to next part of the name, you see **denix**. You can assume from this that your friend has gone to work for the Denix Corporation (or Denix, Inc., or Denix Industries—you can't tell any more from the e-mail address).

The rest of the name, as mentioned previously, is completely arbitrary and up to the company, individual, or organization who set up the machines connecting to the Internet. However, you can make some guesses. Most likely, the **us** part refers to Denix's United States operations. They probably have divisions in other countries, so Denix uses part of the name to signify which machine serves what divisions. There's no way to know what **wimail** is, but most likely it is a machine whose job is to handle incoming mail for Denix and route it to the appropriate person.

That leaves the first part, **mpl@. mpl** is simple. It's your friend's user name, the name they're known by on Denix's computer systems. The **@** is used to separate the user name from the rest of the address. Mail programs (and other programs that handle information on the Internet) use the **@** to find out where the user name ends and the Internet name begins.

How Is the Internet Growing?

The Internet is growing so fast that nobody really knows how big it is. In 1994, it was estimated that a new computer was added to the Internet every 30 seconds, and the growth rate since then has been even greater. Figure 16.1 illustrates the historic and projected rate of growth in the number of computers connected to the Internet.

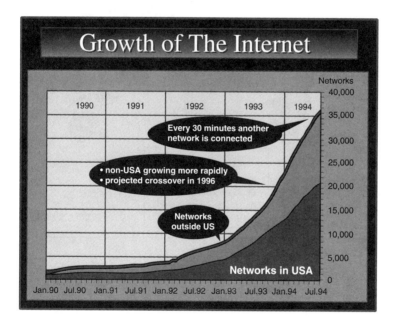

Fig. 16.1
The Internet tends to grow pretty quickly.

Who Controls the Internet?

Officially, nobody governs the Internet. It doesn't belong to anyone, but exists as an agreement among all of its users to stick to the same protocols and naming conventions. Each network on the Internet is a separate entity, and the cooperation of all these entities makes it work.

The Internet Information Center (InterNIC) currently provides the service of registering and tracking individual domain names to make certain there are no conflicts, and the National Science Foundation (NSF) is responsible for doling out IP address numbers.

The Internet is very much self-policing. There is an implicit agreement among its users that it is treated as a resource that is not wasted or abused. So far, this implicit agreement has worked.

Who Can Use the Internet?

Anyone can use the Internet. You can connect from almost anywhere in the world. Figure 16.2 shows how much of the world is Internet-connected as of March, 1995.

Fig. 16.2
Almost the entire world has Internet access.

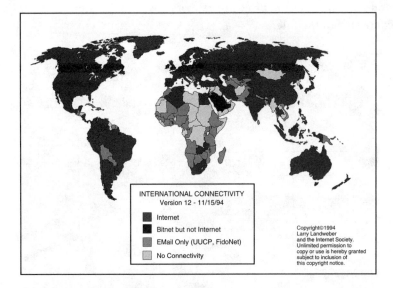

While "anyone" can use the Internet, how you get connected to it varies from individual to individual. Your company might connect to the Internet in order to allow customers access to information, as well as for the exchange of e-mail. Universities are usually connected to the Internet so that students can arrange to have accounts on university computer systems with Internet access. How you connect via a university varies from educational institution to institution.

But, if your company isn't on the Internet (or doesn't allow you to use the Internet connection they are funding for personal use) and you aren't a student at a university with an Internet connection, what can you do? You have two choices: *online services* and *service providers*.

Online services refer to commercial entities like CompuServe, America Online, Prodigy, GEnie, and Delphi. However, online services now can include individual bulletin-board systems (BBSs). All of the major online systems offer Internet e-mail, and most also offer access to the Internet itself, with FTP, the World Wide Web, and UseNet news available for the asking. However, the variety of services available to you varies from online service to online service. Different companies also charge different amounts of money for the usage of the Internet. If you already have an account with one of these companies, you should check to see what they offer and how much it costs to use.

If you don't want to pay CompuServe or America Online more money just to use the Internet, or if you don't have accounts with any of these companies, you can use a service provider. A service provider is a company that provides you with a direct connection to the Internet via their computer systems and phone lines. They have already gone to all the trouble of having high-speed phone lines set up. They've set up all the necessary software for you to use to connect to the Internet. They also will provide a phone number for you to use to establish a connection. Depending on where you live, the phone number may be a local call, it may be a long-distance call, or it may be a 1-800 (toll free) call.

So what's the advantage of a service provider? For one thing, when you use a service provider, you are usually using a system that is designed to provide you with a reliable, dedicated connection to the Internet. Online services like CompuServe have had to retrofit their software and systems to allow you Internet access. Service providers also (usually) let you have free reign on the Internet. They provide most all the services the Internet has to offer. Finally, service providers can be very cheap. While CompuServe and America Online usually charge you by the hour, service providers can offer you access for a flat monthly rate, no matter how much you use their systems. Now, not all providers are that generous, but you may find that a service provider can be much cheaper than the commercial online companies. In addition, service providers usually have less traffic than online services—you spend less time (which equals less money) finding what you want.

How much service providers charge and how you pay for their services vary from provider to provider. Some charge a flat monthly fee for number of hours. Others charge by the hour during certain times of the day. Some let you pay by credit card, while others bill you every month in advance for a certain number of hours. Be sure you understand the terms of a provider before committing yourself!

V

Windows on the Internet

It's interesting that most tiny, remote cities and villages in the world today are getting Internet connections before they get tellphone service. The Internet Society predicted in 1993 that if current trends in Internet growth and world population expansion continue, every person in the world will (theoretically) be on the Net by the year 2004.

How Can I Get Internet Access for My Network?

Internet connections typically come in two forms: dial-up with a modem and direct connections using a leased line from the phone company and a network adapter in a PC on your network.

Each of these has its strengths and weaknesses. In this section, we take a look at both.

Dial-Up Connections

A dial-up connection is the most affordable type of Internet connection. You provide the computer, the modem (at least 14,400 bps—less than that will be too slow for data-intensive applications like World Wide Web browsers), and a phone connection. When you want to get on the Internet, you just call your provider with your computer.

If you only have few users on your local network who are accessing the Internet at the same time and don't expect lots of WWW use, a dial-up connection may be your best bet. You can get a dial-up connection for less than $50 a month and with a low set-up cost.

Dial-up connections work well if you primarily want to send and receive e-mail. You can configure Microsoft Exchange to connect at certain intervals (once an hour, for example) using remote access and download all the mail waiting for your users from your service provider's mail server. Permanent dial-up connections are also available if you want your network to have access to all of the resources on the Internet, including FTP, Gopher (a protocol and suite of applications for viewing Internet data in a hierarchical fashion), and WWW.

Modem connections, even with a 28.8 Kbps modem, are relatively slow. If you plan on more than one user accessing the Internet via your local network at a time, you should probably look at a direct connection.

Direct Network Connections

Most networks connected to the Internet today use a leased line from the local telephone company to make the connection. Leased lines are available at any number of speeds, but most of them are nowhere near the speed of your local network. The most common connection is a 56 Kbps leased line, which is double the speed of a 28.8 Kbps modem. Leased lines are typically connected directly to a service provider and are dedicated for your use only.

The main issue related to connecting your network to the Internet with a leased line is cost. 56K Internet connections typically cost between $800 and $2,000 a month, plus a large one-time set-up charge for the network equipment. Leased lines are typically wired directly into your network, giving you constant access to your service provider.

Leased lines are available in speeds up to 1.5 Mbps (a T1 line) and 36 Mbps (a T3 line) if you need a faster connection. A T1 line runs at about 15% of the speed of your local network and costs several thousand dollars per month.

The Best of Both Worlds

In some cities, there's another option. Some phone companies have begun offering *Integrated Services Digital Network* (ISDN) connections. These are 128 Kbps dial-up connections through a special digital phone line. The line is twice the speed of a 56 Kbps leased line and costs between $25 and $60 a month. If you live in a city that offers ISDN connections, it's probably your best bet for inexpensive but fast Internet access. However, before deciding what type of connection you need, check with your service provider to find out what they support.

Business Resources on the Internet

The Internet is a vast source of information, contacts, communication, software, and services. Chances are good any information you're looking for can be found on the Internet.

The Internet can be broken up into categories by the services offered to help you with your search for information. The most popular services are

- E-mail

- Gopher

- File Transfer Protocol

- World Wide Web

V

Windows on the Internet

Each of these provides a different method of getting information on the Internet. There are a number of others, but these are of the most use to businesses.

E-Mail

You've already learned about using e-mail on your network to communicate with other users. E-mail on the Internet works the same way. You can send messages and files—you can even include sound and video. Additionally, e-mail can be sent to any machine you have an address for (no matter where that machine is), and it's free. Well, not completely free; you have to pay for the phone line to get it out into the Net. However, if you're using a service provider, this is usually included in their normal charges.

Microsoft Exchange has Internet mail capability built-in, so adding global e-mail to your local network e-mail is simple.

Figure 16.3 is an example of e-mail sent over the Internet.

Gopher

Gopher was developed at the University of Minnesota as a way to navigate through lots of information using a hierarchical list. There is some dispute over the name, but the general consensus is that it's called Gopher because it *goes fer* things.

As was mentioned previously, Gopher refers to several pieces of software. Like most Internet services, Gopher software consists of two parts: a Gopher client and a Gopher server. You run the client software on your local computer and tell it to connect to a Gopher server out on the Internet (most Gopher client software contains a built-in list of different Gopher servers that it knows about). The Gopher servers contain all the information that a Gopher client can access. The client asks for this information and presents it to you in a hierarchical fashion.

Like the table of contents of a book, Gopher can present information in a condensed form. When you click on an entry displayed by the Gopher client, you are shown the information associated with that title (much in the same way that Windows Help System shows you information). What makes Gopher so powerful is that a title may or may not point to information on the current Gopher server. It may point to another machine entirely. You, however, don't have to be concerned with this. Just by clicking the entries, you can view information in a logical, ordered manner.

Fig. 16.3
Internet mail
works just like
regular e-mail.

There are thousands of Gopher servers around the world, and they're a terrific place to look for information. Figure 16.4 shows a Gopher server at the University of Missouri with links to a number of different libraries.

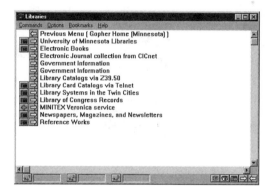

Fig. 16.4
A library Gopher at
the University of
Missouri.

V

Windows on the Internet

File Transfer Protocol

File Transfer Protocol (FTP) is one of the most used services on the Internet. FTP lets you transfer files from one computer to another. Typically, FTP is used to download files from a large archive of software maintained by a company or other organization. There are thousands of megabytes of *freeware* and *shareware* on the Internet for you to download. Freeware is just that: free. You can use it in just about any fashion you like without paying for it. Shareware, on the other hand, is software that you can try for free, but you are expected to pay the author of the software some small fee if you continue to use the software. It's one way for talented software authors to get their creations in your hands without going through the normal distribution channels. Please, if you use a shareware package for more than a few weeks, pay for it!

Unfortunately, the name FTP is confusing. FTP is both a service and a protocol, just like Gopher is a service and a protocol, and the World Wide Web is a service and a protocol. FTP gets its name due to the original program used to connect to another system on the Internet being named *ftp*. It is important to remember that names like Gopher and FTP can refer to both specific software packages as well as services on the Internet.

Windows includes a character-based FTP client built-in that is functional but not very user friendly. Figure 16.5 shows the Windows FTP client transferring a file. As previously discussed, FTP also refers to the software you use to work the FTP service. You must have an "FTP client" to transfer files via the FTP service. Like Gopher, the FTP client connects to an *FTP server* running on the machine you want to connect to. The client and server talk to each other in order to handle the file transfer.

Fig. 16.5

Transferring a file with Windows' character-based FTP client.

Since FTP is so popular, there are a number of graphical FTP clients available that are easier to use than the one included with Windows. Figure 16.6 is an example of one of them being used to get files from a Windows' software archive.

Fig. 16.6

An FTP transfer using a graphical FTP client.

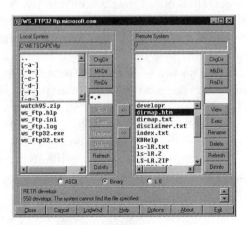

World Wide Web

The World Wide Web (WWW or Web) is one of main reasons for the dramatic growth of the Internet. WWW presents information in an attractive, graphically rich form that is easy to use, which makes it very popular.

"Great!" you're thinking. "Another program for accessing information in yet another form on the Internet!" Well, almost. One thing many people find confusing about the Internet is that there are so many different programs you have to know about. Want to transfer files? Use FTP. Want to connect to a Gopher server? Use a Gopher client. Additionally, Gopher and FTP are not known for being very user-friendly.

The Web attempts to change this (and it does it very well). First, the Web allows you to look at information that is not only text-based, but also graphically-based. It allows people to create *Web pages*, which are nothing more than documents that Web browsers know how to display. Web pages can be any length from one line to several screens long. They can contain graphics and color. They can also contain *hyperlinks*, which are locations you click that can take you to another Web page and that Web page can be on another computer entirely.

To make things even easier, Web browsers also know how to talk to FTP servers, Gopher servers, and even UseNet news servers. This means that one program (a Web browser) can navigate through all the most popular services offered by the Internet. If this wasn't enough, Web browsers are extremely easy to use. If you've used the Windows help system, you can use a Web browser.

One of the the most popular WWW browsers is Netscape Navigator (see fig. 16.7). Netscape, like most WWW browsers, displays formatted text, graphics, sounds, animations, and video. Netscape also allows elements from different pages—or even different computers—to be linked together so that you can jump from one to the other with the click of a mouse.

Today, you can find almost anything on the WWW. Figure 16.8 shows WWW clients displaying a variety of media-rich content.

V

Windows on the Internet

Fig. 16.7
Netscape is one of
the most popular
Web browsers.

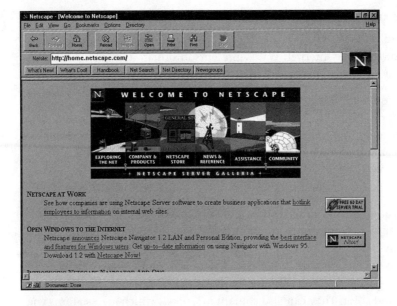

Fig. 16.8
A WWW page with
information about
Windows 95.

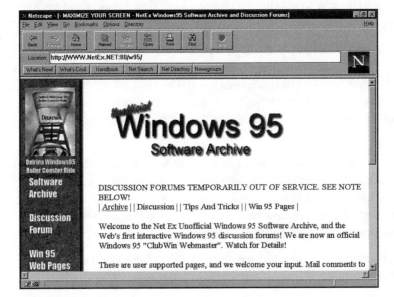

From Here...

In this chapter, you learned about the Internet's origins, what the Internet is,
how to get connected, and what services are available for your network.

For more information on the Internet see

- Chapter 17, "Connecting to the Internet," discusses how to connect to the Internet.

- Chapter 18, "Using Internet Services in Windows," discusses how to use the different Internet services with Windows.

- Appendix D, "Internet Access Providers," is a list of Internet access providers.

V

Windows on the Internet

Chapter 17

Connecting to the Internet

In chapter 16, you were given a brief introduction to the Internet. This chapter incorporates what you learned there to take you through the necessary steps to connect to the Internet using the software supplied with Windows.

Specifically in this chapter, you learn

- The steps to install the networking software

- The steps for installing the TCP/IP drivers

- The process of setting up the TCP/IP drivers to connect to the Internet

- To test the Internet connection to make sure everything is working the way it should

If you've worked with TCP/IP drivers under previous versions of Windows, you'll quickly notice that Windows 95 comes with all the necessary software to get on the Internet quickly. Quite simply, Windows 95 was born to network. Earlier versions of Windows required you to go to other vendors for the necessary software, which was usually rather difficult to install. With Windows 95, the drivers are tightly integrated into the system itself.

What You Need To Get Connected

In chapter 16, "Introduction to the Internet," you learned what you need to have before you can configure your system to connect to the Internet. This included contacting a service provider for an account and having them provide you with the necessary information in order to set up Windows.

This chapter makes several assumptions about your system. Make sure you have the following information before proceeding:

- You have contacted a service provider and have set up an account. Your service provider provides you with several key pieces of information about their system that you'll need to have before you can connect. Specifically, you'll need your login name and password, the phone number to dial to connect to your provider, your IP address (if your provider uses fixed IP number assignment), and what protocol your provider wants you to use (PPP or one of the SLIP protocols).

- You have already purchased and installed a modem on your computer. For your own sanity's sake, make sure your modem is at least 14,400 bits per second (bps) (28,800 is even better). Many Internet applications (especially the World Wide Web browsers) transfer a lot of data to your computer over the phone line. Anything slower than 14,400 bps will be unbearable.

- You are going to use PPP (Point-to-Point Protocol). Most providers offer you the option of using SLIP, CSLIP and PPP. If you have a choice, pick PPP. It's faster and more reliable than SLIP or CSLIP. While Windows does support SLIP and CSLIP, it's more work to install and set up. Installing SLIP support is briefly covered, but the main thrust of the discussion assumes a PPP connection.

- You are using a service provider and not an online service. Yes, CompuServe, America Online, Prodigy, and Delphi all let you get to the Internet. However, they don't use any of the networking features of Windows. They use Windows as a glorified terminal. CompuServe does offer a direct Internet connection option, but it uses CompuServe's own TCP/IP drivers, which are not installed the same way (or with the same ease) as Windows drivers.

To help make this subject more palatable (and hopefully, a bit clearer), I'll be using my provider as an example when you get to that part of the process. And while each provider does things a bit differently, it should not be too difficult for you to handle any minor differences between my provider and yours.

Why Use Windows Internet Drivers?

If you look through any computer-related magazine, you'll be flooded with advertisements from companies offering you complete turnkey solutions to accessing the Internet. Is there an advantage to using any of these packages?

In truth, it depends on how you look at it. Yes, these packages offer you a suite of applications that will give you e-mail capabilities, let you read UseNet news, surf the World Wide Web, and all sorts of other wonderful activities. However, you'll pay a price ranging anywhere from $100 to more than $500. You'll also have to deal with installing and setting up these somewhat complex pieces of software.

One nice feature of the Internet is that many of the best tools are available for free or for a modest shareware fee. You simply have to know where to look and what to look for. One reason these software packages are so popular is that Windows 3.1 didn't come with any support for accessing the Internet.

Windows 95 changes that. Microsoft now has TCP/IP support—the protocol needed to connect to the Internet—available as part of Windows 95. All you have to do is install and configure it.

The Benefits of Windows Internet Drivers

There are certainly advantages to using Windows TCP/IP drivers. While the fact they're included with Windows is one of the more obvious reasons, the real reasons are much deeper:

- Windows TCP/IP drivers are 32-bit drivers, unlike many of the currently available TCP/IP (Winsock) drivers. While everyone touts the wonders of being 32-bit, in this case it makes a big difference because low-level networking drivers can be a bottleneck.

- The drivers are integrated into Windows' shell. This means that they interact with you via Properties sheets, making them easy to set up.

- Microsoft's drivers are completely Winsock-compliant and enable you to use 32-bit and 16-bit applications. Many of the most popular freeware and shareware Internet applications are available as 32-bit applications (with Windows 95-specific versions in the works). The 32-bit versions are much more efficient than their 16-bit counterparts. However, if there is a 16-bit application you like, it should work just fine with Microsoft's TCP/IP drivers. If it doesn't, look for an application that does. Windows users on the Internet are a picky lot, and Windows 95 has people excited enough to guarantee a veritable glut of Windows 95-specific Internet applications. If an application doesn't work with Microsoft's 32-bit Winsock drivers, most likely it'll be updated soon.

You'll go through the necessary steps to install the proper drivers, set up your TCP/IP connection, and get connected to the Internet. This will get us ready

V

Windows on the Internet

for the next chapter, where you'll go out onto the Internet and grab a bite of software for your use.

Installing TCP/IP on Windows 95

To connect to the Internet via your modem, you must first install Windows Dial-Up Networking. Dial-Up Networking is an accessory provided with Windows that allows your system to connect to other computers via a phone line, with the connection resembling a direct network connection. Dial-Up Networking provides the connection the TCP/IP drivers need because TCP/IP expects a direct connection. TCP/IP doesn't understand how to talk to your modem or how to log in to your provider, but Dial-Up Networking does.

Installing Dial-Up Networking

Installing the necessary drivers to access the Internet is a three-step process. The first step is to install a Windows component known as Dial-Up Networking. This software enables (among other things) your computer to be a part of a Windows network over a phone line. It's also required by the TCP/IP drivers. Go to the My Computer icon on your desktop and double-click it. A window opens up, showing you the current drives on your system. It probably looks very similar to figure 17.1.

Fig. 17.1
My Computer shows your drives and other important folders.

If you see a folder named Dial-Up Networking, you've already installed the first piece of software. In that case, skip ahead to the next section. If you don't see a Dial-Up Networking folder, you need to install Dial-Up Networking. Here's what you do.

1. Open the Start menu and choose Settings, Control Panel. You see a window showing all the Control Panel applets.

2. Double-click the Add/Remove Programs icon and select the Windows Setup tab in the Add/Remove Programs Properties sheet (see fig. 17.2).

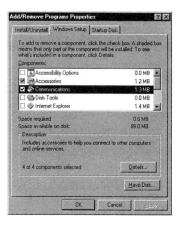

Fig. 17.2
The Windows 95 Add/Remove Programs Properties sheet for adding and removing software.

3. Click the Communications entry and then click the Details button. The Communications dialog box appears. This dialog box shows the pieces of software that Windows classifies as dealing with communications (see fig. 17.3).

Fig. 17.3
Software in Windows 95 that deals with communications and networking.

Now, click the checkbox next to Dial-Up Networking so that a checkmark appears in the box. When you've done this, click the OK button. The Communications dialog box closes, and you'll once again be looking at the Add/Remove Programs Properties sheet. Click OK.

Windows now begins copying the necessary files from your installation CD-ROM to your hard drive. You'll be kept up-to-date on how many files have been copied via a progress meter.

V

Windows on the Internet

After all the necessary files have been copied, you'll get a dialog box instructing you to shutdown the computer when you're done in order for the new software to take effect. Just click the OK button since you've got more software to install.

Now you're ready to install the TCP/IP drivers themselves.

Installing the TCP/IP Drivers

Now that you have Dial-Up Networking installed, you're ready to install the TCP/IP drivers. Remember, Dial-Up Networking gives your computer the ability to connect to your provider via a modem. The TCP/IP drivers provide the support for the Internet connection itself. The TCP/IP drivers handle the packets that Internet uses; Dial-Up Networking handles the dirty details of dealing with your modem and COM ports.

The following discussion assumes you are going to use a PPP (Point-to-Point Protocol) connection with your provider. If you need SLIP (Serial Line Interface Protocol) or CSLIP (Compressed SLIP), you still need to install the TCP/IP drivers. However, you'll need to perform an extra step later on in this chapter. By default, when you install the TCP/IP drivers, the installation routines assume you're going to use PPP.

You'll need to install SLIP support, which is discussed in the section "Installing SLIP/CSLIP Support." The good news is that it's easy to install because that support is on the CD-ROM.

The following are the steps to install the built-in TCP/IP drivers:

1. Open the Start menu and choose Settings, Control Panel.

2. Double-click on the Network icon in the Control Panel window.

3. Open the Start menu and choose Settings, Control Panel. If you are continuing from the last section, this dialog box is already open.

   The Network applet appears, showing you the current networking options that are installed. Depending on what you installed when you set up Windows, you may or may not have any entries displayed. In any case, you see something similar to figure 17.4.

4. Click the Add button. This displays the Select Network Component Type dialog box, asking you what exactly you want to add (see fig. 17.5).

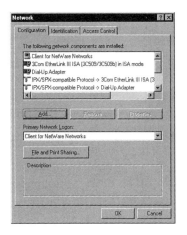

Fig. 17.4
The Network applet is used to add network components.

Fig. 17.5
Adding a network component is done by category.

V

Windows on the Internet

5. Select Protocol and click the Add button.

After you click the Add button, you see the Select Network Protocol dialog box.

6. Click the Microsoft entry in the Manufacturers list box. The items listed in the Network Protocols list box change to match the list in figure 17.6.

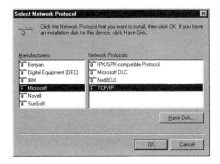

Fig. 17.6
Selecting the TCP/IP protocol for installation.

7. Select TCP/IP and click OK. The dialog box closes, and you'll be back at the Network dialog box. However, there is a new entry marked TCP/IP.

8. Click OK. The system installs the TCP/IP drivers.

Before continuing, make sure to bind the Dial-Up Adapter to the TCP/IP drivers. *Binding* makes sure that the TCP/IP drivers automatically use Dial-Up Networking and not another NIC in your system (if you have any NICs installed). For example, if you had an NIC installed in your computer, the TCP/IP drivers could use Dial-Up Networking and your NIC connection to connect to the Internet (assuming your NIC was connected to a network that had an Internet connection). Binding just tells the TCP/IP drivers what connections to work with when connecting to the Internet. To do this, follow these steps:

1. Click the Dial-Up Adapter entry and click Properties.

2. The Dial-Up Adapter Properties sheet appears; click the Bindings tab and make sure that there is a checkmark next to the TCP/IP entry (see fig. 17.7).

Fig. 17.7
Selecting the network protocols to bind TCP/IP to.

You can clear the checkmarks next to IPX/SPX-compatible Protocol and NetBEUI if you're not planning to connect to either a NetWare server or the Microsoft Network via a phone line. Leaving these boxes marked won't hurt anything, but it may slow down connecting to the Internet because Windows tries to verify what type of network you're connecting to over the Dial-Up Adapter.

3. After setting the bindings, click OK and you'll be back at the Control Panel window. At this point, Windows asks you if you want to reboot your computer. In this case, you do (so that the bindings are in effect for the next step), so let Windows reboot by clicking Yes. Make sure all of your work is saved!

4. After Windows has reloaded, double-click the Network icon in Control Panel. If you had Control Panel open when you rebooted your computer, it should open again automatically. If it didn't, open the Start menu and choose Settings, Control Panel.

Once the Network Properties sheet appears, select TCP/IP and click the Properties button. If there is more than one entry marked TCP/IP, select the one that says TCP/IP->Dial-Up Adapter. You'll see the TCP/IP Properties sheet with quite a few options (see fig. 17.8). Here is where you'll need the information sent to you by your provider.

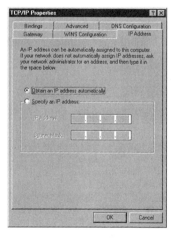

Fig. 17.8
The options available for configuring the TCP/IP drivers.

The first piece of information you need to supply to Windows is your TCP/IP address. There are two possibilities here. Some providers assign you a unique IP address each time you connect. Others assign you an IP address that never changes. Your service provider should tell you which type of IP address connection you need to use to access their service.

■ If your service provider instructed you it assigns an IP address automatically each time you connect, choose Obtain an IP Address Automatically.

V

Windows on the Internet

■ If your service provider tells you to use an IP address that never changes, choose Specify an IP Address. Enter the IP address in the IP Address text box. If your service provider uses a subnet mask address, enter it in the Subnet Mask text box. Both pieces of this information should have been supplied to you when your service provider set up your account. IP addresses use the format of **123.456.789.01**

Depending on your provider, this may be all the information you need to enter. If so, skip ahead to the "Setting Up a New Connection" section, which describes the final necessary step to have Windows call your provider and set up the TCP/IP connection. The rest of this section covers the other tabs on the TCP/IP Properties sheet.

Entering Your WINS Resolution

The next tab is marked WINS Configuration (see fig. 17.9). WINS (Windows Internet Naming Service) is a way for one computer to find out the IP address of another computer on the Internet. However, WINS is not used by a lot of providers (most use DNS). WINS has some advantages over DNS, the main advantage being that WINS servers are much simpler to set up than DNS servers. However, WINS is specific to Windows, while DNS is supported by almost every implementation of UNIX available. Because most providers use DNS, this section focuses on DNS. If your provider uses WINS, they can help you fill in the necessary information. DHCP for WINS Resolution is used if you are using WINS and your provider automatically assigns your IP address when you connect. If your provider uses DHCP (Dynamic Host Configuration Protocol), mark the Use DHCP for WINS Resolution checkbox.

Fig. 17.9
Setting up TCP/IP to use WINS for name resolution.

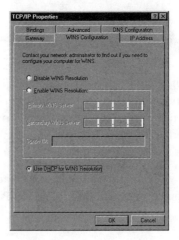

Entering Your Gateway Address

The next page is the Gateway page (see fig. 17.10). If your provider gives you a remote gateway IP address, you need to enter it in the New Gateway text box and click Add. A gateway is simply the IP address of a machine that takes IP packets sent to it and decides where in the network they should go.

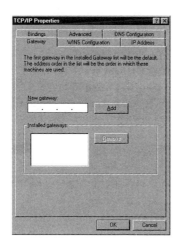

Fig. 17.10

Specifying a gateway address for your Internet connection.

In reality, "where they should go" is a relative phrase. Most gateway machines simply look at packets to see if they should be sent to one of a limited number of destinations. The destinations are usually other machines that go through the same process all over again. In this roundabout fashion, IP packets end up where they belong. For example, if you want to set up an FTP session with a site in another state, the gateway machine looks for the best way to establish the connection outside of your provider's network. If you're connecting to a computer in Washington, the gateways set up the connection route. It may go from my house to my provider to another California site to a site in Oregon (or Nevada—or some other place) to Washington.

Entering Your DNS Host

The next page is the DNS Configuration page (see fig. 17.11). As discussed in chapter 16, DNS (Domain Name System) is a software package used by machines on the Internet that enables you to use easy-to-remember names instead of hard-to-remember IP address numbers. If your provider provides you with IP addresses of name servers, these are most likely machines running DNS. Some service providers have more than one name server available.

◀ See "How Are All the Networks Organized?," p. 274

V

Windows on the Internet

Fig. 17.11
Setting up DNS
allows you to use
names, not IP
addresses.

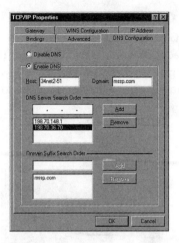

The Host and Domain text boxes and the Domain Suffix Search Order section
are usually provided by your provider if they are needed. Host and Domain
are simply places to name your machine. When the two are combined, they
form your complete Internet address. The Domain Suffix Search Order section enables you to specify multiple domains (if they are needed) that can be
sent to DNS when it's trying to match a name to an IP address.

Entering Advanced and Bindings Information

The remaining two tabs, Advanced and Bindings, usually do not need to be
updated. Advanced has no entries you can alter (for the simple reason that
Windows TCP/IP drivers don't have any Advanced properties; other vendors'
software might make entries here for you to change).

Bindings specifies what networking clients are bound to TCP/IP. Bindings
does have an entry, File and Printer Sharing, that appears on the Networks
dialog box. Click this button and deselect the two options that appear so that
printer and file sharing are disabled. Remember, when you are connected to
the Internet, you're part of a global computer network, and Windows can
make some of the devices on your system visible to the outside world. Unless
you want people to be able to print to your printer, you should disable this
checkbox (if it is available).

Installing SLIP/CSLIP Support

If you are planning on using PPP to connect to your provider, skip to the
next section. If you need to install SLIP support, read on. Your service
provider tells you what type of communication support you need to use to
connect to their service.

To install SLIP support, first display Control Panel and double-click the Add/Remove Programs icon. Click the Windows Setup tab. You'll see the familiar Setup page you saw in figure 17.3.

Click the <u>H</u>ave Disk button. You'll be asked for the location of the disk you want to install from. You should either enter the following path or use the <u>B</u>rowse button to locate the RNAPLUS.INF file in the ADMIN\APPTOOLS\ DSCRIPT directory on the CD-ROM.

> **Note**
>
> Don't be confused by the fact that there is a subdirectory under ADMIN\APPTOOLS called SLIP. It just contains a text file pointing you to the DSCRIPT directory. By the way, the Windows 95 Resource Kit also has the path wrong.

Click OK and you see the Have Disk dialog box, where you can select what software you'd like to install that is referenced in the RNAPLUS.INF file. There is only one package to choose, so select the checkbox next to the item (see fig. 17.12).

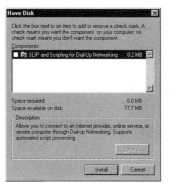

Fig. 17.12
Select the SLIP package to install SLIP support.

Click the <u>I</u>nstall button and let the system install the necessary files. After that's done, click OK to close the Add/Remove Programs Properties sheet, and SLIP support is now installed.

Setting Up a New Dial-Up Connection

At this point, you've installed Dial-Up Networking and the TCP/IP drivers. You've also configured the TCP/IP drivers with the necessary information provided by your service provider (IP addresses, DNS parameters, and so on).

V

Windows on the Internet

Now that TCP/IP is installed and configured, create an entry under Dial-Up Networking that instructs Windows to call your service provider.

Open the My Computer window; then double-click Dial-Up Networking. You see a window with one icon, titled Make New Connection (see fig. 17.13).

Fig. 17.13
Your Dial-Up Networking window has one new icon.

Double-click the Make New Connection icon. The Make New Connection Wizard appears and asks you questions about your new connection. The first dialog box asks you about the name of your connection and which modem you'd like to use for the connection (see fig. 17.14). You can name it anything you like, but it's probably a good idea to pick a name that means something to you. Here, I chose Internet because I'm setting up a connection to my Internet service provider. Because I only have one modem, it's selected as the default.

Fig. 17.14
The Make New Connection Wizard guides you through the dial-up process.

Click Next to go to the next step. On the next dialog box, you specify the phone number for your service provider (see fig. 17.15). Enter the phone number that your provider gave to you, and click Next.

When you click Next, you'll be presented with the final dialog box, asking you to confirm that you're done (see fig. 17.16).

Now, your Dial-Up Networking window has a new icon for the connection you just created.

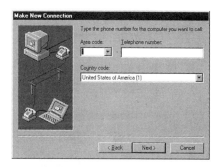

Fig. 17.15
Here's where you enter your service provider's phone number.

Fig. 17.16
The last Make New Connection Wizard step.

V

Windows on the Internet

Configuring SLIP/CSLIP Dial-Up Information

If you are going to use PPP to connect to your provider, you are done. Skip ahead to the next section where you can quickly test the TCP/IP drivers.

If you're going to use SLIP or CSLIP, you need to make a change to your new connection because Microsoft's TCP/IP drivers assume PPP. Go to your newly created connection icon, Internet in this example, and right-click. From the pop-up menu, select Properties. You'll see the Internet dialog box (see fig. 17.17).

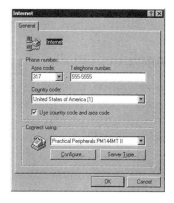

Fig. 17.17
The Internet dialog box lets you specify the specific details of your connection.

Click the Server Type button so that you can select SLIP instead of PPP. You see the Server Types dialog box (see fig. 17.18).

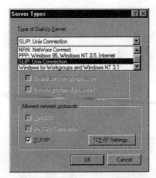

Click the arrow button at the end of the line that reads PPP: Windows 95, Windows NT 3.5, Internet, and from the resulting drop-down list, click SLIP: Unix Connection. If you are using plain SLIP, unmark Enable Software Compression checkbox; if you're using CSLIP, make sure that this checkbox is marked. Click OK.

By the way, if you (out of curiousity) click the TCP/IP Settings button, you'll see that none of the options are set. Don't panic! By default, the local settings for this connection are set to their default values, not the values you specified earlier when you configured TCP/IP. You only need to change these settings here if you want to have settings that are different from the system-wide settings you made earlier.

Now, test your connection.

Testing Your New Connection

Once your connection is set up, all you have to do to activate it is double-click your connection icon. Before you test your new connection, the following are a few things to consider when connecting to a service provider:

■ Different Internet providers have different ways of establishing a connection. Some service providers log on to their UNIX machine. Once that has happened, the PPP connection is automatically established. Not every provider works this way. Some providers have you log on and then select from a menu. Others have a special command you must issue to start a SLIP or PPP connection.

■ Microsoft's SLIP drivers do not work well with providers that use dynamic IP addressing assignment (where your IP address changes each
time you connect). If your provider works this way, you'll have to
change your configuration each time you call, which is another reason
why you should use PPP if at all possible. If you need to interact with
your provider's UNIX system before the PPP drivers can take over the
session, click the Configure button in the Internet dialog box (refer to
fig. 17.17) to instruct the drivers to open a terminal window for you at
the appropriate time so that you can interact with your provider.

If you double-click the Internet icon, you see the Connect To dialog box (see
fig. 17.19).

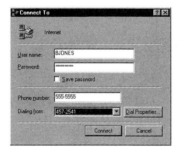

Fig. 17.19

The Connect To
dialog box lets you
specify your user
name and
password.

Here is where you specify your user name and password that your provider
assigned to you. You are asked for the password each time you try to connect
unless you type your password in and mark the Save Password checkbox.
Here, you enter your user name and password, and click Connect.

When you do that, Windows dials your provider, logs you on, and establishes
a PPP connection. You'll see several progress dialog boxes as this happens.
When the connection is established, you'll get a duration window. This window just shows you that a dial-up connection is active and for how long it's
been active.

So how do you know it's working and that all the parameters you specified to
TCP/IP are right? Well, Microsoft supplied you with a couple of utilities to
allow you to do just that.

When you installed the TCP/IP drivers, a few bare-bones utilities were also
installed. Now that you have a connection going, you can use these utilities
to test your setup.

▶ See "Using the PING Command," p. 389

To test out your setup, you use a utility with a long history in the UNIX world, Ping. Ping has one job. Given an address or a machine name, Ping sends out a packet to the address, asking the machine at the destination address to send a response packet back. Ping then waits for response packets and shows the amount of time it took for the packet to return. Ping is also a quick and easy way to test your DNS setup. If you specify a numeric IP address and Ping reports success, then your packets are getting out into the Internet. If you Ping a machine by name and don't get a response or Ping reports that it couldn't resolve the name, then your DNS parameters are not right. Most of the utilities supplied by Microsoft are command-line utilities. Ping doesn't have a fancy windowing front end.

Troubleshooting

If things didn't work the way you expected, go back and make sure you entered all the data correctly. Transposing a number can cause TCP/IP to fail, with little explanation as to what the problem is.

Also, if you can't connect, make sure your modem is working properly. If you know it is, use the Windows HyperTerminal application to call your provider. Make sure you can connect normally before setting up a TCP/IP connection. If your provider has special instructions for setting up a connection, make sure you understand them. Take advantage of the Dial-up Scripting Tool (available under the Programs, Accessories menu) provided by Microsoft. You can use it to help automate complicated connection sequences.

From Here...

In this chapter, you learned how to get your system configured to start talking to the Internet. Setting up a Dial-Up Network icon with the appropriate TCP/IP settings makes getting connected to your service provider easy.

From here, some of the other chapters in this book will help you understand networking and the Internet more:

- Chapter 4, "Understanding How Networks Work," provides you with the basics to understanding networks in general—even the Internet.

- Chapter 16, "Introduction to the Internet," tells you more about what the Internet has to offer and how it is organized.

- Chapter 18, "Using Internet Services in Windows," where you connect to your provider, retrieve some software for using the Internet with Windows from an FTP site, and install it.

Chapter 18

Using Internet Services in Windows

In the last chapter, I went through the involved but straightforward process of setting up TCP/IP under Windows 95 and getting connected to an Internet provider. If you were successful, pat yourself on the back! The hardest part of using the Internet is setting up your original connection. One thing to keep in mind: if it seemed like an obtuse process, remember that it's easy under Windows. If you were going to do this on a UNIX system, you would be in for a very complicated sequence of actions. Trust me on this; I've done it several times.

So you're connected. Now what? In this chapter, you're going to learn to use your new connection to link to an Internet site, retrieve one of the most popular programs for use with the Internet, and go through the process of installing and using this new program. This will give you a feel for using two of the most popular tools available to Internet users: using FTP to transfer files from one computer to another and browsing the World Wide Web.

In this chapter, you will learn about these topics:

- Using the FTP application included with Windows

- Downloading files with the FTP application

- Installing the application that you downloaded: Netscape

- Using Netscape to surf the World Wide Web

The Basics of FTP

Let's take a look at where chapter 17, "Connecting to the Internet," left off. You've got a Dial-Up Networking icon that you can double-click. When you do that, Windows 95 uses your modem to dial the phone number of your provider. It then proceeds to log on to their system and starts a PPP (or SLIP) session. Isn't that thrilling? But, where's all the fun stuff the Internet is supposed to offer?

It would seem that you're kind of stuck here. You can stop checking the back of the book to see if there is a CD-ROM or floppy that is chock-full of goodies for use with the Internet. It's not there. So how are you supposed to use the Internet if there's no software supplied with this book? You're also probably thinking to yourself, "Well, this is nice. Microsoft goes and gives me these wonderful drivers to set up an Internet connection and no software to use with them! So I can connect and disconnect from my provider."

If you're really ambitious, you've probably gone into the Windows help system and looked for words and entries that resemble Internet, FTP, PING, and WWW; the only thing you found was a topic concerning what you went through in chapter 17, "Connecting to the Internet."

However, it probably just occurred to you that you tested your connection with something called PING. How come that's not documented?

Microsoft was kind enough to supply several sparse, but functional, tools with the TCP/IP drivers, of which PING is one of them. They also provide you with a way to get the software you need to work with all the fun stuff you've read about. Unfortunately, they don't document any of these tools. You'll have to buy the *Windows 95 Resource Guide* in order to read about them.

You've used Microsoft's drivers to get connected. You're going to use one of these tools to get some software. That tool is called FTP.

Introduction to File Transfer Protocol

FTP is the abbreviation for File Transfer Protocol. It's the Internet equivalent to downloading and uploading from or to a BBS or online service. With FTP, you connect to an Internet site and if that site allows FTP, you can exchange files with that site. Unfortunately, FTP was designed to be functional and not pretty. It was also designed originally for the UNIX operating system (OS), and it shares the sparseness of that powerful OS's command set. Microsoft's version of FTP is basically a clone of the UNIX tool in every respect.

Don't let the sparseness of Microsoft's version of FTP scare you. While Microsoft's version of FTP may be obtuse and not very pretty, it's free and it's enough to get you started. There are several wonderful versions of FTP for Windows that take full advantage of the Windows interface.

The mechanics of FTP are very complex and would take a whole book to explain. However, it does help to know how to use this tool, and you will use it as a bootstrap for your Internet exploration. The best way to learn a little bit about FTP is to use it, so let's do that. Just remember, FTP is a way to transfer information from one computer on the Internet to another. Once you learn how to use FTP, you'll have the ability to use one of the most powerful and useful features of the Internet.

Establishing an FTP Session

First, establish a connection to your provider. This is done by double-clicking the new Internet connection that you created in chapter 14, "Using Electronic Mail with Windows." Once you've established a dial-up connection to your Internet service provider, open an MS-DOS prompt session (either full-screen or windowed). The site you want to connect to is called **ftp.mcom.com**. Where did the site name come from? In this case, I just happen to know it. There are many books that list the various FTP sites around the Internet, and you should definitely consider picking one up at some point. However, once you start using other Internet tools (like the World Wide Web), you don't have to know exact site names. The tools help point you in the right direction.

Once you are connected, you can make sure everything is okay by pinging **ftp.mcom.com** (type **ping ftp.mcom.com** at your DOS prompt). You'll see something similar to figure 18.1. By pinging **ftp.mcom.com**, you can be sure that your DNS parameters are correct, your Internet connection is active, and you are ready to begin using the tools that this chapter discusses. By the way, don't be confused by the use of an MS-DOS session. Once you've connected to your provider, all programs that use TCP/IP will see a connection, even programs that run under MS-DOS. Also, if the PING command works, then you know that **ftp.mcom.com** is up and accepting connections via the Internet.

Fig. 18.1
Pinging
ftp.mcom.com.

At this point, you're connected and you know that **ftp.mcom.com** is alive and well at IP address **198.95.249.66**. Now let's run FTP. The FTP application included with Windows is easy to start: type **ftp** at the DOS window's C:\ prompt. When you invoke FTP without any command-line arguments, you don't get much. You just get the ftp> prompt. The title bar text in the window also turns from MS-DOS prompt to FTP.

You can get a list of commands for FTP by entering **?**. As you can see, FTP supports over 40 commands. The command you issue to connect to a site is the open command. This command opens an FTP connection to an FTP site, allowing you to list the files stored at that site and select files you want to download. Enter **open ftp.mcom.com** at the ftp> prompt. You'll be asked to identify yourself via the User: *prompt*.

FTP will connect to the site that you requested and attempt to open a connection. Once this has been done, the remote system identifies itself via the line that starts with the 220. FTP messages tend to always start with a number that identifies the message (if you had documentation for FTP, you could look this up).

Logging On to Your FTP Site

You've connected, and now you're being asked for a user ID. What should you type? Your Internet account name? If you actually had an account on this system, you would already have an ID to type in. However, in this case, you're going to use *anonymous FTP*, which means that you can log in to **ftp.mcom.com** without having an ID. Not all computers on the Internet allow anonymous FTP. However, all FTP sites available to the public do.

Since you're going to use anonymous FTP, enter **anonymous** for your ID. After you press Enter, one of two things will happen.

FTP sites can handle many, many users at once, all connecting via the Internet to retrieve files and software packages. However, there are limits to the number of simultaneous connections a site can accept. If there are no free connections available for anonymous FTP, you'll get a polite message like the one shown in figure 18.2.

Fig. 18.2
Too many connections message.

In the case of **ftp.mcom.com**, it can handle only 250 anonymous users at once, and at this time, there are that many using anonymous FTP. Different systems produce different messages, ranging from the terse "no anonymous connections available" to **ftp.mcom.com**'s lengthy message explaining the problem and providing pointers to other sites where you can find the software you're looking for. Keep in mind that not all FTP sites can handle as many as 250 simultaneous users; with some sites, it can be as few as 20 at a time.

On the other hand, if there is an available connection, you'll be asked for a password. While you can enter anything you like for a password when using anonymous FTP, it's customary to enter your e-mail address.

Once you enter your e-mail address, you'll get a welcome message from the FTP software running on the remote system followed by another ftp> prompt (see fig. 18.3).

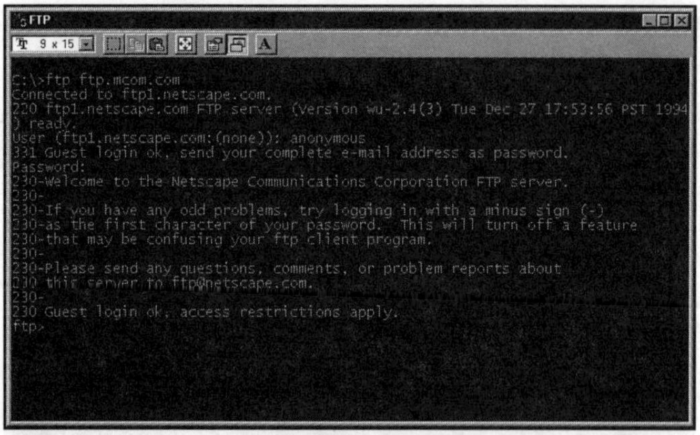

Fig. 18.3
Welcome
message from
ftp.mcom.com.

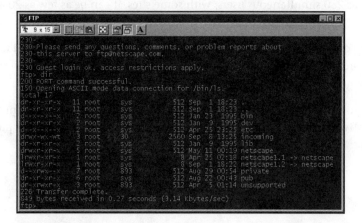

Listing Files Located on an FTP Site

You can now issue commands to the remote system and have it respond. You can think of the ftp> prompt as a simple command shell where you can look at directories, move to different directories, etc. If you like, you can even think of the ftp> prompt as being exactly like DOS's C:\> prompt, although the commands available to you are limited when compared to DOS.

So what are you looking for? You're looking for Netscape's World Wide Web browser software, which is also called Netscape. Netscape actually makes versions of their browser software available for Windows (both 16- and 32-bit), the Macintosh, and various flavors of UNIX. Netscape has a version of Netscape specifically for Windows 95, so that's what you'll grab.

At the ftp> prompt, type **dir**. FTP shows you a list of files in the current directory (see fig. 18.4).

Fig. 18.4
Issuing the first
dir command.

While it's not always the case, Netscape's FTP software site is on a UNIX system. As with all UNIX systems, you see directories called bin, dev, etc, and pub. The dir command produces several messages about PORTs and connections for /bin/ls. These are just informative messages from the FTP software telling you it's sending ASCII (instead of binary) data to your computer.

The output from the dir command may look a little strange if you've never seen UNIX before. The first five columns are various pieces of information about each file: the permissions (r for read, w for write, etc.), the owner of the file, its size, and so on. You don't really need to care about this. However, you do want to look at the entries that begin with the letter d. These are subdirectories (just like in MS-DOS) that you can access. On most FTP sites, anonymous FTP lets you go into the pub (for public) directory. Freely available software is usually kept there.

In this case, however, you want to go to the netscape directory, which is where Netscape keeps copies of their browser. It's free for the taking; however, if you use it for any amount of time, you might consider purchasing a copy directly from Netscape. It's not expensive, around $50, and you get a very nice printed manual (as well as support).

So to go to the netscape directory, enter **cd netscape**. Then issue another dir command to see what's there. You'll see a screen similar to that shown in figure 18.5.

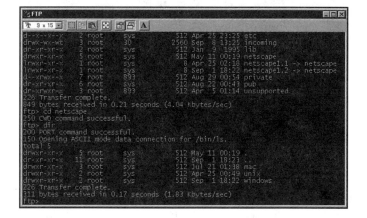

Fig. 18.5
Going into the netscape directory.

You can see that there are several subdirectories in the netscape directory, one for each operating system supported by Netscape. You obviously want the windows directory: enter **cd windows**. You'll be rewarded with a message about the software you're about to download (see fig. 18.6).

V

Windows on the Internet

Fig. 18.6
Going into the
`windows` directory.

Fig. 18.6
Going into the
`windows` directory.

You should read this message when you see it on your own, but basically, it's warning you that the software you're about to retrieve is licensed and may not be exported to certain countries. If you download it, you are agreeing to Netscape's terms.

Okay, so do another `dir` and see what's here (see fig. 18.7).

Fig. 18.7
Issuing `dir` in the
`windows` directory.

Finally! Here is where the software you're looking for lives. There are five files here. The two executables (`n16e12n.exe` and `n32e12n.exe`) are two different versions of Netscape for Windows. The `12n` in the name refers to the version number, which is 1.2n. If this were a beta version, the `n` would be replaced by a `b`. This is not a rule, it's just the way Netscape does it. The `16` and `32` refer to the platform that each executable is meant for. `16` is for 16-bit Windows (Windows 3.x), and `32` is for 32-bit Windows (Windows NT and Windows 95).

Downloading an FTP Site File

Now that you have found the file, download it to your system's hard drive. So how do you get it? There are two commands you have to issue.

The first sets the mode for the FTP transfer. There are two modes: ASCII and binary. The default mode is ASCII. ASCII is used by the FTP software itself to send text to your machine. It's useless, however, for transferring executables. If you just issued the command to transfer n32e12n.exe to your system, FTP would obey your command, but what you would get wouldn't be of any use since ASCII transfers strip information from the data stream. You want to do a binary transfer, so issue the binary command to set the proper mode (see fig. 18.8).

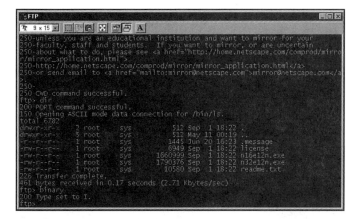

Fig. 18.8
Issuing the binary command.

The second command retrieves n32e12n.exe. The command is get. Just enter **get n32e12n.exe**. You can see from the output of the dir command that this file is over a megabyte in size, so it will take a while for it to transfer to your PC. Enter **get n32e12n.exe**. Unless there is a problem, **ftp.mcom. com** sends the file to your machine (see fig. 18.9).

When the file has been transferred to your computer, the FTP software will give you a summary of how long it took and how much data was transferred. In this case, it took about 750 seconds (or 12 minutes), using a 14.4Kbps connection, for the file to be transferred.

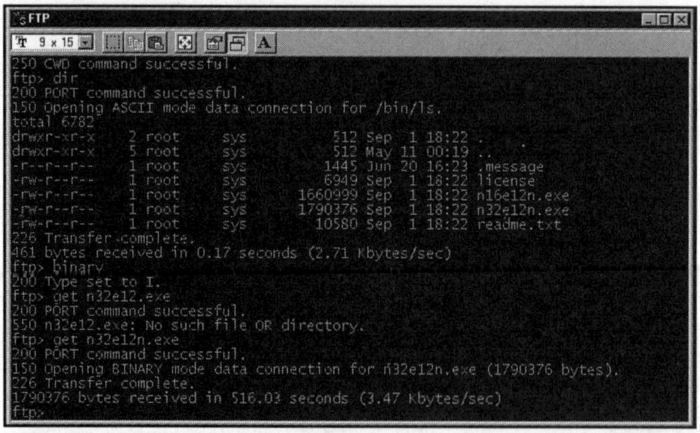

Fig. 18.9
File transfer
messages.

Now that you're done with that, close the FTP connection so someone else can get in. Enter **close** and **quit** to exit the FTP program (see fig. 18.10). You now have n32e12n.exe in the directory you started out from, namely C:\. If you want to specify where the files you are retrieving go on your local machine, you can use the **lcd** (Local Change Directory) command before you issue the **get** command. Just enter **lcd** *directory*, where *directory* is the location on your machine you want to change to.

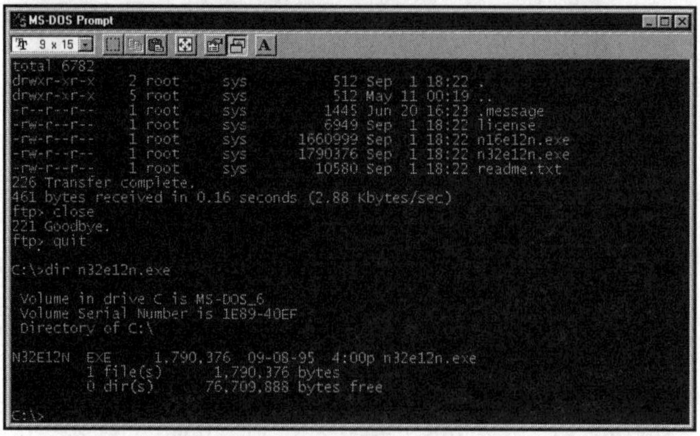

Fig. 18.10
Ending the FTP
program.

Let's go set up Netscape's software and try it. You should probably disconnect from your provider while doing this, but you don't have to.

Installing Netscape

Netscape is a Windows application, and like most Windows applications, it has a SETUP.EXE application that you must run before you can use Netscape. However, don't go run `n32e12n.exe` just yet. It won't install Netscape.

The application `n32e12n.exe` is a special type of executable, commonly called a *self-extracting executable*. It is a collection of files, compressed and bound together in one piece. When you run `n32e12n`, it expands into the various files needed to set up and install Netscape.

The first thing you need to do is create a temporary directory to put the pieces into. You can't save it to a floppy because it won't fit. So open an MS-DOS prompt session, pick a drive that has some free space on it, and create a directory. For simplicity's sake, name that directory JUNK and put it on drive C. Then make JUNK the current directory by entering the **CD \JUNK** command (see fig. 18.11).

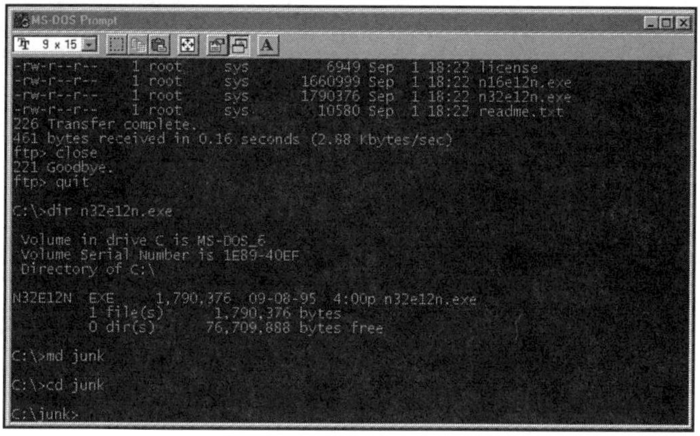

Fig. 18.11
Creating a directory.

Next, enter the path to wherever you put `n32e11n.exe`, followed by **n32e11n.** The various files are extracted automatically as `n32e11n` executes. If you then enter **dir**, you'll see all the files necessary to set up Netscape including the SETUP.EXE installation program (see fig. 18.12).

You can see that the second-to-last line printed by `n32e12n.exe` is SETUP.EXE. Now, just enter **SETUP** at the MS-DOS prompt, and Netscape's installer executes (see fig. 18.13).

Fig. 18.12
Executing n32e11n.

Fig. 18.13
Netscape's
installer.

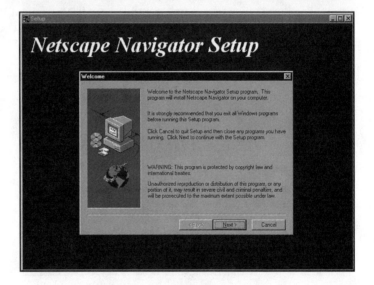

Netscape 1.2 uses a new installation program known as the Installation Wizard. The first screen you'll see just tells you about Netscape, so choose the Next button. By default, Netscape installs itself in the PROGRAM FILES directory that Windows uses for its own programs (such as Accessories and Plus!). Unless you have a pressing need to select another directory, it's best to accept the default.

After Netscape finishes its installation, it will create an entry on the Programs menu called, appropriately enough, Netscape Navigator (see fig. 18.14). By default, it leaves the Windows program group it creates open on the desktop. It also creates a shortcut on your desktop.

Fig. 18.14
Netscape's group.

You should take a look at the Read Me file at some point. It contains another copy of the License Agreement along with instructions on installing and getting started with the various versions of Netscape.

Setting Up Netscape and Understanding What You See

Now you need to do a little configuration of Netscape. Connect once again to your provider and when you're connected, double-click the Netscape Navigator icon to execute Netscape. After getting another chance to examine Netscape's license agreement, which you must accept in order to run the program, click the Accept button; you'll start to see graphics and text in Netscape's window after a moment. While it's working, Netscape's moonrise N will have comets floating slowly by it, along with the word Netscape in the status bar at the bottom of the window. When the comets stop moving and the words Document: done appear in the status bar at the bottom of the window, Netscape has finished connecting to its default startup page, the Netscape Home Page (see fig. 18.15).

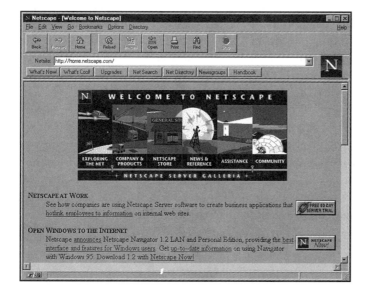

Fig. 18.15
Netscape in action.

V

Windows on the Internet

Congratulations! You just went to your first World Wide Web page! This is the default starting point for surfing the Web with Netscape.

Netscape (and the World Wide Web) are rather complex and have a lot of depth. Indeed, whole books have been written about the Web and Netscape. While this chapter can't begin to cover Netscape and the Web, it can help you set up a few things so you can get started.

First off, notice the line at the top of the window that reads **http://home.netscape.com**. When you see a line that begins with http or ftp, you are looking at a *Uniform Resource Locater* (or URL, for short). It's just another way of specifying a machine and a location on a machine on the Internet. In this case, http means that you want to connect to a World Wide Web page (http is short for *hypertext transport protocol*) and **home.netscape.com** is the machine you want to connect to.

Move your mouse over the blue underlined text and notice that it changes to a finger. This means that the blue underlines are *hyperlinks* and that if you click while the mouse pointer is a finger, you'll be taken to wherever that hyperlink points to (which is shown in the status bar at the bottom of the Netscape window). What makes the Web so powerful is that the place you jump to doesn't have to be on the same machine on the Internet. It may be on another machine in the same company or in another state or even in another country.

You might also notice that when you moved the mouse over the graphics at the top of the window, it also changed to a finger. Pictures can also be pointers to other locations. Many Web pages use graphics to make their content easier to comprehend. If you click a hyperlink and go somewhere that you don't like and want to go back to where you were, use the Back button at the top of the window. Likewise, if you want to go back all the way to your starting point, click the Home button.

Using Netscape as an FTP Client

Most people use Netscape to browse the Web, but it can do many other things. For example, it is an FTP client. In other words, it can do the same job that FTP.EXE did earlier, but in a friendlier fashion. If you want to try it out, go to the text entry area at the top of the screen, delete the text **http://home.netscape.com** and enter **ftp://ftp.mcom.com**. Presto! Netscape will become an FTP client (see fig. 18.16).

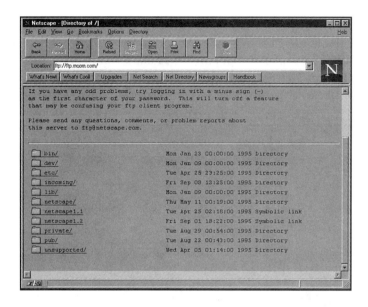

Fig. 18.16
Netscape and FTP.

If you'd like to try this (and you can get to the **ftp.mcom.com** site), then just point and click to retrieve files. Netscape gives you a list of files just like FTP.EXE did, but you'll notice that directories have small folder icons next to them, while other types of files have different icons to show what they contain. Double-click a directory name to show that directory; double-click a file to view it (if Netscape knows how to show it to you) or download it.

There is one thing to keep in mind when using Netscape as an FTP client. Just because Netscape can connect to an FTP site doesn't mean the connection will *stick*. Take FTP.EXE for example. When you use FTP.EXE to connect to an FTP site, the connection is *locked*—that is, once you are connected, that connection stays active and open until you either exit FTP.EXE, close the connection with the **close** command, or disconnect from your provider. Netscape doesn't work that way. When you use Netscape as an FTP client, it opens a connection, gets the information necessary to show you what you've asked for, and then it closes the connection. So it is possible that you could jump to **ftp.mcom.com**, get a directory listing, and then get the familiar too many anonymous connections when you double-click on a folder or file. This is because Netscape has to open a new connection to satisfy your request.

Using Netscape as a Newsreader

Netscape also knows how to read UseNet news. You'll have to tell Netscape the IP address (or name) of your provider's news server in order to do this. Choose Options, Preferences. You'll get a tabbed dialog box. Click the Mail and News tab. You'll see the Mail and News page shown in figure 18.17.

Fig. 18.17
Configuring mail and news.

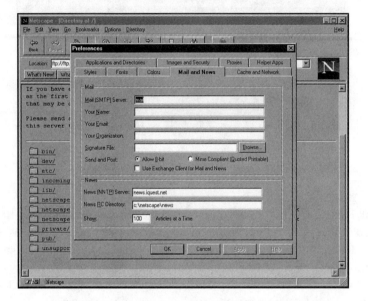

Fill in the names of the necessary servers and choose OK. Your provider should have given you the name of your mail server. If not, ask. You'll need it for any Windows-based Internet mail program you use. Whether or not you have news access depends on your provider.

Once you've typed in the appropriate information, click OK. You'll be taken back to the Netscape main window. If you've got access to a news server, choose Directory, Go to Newsgroups. Netscape will connect to your news server and become a very nice UseNet newsreader (see fig. 18.18).

Netscape's Directory and Help Menus

Finally, take a look at the Directory menu. Each item on there can help you find resources on the Internet. Netscape has links to various WWW directories, as well as search engines for the vast resources of the Internet.

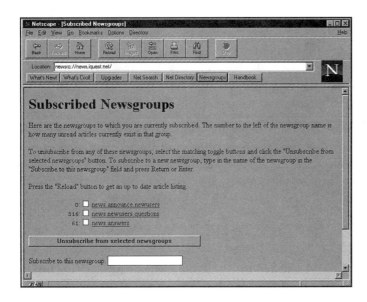

Fig. 18.18
Netscape as a
newsreader.

One more thing. Don't overlook the Help menu. It can show you complete documentation on Netscape. It even has a tutorial. Before you try it, remember this: Netscape's manuals and tutorial are all on the Internet as Web pages. Yes, if you choose Directory, Tutorial, you won't get a Windows 95 help session; you'll get a Web page that will tell you all you need to know about Netscape!

Now, go explore. You can't hurt your computer with Netscape. If you get lost, use the Home button to start over. Use the online tutorial to learn more. And, yes, buy a book on the World Wide Web. Just don't get your family upset because you're keeping the phone line tied up for hours at a time!

Internet Troubleshooting

The Internet is a complex system and is prone to a number of problems. Windows goes a long way toward making it as painless and trouble-free as possible, but you may still run into pitfalls. Here are come common problems and their solutions.

I get a `cannot find winsock.dll` *message whenever I try to start an Internet program.*

This means you probably don't have TCP/IP installed correctly. Open the Network Neighborhood Properties sheet and see if you have the TCP/IP protocol installed. If not, click Add and install it.

I get an unknown host error when I try to connect with FTP or Telnet.

This could be the result of a couple of things. Easy one first: make sure you have typed the name of the host correctly. The message means that Windows asked the Internet for a connection to a machine and the Internet said it couldn't find one by that name.

The more difficult one: it's possible that your Domain Name Server isn't set up correctly. You need to check with your network administrator to see what the address is for the DNS you should be using and make sure you have it entered in the DNS tab of the TCP/IP Properties sheet in the Network Neighborhood.

I transferred a file using FTP. The system said the transfer was successful, but the file seems to be corrupted.

Make sure you transferred the file in binary mode (by entering **bin** before starting the transfer). Any file can be transferred in binary mode, but only text files can be transferred in ASCII mode, so it's a good practice to switch to binary mode each time you do a transfer.

From Here...

This chapter covered the basics of connecting to the Internet, and you retrieved one of the most popular Internet tools, Netscape, which can be used to surf the World Wide Web, transfer files from FTP sites, and read and respond to UseNet news. A detailed discussion of the Internet is beyond the scope of this book, but there are a number of good guides to the Internet available.

For more information:

- Chapter 17, "Connecting to the Internet," gives more information on the technical aspects of using Windows 95 with the Internet.

- Chapter 19, "Connecting to Other Networks," tells you more about configuring the many other Windows connectivity options.

- Appendix D, "Internet Access Providers," helps you find an Internet connection in your area.

Part VI

Connecting Windows to Other Networks

Chapter 19

Connecting to Other Networks

Up until this point we've covered networking from the standpoint of connecting to other Windows workstations. This chapter broadens the scope of the networking environment to cover connecting to other types of servers.

Unless your company is just getting started in networking, you probably already have an existing server that contains vital information for your business. In order to attach to other servers, you have to load additional client software to make the connection. This chapter covers

- Installing network client software for other networks

- The different types of networking clients

- How to configure the right protocols for a particular network

- Troubleshooting when something goes wrong

Understanding Network Client Types

Windows is built to handle networking as an integrated part of its operating system. However, the architecture designed for handling networking is also designed for compatibility with most of the older network client software. *Client software* is a set of drivers that allows Windows to communicate with network resources that rely on a particular architecture to advertise their services. To understand how Windows can support both new and old client software, you need examine the differences between each type of client.

Before Windows 95, you needed to install DOS software to connect to a network. The software you loaded allowed DOS and Windows 3.x to use the network hardware to connect to a server. This software tricked DOS into thinking that you had an external hard drive with a drive letter like Q, which you knew was really a directory on your network server. Under DOS and Windows 3.x, this software was an external add-on to Windows. For example, to connect to a NetWare server, you needed to load LSL.COM, the NIC driver (e.g., NE2000.COM), IPXODI.COM, and NETX.EXE. All of these you tried to load into high memory to conserve as much conventional memory as possible. You also needed to maintain your NET.CFG file to ensure all protocols were loaded correctly.

Under Windows 95, the network drivers are an integrated piece of the operating system. Your conventional memory usage by network drivers is reduced to nothing because they are loaded as part of Windows. Before, each network protocol had to be loaded through conventional memory. Now, the network functions all blend into the Network Neighborhood where many different networks can be running simultaneously. This integration of the network clients makes Windows an excellent network client operating system.

The functions described here show the differences of the older-style network drivers next to the newer, integrated network clients under Windows. The remainder of this section discusses the important performance and resource differences between the native Windows protected-mode network clients and the older-style real-mode network clients. We'll also take a look at selecting, loading, and configuring protected-mode network clients.

Protected-Mode Network Clients

The protected-mode network client is network software that has been designed for the Windows 95 architecture. This software capitalizes on the 32-bit operating system by very closely integrating the 32-bit network software to the networking framework of Windows. With protected-mode network software, up to ten network clients can be loaded to allow access to ten different vendors' servers on the same network. Figure 19.1 shows an overview of the networking architecture of Windows, highlighting the protected-mode networking clients.

The word *protected* in protected-mode network client, means that the 32-bit application can fit in with the 32-bit operating system and run in the fast protected-mode of the Intel 386, 486, and Pentium CPUs. Also, the network clients using protected-mode are shielded from halting the entire system if they fail and allowing the network software to be protected from any other application that fails. This means you can continue to communicate with the Novell or other servers if another application crashes.

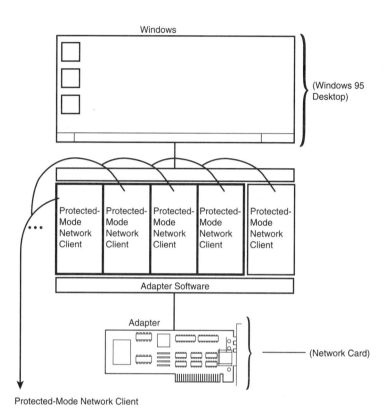

Windows

(Windows 95
Desktop)

...

Protected-
Mode
Network
Client

Protected-
Mode
Network
Client

Protected-
Mode
Network
Client

Protected-
Mode
Network
Client

Protected-
Mode
Network
Client

Adapter Software

Adapter

(Network Card)

Protected-Mode Network Client

Fig. 19.1
Windows sup-
ports up to ten
protected-mode
network clients
to support many
different network
servers.

In addition to the tight integration with Windows and the faster 32-bit
operation, the protected-mode network clients also benefit from the network
caching that takes place within the operating system. A *cache* is a temporary
storage area that allows the computer to store frequently accessed information in memory. By keeping this frequently used information in memory, the
computer does not have to reload it from the network. Novell, LANtastic,
Banyan-Vines, and UNIX servers all reap the performance benefits from network caching.

Now that you know more about protected-mode network clients, here's the
best part: they make getting connected to other networks easy because they
are built right into Windows! Windows manages the configuration details of
your protected-mode clients, so you can focus on the tasks you need to perform. You'll learn how to install protected-mode network clients later in this
chapter.

Real-Mode Network Clients

In the discussion earlier in the chapter, we talked about the way network
drivers worked with previous versions of Windows and DOS. Under the old

VI

Connecting to Networks

way, the drivers were loaded before Windows; then they tricked DOS/ Windows 3.x into thinking there was another hard drive. These real-mode network clients are designed for DOS but work under Windows. These drivers are built using 16-bit technology. While they may offer adequate networking speed, they may not be as fast as the integrated 32-bit network clients for Windows 95.

In other words, real-mode network clients are not part of Windows. They must be loaded before Windows is started, forcing you to have an AUTOEXEC.BAT and a CONFIG.SYS. They do not run in protected-mode and, therefore, do not benefit from memory protection or 32-bit CPU processing.

Additionally, the real-mode networking client is loaded before the Windows 95 operating system takes control of the system. When the system starts, the 16-bit real-mode network drivers are loaded through the CONFIG.SYS and AUTOEXEC.BAT files. Because these drivers are designed for DOS, you cannot typically load more than one of these real-mode network drivers at a time. Figure 19.2 highlights how Windows 95 supports one real-mode network client in its networking architecture.

Fig. 19.2
Windows supports one real-mode network client along with the protected-mode network clients.

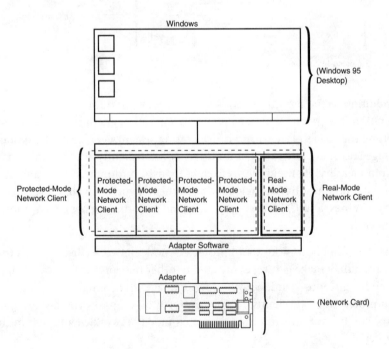

The real-mode driver also does not permit you to make use of Windows' single logon procedure that attaches to other servers automatically. You must logon during your AUTOEXEC.BAT, connecting to the server to complete your drive mappings. If you don't do this before Windows starts, you won't be able to access the services of the real-mode network client.

Now that you know the difference between the two types of network clients, you can move on and see how to connect to servers using the network clients. When you see that a particular network uses a real-mode or protected-mode client, you'll know ahead of time what inherent weaknesses and benefits it already has.

Microsoft Networks

The Client for Microsoft Networks is one of the two protected-mode network clients shipped with Windows 95. This client allows your Windows workstation to connect to any server that is built on the Microsoft server foundation. Several different servers are built on this platform. They are

- Microsoft Windows for Workgroups

- Microsoft Windows NT Workstation

- Microsoft Windows NT Server

- Microsoft LAN Manager

- IBM OS/2 LAN Server

- DEC Pathworks

Installing the Client for Microsoft Networks

Before you can connect to any of the Microsoft network types, you must first install the client itself. The Client for Microsoft Networks is the basis for connecting to Windows for Workgroups, Windows NT, LAN Manager, or DEC Pathworks servers.

Perform the following steps to install the client for MS Networks:

1. Open the Start menu and choose Settings, Control Panel.

2. Double-click the Network icon. The Network dialog box appears as in figure 19.3.

3. Click the Add button on the Configuration tab of the Network dialog box.

4. Click Client in the Select Network Component Type dialog box.

Fig. 19.3
To install the
Client for
Microsoft
Networks, click
the Add button.

5. From the Select Network Client dialog box (see fig. 19.4), select Microsoft from the list of Manufacturers, and Client for Microsoft Networks from the list of Network Clients.

Fig. 19.4
Select Client
for Microsoft
Networks to install
the software.

6. Click OK to install the client software. When prompted to restart your computer, click OK to complete the installation.

Now that you have installed the Client for Microsoft Networks, many of the following types of networks are easy to connect to. In fact, you have already done all the steps to get connected to some of the following network types.

Windows for Workgroups

While Windows for Workgroups is not a network operating system, it should be mentioned that any workstation using Windows for Workgroups can share files and printers with your Windows workstation. However, some of the more advanced features, such as fax-modem sharing, don't operate properly without Windows 95.

You do not need to install any additional software to connect to Windows for Workgroups workstations on your network. These workstations use a similar file-sharing protocol as Windows 95 to share their files. However, you may want to upgrade these workstations to Windows 95 to take advantage of the more advanced networking features like fax sharing.

You'll know you're connecting to a Windows for Workgroups server by viewing the properties of the server. In the Network Neighborhood, right-click the server name and choose Properties from the pop-up menu. The Type of server will be shown as Windows for Workgroups on the server's Properties sheet. An example is shown in figure 19.5.

Fig. 19.5
The Type identifies this server as a Windows for Workgroups peer server.

Connecting to Microsoft LAN Manager

Microsoft LAN Manager has largely been replaced by Windows NT Server; however, there are many installed servers that use the OS/2 v1.2 version of the Microsoft network operating system. You will not need to install any additional software to access the basic file and print services on your LAN Manager server.

> **Note**
>
> The IBM OS/2 LAN Server and Microsoft's LAN Manager software were basically the same network operating system several years ago until IBM and Microsoft began to differ on the direction of OS/2. Microsoft LAN Manager is based on an older version
>
> (continues)

(continued)

of OS/2, is no longer sold by Microsoft, and contains fewer enhancements than IBM's LAN Server, which is based on OS/2 Warp.

Also, DEC Pathworks is a specially licensed version of Microsoft's LAN Manager software that runs on the DEC VAX system. This allows PCs to connect to mainframe and minicomputers that act as network servers.

Windows NT Server

The Windows NT Server connectivity with Windows 95 is excellent since both of these operating systems grew up together. Your Client for Microsoft Networks can also connect you into the advanced security offered by Windows NT Server, like encrypted passwords.

You can tell if you have access to a Windows NT Server by double-clicking the server's icon in the Network Neighborhood. If you have access to any of its resources, they'll be displayed in the server's window. If you don't have rights to anything, the window will be empty.

You can't tell what kind of server each computer is by the icon in the Network Neighborhood unless you inspect its Properties sheet. To find out if a server is a Windows NT Server, right-click the name of the server and choose Properties from the pop-up menu. This displays the server's Properties sheet. If it is a Windows NT server, the type will be identified as Microsoft Windows NT (see fig. 19.6).

Fig. 19.6

If you're connecting to a Windows NT Server, its Properties sheet will identify the type as a Microsoft Windows NT Server.

DEC Pathworks

DEC Pathworks is a Windows LAN Manager network operating system that
runs on a DEC VAX. DEC plans to provide a 32-bit network client in the very
near future to access DEC Pathworks servers. Until that time, you'll need to
perform some special steps to access a DEC Pathworks server. To connect to
a DEC Pathworks v5.x server, you must install the Client for Microsoft Networks and the DEC Pathworks protocol. Follow these steps to configure your
computer to access the server.

> **Note**
>
> If you want to access a DEC Pathworks v4.1 server and you don't have the 32-bit
> network client from DEC, you must first install Windows for Workgroups 3.11 on the
> computer before installing Windows. The drivers are available on CompuServe in the
> DECPI forum. You don't need to do this if you plan to access a Pathworks v5.x server.

1. Right-click the Network Neighborhood icon and select Properties from
   the pop-up menu. This displays the Network dialog box.

2. Select Add from the Network dialog box.

3. Select Protocol from the Select Network Type dialog box and click Add.

4. Select Digital Equipment (DEC) from the Manufacturers list as figure
   19.7 shows.

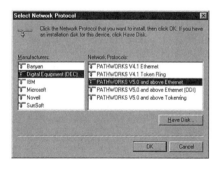

Fig. 19.7

Select Digital
Equipment (DEC)
from the Manufac-
turers list and the
Network Protocol
appropriate for
your configura-
tion.

5. Select the appropriate Pathworks protocol version from the Network
   Protocols list.

6. Click OK to add the Pathworks protocol.

VI

Connecting to Networks

Once complete, use the following table to ensure that your configuration files have the appropriate entries to support a DEC Pathworks real-mode network client.

Table 19.1 Required Entries in Configuration Files for a DEC Pathworks Network Client	
Configuration File	**Entries**
AUTOEXEC.BAT	C:\WINDOWS\NET START
	C:\PW\STARTNET.BAT
CONFIG.SYS	REM - By Windows 95 Setup - Stacks=9,256
	FILES=100
	REM - By Windows 95 Setup - buffers=30
	FCBS=16,8
PROTOCOL.INI	[DLL$MAC]
	drivername=DLL$MAC
	lanabase=0
	bindings=DEPCA$[NWLINK$]
	drivername=NWLINK$
	frame_type=4
	cachesize=0
	bindings=DEPCA$[NETBEUI$]
	drivername=NETBEUI$
	lanabase=1
	sessions=10
	ncbs=12
	bindings=DEPCA$[DEPCA$]
	drivername=DEPCA$

Configuration File	Entries
	`maxmulticast=8`
	`maxtransmits=16`
	`adaptername=DE100`
	`interrupt=5`
	`ioaddress=0x200`
	`ramaddress=0xd000[PROTMAN$]`
	`priority=ndishlp$`
	`drivername=protman$[NDISHLP$]`
	`drivername=ndishlp$`

Connecting to a Novell NetWare Network

If you are one of the estimated 70% of networked users who connects to a Novell NetWare server, you are in luck. The other protected-mode client software that comes with Windows 95 is the Client for NetWare Networks. This allows you to take advantage of the high-speed protected-mode network client software while connecting you to current Novell NetWare servers.

Some initial tests of the Client for NetWare Networks under Windows showed a 200% increase in speed over the standard Novell NetWare software running on DOS. Now you may not see this dramatic improvement in everything you do, but the vast majority of your work will see an improvement when you are connected to the NetWare server using the Client for NetWare Networks.

In addition to the speed increases, the Client for NetWare Networks allows you to maintain the current level of integration with your login scripts. Some network administrators have set up sophisticated login scripts that provide virus-scanning, drive-letter mappings, and other configuration options to enhance your connection to the network. The Client for NetWare Networks

VI

Connecting to Networks

allows Windows to automatically run the login scripts when you attach to your NetWare server. The login script performs everyday duties each time you log into the server, like map drive letters to network resources and map DOS printer ports to network printers for DOS sessions.

> ### Note
>
> To learn more about the options related to login script processing or other connection options for Novell NetWare servers, see the "Logging On to a Novell NetWare Network" section of chapter 20, "Using Windows with Corporate Networks."

To install the Client for NetWare Networks, follow these steps:

1. Right-click the Network Neighborhood icon and select Properties from the pop-up menu. This displays the Network dialog box.

2. Select Add from the Network dialog box.

3. Select Client from the Select Network Type dialog box and click Add.

4. Select Microsoft from the Manufacturers list.

5. Select Client for NetWare Networks from the list of Network Clients.

6. Click OK.

Windows adds the default protocols for connecting to a Novell NetWare server automatically. These default protocols should work in most situations, but the following sections describe situations in which the defaults may need to be changed.

Connecting to a NetWare 3.x Network

When you install the Client for NetWare Networks on your Windows workstation, the default setup will be configured to attach to a NetWare 3.x server. If you don't know which version of NetWare server you will be connecting to, try using this default installation. Most network administrators will maintain the default installation unless there is a compelling reason to do otherwise. Check with your network administrator to find out which protocol you should be using to connect to your NetWare 3.x server if you are unsure.

Since your Novell NetWare servers will appear in the Network Neighborhood, you can connect to them as you connect to any other Windows workstation.

> **Note**
>
> To find out more about connecting to servers through the Network Neighborhood, see the "Finding Machines and Resources on the Network" section in chapter 8, "Using the Network Neighborhood."

Connecting to a NetWare 4.x Network

NetWare 4.x servers are built somewhat differently than the NetWare 3.x servers. While the 4.x servers can be accessed in the same way as their earlier counterparts, the default installation for a NetWare 4.x server will not be visible to your Windows workstation unless you make some changes to your configuration.

The NetWare 4.x servers have a built-in system called NetWare Directory Services (NDS) that allow you to log in to the network once and gain access to each of the various servers to which you have been granted rights. This feature of the Client for NetWare Networks was still in development when this book was written but may already be available by the time you read this. The Client for NetWare Networks can currently only log in to individual servers on the network whether they are running NDS or not.

In addition to the NDS feature, NetWare 4.x servers use a slightly different protocol when running on an Ethernet network. This will prevent your Windows 95 workstation from seeing a NetWare 4.x server on the network.

If you cannot see any NetWare 4.x servers after installing the Client for NetWare Networks, try changing the following settings:

1. Open the Start menu and choose Settings, Control Panel.
2. Double-click the Network icon to view the Network dialog box.
3. Select File and Printer Sharing for Microsoft Networks from the list of The Following Network Components Are Currently Installed.
4. Select IPX/SPX-Compatible Protocol from the list of The Following Network Components Are Currently Installed.
5. Click the Properties button.
6. Select the Advanced tab in the IPX/SPX-Compatible Protocol Properties sheet.
7. Select the Frame Type option from the Property list.

8. Change the Value option from Automatic to Ethernet 802.2.

Fig. 19.8
Change the Value
of the Frame Type
Property to
Ethernet 802.2.

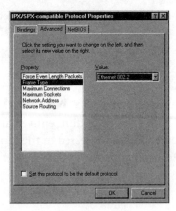

9. Click OK to save your frame type changes.

10. Click OK on the Network dialog box to save your networking options.

11. When prompted, answer Yes to restart Windows to allow these changes to take effect.

Once you make these changes, a NetWare 3.x server will look and act no differently than a NetWare 4.x server or any other Microsoft server. You will be able to access the printers and files shared by the server.

Connecting to an IBM OS/2 LAN Server

You can connect to an IBM OS/2 LAN Server versions 1.2, 1.3, 1.3 CSD, 2.0, and 4.0. While this may seem like a wide range of compatibility, you need to be aware of some special issues when connecting to an IBM LAN Server. These issues depend on the type of network client loaded and the manner in which you wish to locate the server.

If you want to access other network services besides the IBM OS/2 LAN Server, see the following section, "Accessing Other Servers with Client for Microsoft Networks." If you want to use the Network Neighborhood to see and connect to the resources available from IBM OS/2 LAN Servers, "Browsing IBM OS/2 LAN Servers" will teach you how to configure your network to do just that.

Accessing Other Servers with Client for Microsoft Networks

If you installed Windows with the IBM OS/2 LAN Server real-mode network client in your CONFIG.SYS and AUTOEXEC.BAT, you may have noticed that you can't install support for any other network clients or protocols within Windows. If you don't need to access network services other than the OS/2 LAN Server, you're all set. However, if you need to access NetWare, Windows NT, Windows 95 peer servers, or others, you need to perform some additional work to set up your computer. That's because the real-mode IBM OS/2 LAN Server network client doesn't support any other networks being loaded at the same time—not even after Windows starts. You can work around this. You'll be able to set up your computer to access servers via Client for Microsoft Networks, Client for NetWare Networks, and access an IBM OS/2 LAN Server at the same time.

To begin configuring your computer to simultaneously access an IBM OS/2 LAN Server and other server types, you need to deactivate the existing drivers that are accessing the OS/2 LAN Server. To do this

1. Remove the existing lines in your CONFIG.SYS file. You should comment out the DEVICE lines used when loading the network drivers. This can be done by placing the word REM before each entry. When finished, the lines should look something like this:

   ```
   REM DEVICE=C:\LS20\DRIVERS\PROTMAN\PROTMAN.DOS /i:c:\LS20
   REM DEVICE=C:\LS20\DRIVERS\PROTMAN\PROTMAN.EXE /i:c:\LS20
   REM DEVICE=C:\LS20\DRIVERS\DXMEOMOD.SYS
   REM DEVICE=C:\LS20\DRIVERS\ETHERNET\ELNK\ELNK.DOS
   ```

2. Comment out the lines in your AUTOEXEC.BAT which load the real-mode network drivers. This can be done by placing the word REM at the beginning of each line. When complete, the two lines should look like the following:

   ```
   REM LOAD NETBEUI
   REM NET START WORKSTATION LANServer_domain
   ```

   LANServer_domain is the name of the domain for the LAN Server. You should write this name down to use later when you identify your workstation as part of a workgroup.

3. Restart the computer by opening the Start menu and choosing Shut Down.

Once your computer restarts, you are ready to begin configuring your computer to access more than one type of network server. To learn how to do this, follow these steps:

VI

Connecting to Networks

1. Install the Client for Microsoft Networks as described at the beginning of this chapter, "Installing the Client for Microsoft Networks."

2. Right-click the Network Neighborhood icon and select Properties from the pop-up menu. This displays the Network dialog box.

3. Select the Identification tab and enter the LAN Server domain name in the Workgroup text box as seen in figure 19.9.

Fig. 19.9

Enter the domain name of the IBM OS/2 LAN Server in the Workgroup field.

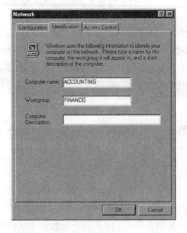

4. Click OK to save your changes.

5. When prompted, click Yes to restart your computer.

To access the IBM OS/2 LAN Server, you can use the Map Network Drive command within the Windows Explorer. To do this:

1. Start an Explorer session by opening the Start menu and choosing Programs, Windows Explorer.

2. Select Tools, Map Network Drive. This displays the Map Network Drive dialog (see fig. 19.10).

Fig. 19.10

Select the Drive letter and enter the Path name to map to the IBM OS/2 LAN Server.

3. Select the local drive letter you wish to use from the Drive drop-down list to map to the server drive.

4. In the Path text box, enter the server name and shared resource name of the IBM OS/2 LAN Server you want to connect to the drive letter. Remember to use UNC format when specifying the path. For example, if the server name is LAN_SRV1 and the shared drive is PROJECTS, you would enter **LAN_SRV1\PROJECTS**.

5. Click OK to complete the mapping.

The selected drive letter now gives you access to the server drive you specified.

> **Note**
>
> When you connect a drive letter via the Windows interface, that drive letter is available for all DOS sessions. If you use the command-line utilities in a DOS session to map a drive letter to an IBM LAN Server drive, that drive letter can only be used by that specific DOS session.

If you would like to use the Network Neighborhood to browse for IBM LAN Servers, you must configure a workstation in a special manner in order for anyone to find the LAN Server on the network. The next section explains in detail how to set this up.

Browsing an IBM OS/2 LAN Server

If you would like to use the Network Neighborhood to browse for shared resources on an IBM OS/2 LAN Server, you'll need to modify a single workstation within its domain. In order for the Windows network workstations to see the IBM OS/2 LAN Server, a workstation must have File and Printer Sharing for Microsoft Networks installed with LM Announce enabled.

What this means is that you'll need to have one workstation within each LAN Server domain help advertise the server's resources to the other Windows workstations. The regular Windows workstations don't have a road map to get to the LAN Server. But, once they've found the way, the workstation and server can communicate without a problem.

To configure a workstation to perform this advertising service for the IBM OS/2 LAN Server, follow these steps:

1. Ensure that the Client for Microsoft Networks is installed. If you aren't sure, review the procedures described at the beginning of this chapter, "Installing the Client for Microsoft Networks."

2. Right-click the Network Neighborhood icon and select Properties from the pop-up menu. This displays the Network dialog box.

3. As seen in figure 19.11, change the Primary Network Logon to Client for Microsoft Networks. This tells Windows that you'll be wanting to access the IBM OS/2 LAN Server on a daily basis.

Fig. 19.11
Change the Primary Network Logon to Client for Microsoft Networks.

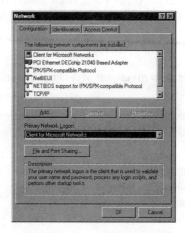

4. Select File and Print Sharing from the Network dialog box and choose I Want To Be Able To Give Others Access to My Files from the File and Print Sharing dialog box (see fig. 19.12). Click OK to accept your choice.

Fig. 19.12
To install File and Print Sharing for Microsoft Networks, choose I Want To Be Able To Give Others Access to My Files.

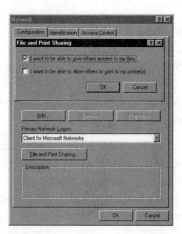

5. Click OK on the Network dialog box to save your changes. At this time, Windows installs the File and Printer Sharing for Microsoft Networks.

6. When prompted, choose Yes to restart your computer to complete the installation.

Now you're ready to turn on the LM Announce feature for this workstation. To perform this task, follow these steps:

1. Right-click the Network Neighborhood icon and select Properties from the pop-up menu. This displays the Network dialog box.

2. Select File and Printer Sharing for Microsoft Networks from the list of The Following Network Components Are Currently Installed.

3. Click the Properties button to display the Advanced tab of the File and Printer Sharing for Microsoft Networks Properties sheet (see fig. 19.13).

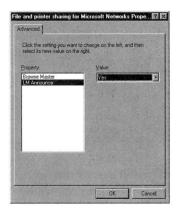

Fig. 19.13
Select the LM Announce Property and change its Value to Yes.

4. Select LM Announce from the Property list.

5. Change the Value option to Yes.

6. Click OK to save the change to the LM Announce value.

7. Click OK on the Network dialog box to save your network settings.

8. When prompted, choose Yes to restart Windows to enable the change.

Now that you've configured a workstation within the LAN Server's domain to perform the LM Announce function, all Windows workstations on the Windows network will be able to browse for the LAN Server using the Network Neighborhood.

You can tell you've connected to an IBM LAN Server by right-clicking the name of the server in the Network Neighborhood. Choose Properties from the pop-up menu and check the type on the server's Properties sheet. If it reads IBM LAN Server similar to figure 19.9, then you'll know it's an IBM OS/2 LAN Server.

Connecting to a UNIX-Based Network

There are many varieties of UNIX that exist for many different computers. There is no blanket statement that can be said about connecting your Windows workstation to a UNIX server, so I'll cover a few examples that should get you started in the right direction.

The three basic types of connectivity to UNIX servers that exist for Windows are

■ NetWare server emulation

■ NFS network connectivity

■ Terminal emulation

Because most of the UNIX-related client software is not part of the Windows installation materials, you'll need a disk from the company that makes the UNIX server to perform the installation steps below.

The following sections describe each of the three connection types.

NetWare Server Emulation

UnixWare has a built-in NetWare server emulation feature that allows it to appear as another NetWare 3.x server to the clients on the network. For this type of installation, the UNIX system administrator has to set up UnixWare to provide this service on the network. You will be able to use the Client for NetWare Networks as described in the section "Connecting to a Novell NetWare Network" in this chapter to connect to this type of server.

> **Note**
>
> Other UNIX vendors may offer this type of connectivity feature as an add-on product to their operating system. Check with your UNIX system administrator to see if your company is using a UNIX system that supports NetWare server emulation.

NFS Network Connectivity

The Network File System, commonly called NFS, allows UNIX systems to share data over the network by virtually grafting directories from a remote

UNIX system into the directory tree of the local UNIX system. Windows can take advantage of the NFS file sharing by loading an NFS network client for the appropriate version of UNIX.

As an example of installing an NFS network, we'll use SunSoft PC-NFS. But any NFS client generally follows these steps:

1. Ensure that the Client for Microsoft Networks is installed. If you aren't sure, review the procedures described at the beginning of this chapter, "Installing the Client for Microsoft Networks."

2. Right-click the Network Neighborhood icon and select Properties from the pop-up menu. This displays the Network dialog box.

3. Select Add from the Network dialog box.

4. Select Client from the Select Network Type dialog box and click Add.

5. If your manufacturer is not listed, click the Have Disk button and insert the Windows 95 network client disk provided by your NFS vendor.

6. If your manufacturer is listed, select it from the list of Manufacturers and the appropriate client from the Network Client list. In our example, select SunSoft from the Manufacturers and SunSoft PC-NFS (version 5.0) from the list of Network Clients.

7. When prompted, answer Yes to restart Windows to complete the installation.

If you've installed the SunSoft PC-NFS network client with the Client for Microsoft Networks, be sure your configuration files contain the entries as shown in table 19.2. If they don't, your SunSoft client won't work correctly.

Table 19.2   Required Entries in Configuration Files for a SunSoft PC-NFS Network Client

Configuration File	Entries
AUTOEXEC.BAT	`C:\WINDOWS\NET START`
	`SET TZ=PST8PDT` (or similar time zone code)
	`SET PATH=C:\NFS;C:\NET;%PATH%`
	`SET NFSDRIVE=C`
	`SET NFSPATH=C:\NFS`

(continues)

VI

Connecting to Networks

Table 19.2 Continued	
Configuration File	**Entries**
	SET TN_DIR=C:\NFS\TELNET
	C:\NFS\PRT *
	C:\NFS\NET INIT.
	C:\NFS\RTM
CONFIG.SYS	REM DEVICE=C:\NET\IFSHLP.SYS
	LASTDRIVE=Z

Since there are many NFS vendors that will be providing Windows network clients, you need to consult the UNIX software's manuals for specific installation instructions.

Note

Most UNIX servers will not allow you to browse their resources using the Network Neighborhood. Instead, you'll have to map a network drive using the Explorer.

Terminal Emulation

Most vendors' UNIX systems provide a terminal access mechanism called Telnet which can be accomplished over the network. To establish a Telnet session with a UNIX system, you need to install the TCP/IP protocol on which the Telnet terminal emulation software runs.

To install the TCP/IP protocol and Microsoft's Telnet client, follow these steps:

1. Right-click the Network Neighborhood icon and select Properties from the pop-up menu. This displays the Network dialog box.

2. Select Add from the Network dialog box.

3. Select Protocol from the Select Network Type dialog box and click Add.

4. From the Select Network Protocol dialog box shown in figure 19.14, select Microsoft from the Manufacturers list.

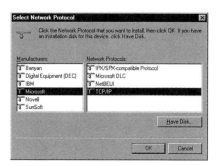

Fig. 19.14
Select Microsoft
from the Manufac-
turers and TCP/IP
from the Network
Protocols.

5. Select TCP/IP from the Network Protocols list.

6. Click OK to add the TCP/IP protocol.

7. Select the TCP/IP protocol from the Installed Components list on the
   Network dialog box and click the Properties button.

8. On the IP Address tab, select the Specify an IP address option and enter
   your IP Address and Subnet Mask. These should be obtained from your
   UNIX system administrator.

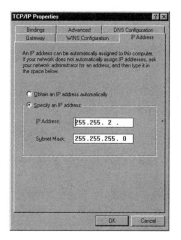

Fig. 19.15
Enter your
assigned IP address
and subnet mask
in the text boxes
provided on the IP
Address tab.

9. Choose the Gateway tab of the TCP/IP Properties sheet.

10. If you can access the Internet or have other internal TCP/IP networks,
    you may add the TCP/IP gateway addresses here. Again, these can be
    obtained from your UNIX system administrator.

11. Choose the DNS Configuration tab of the TCP/IP Properties sheet.

VI

Connecting to Networks

12. Choose the Enable DNS option if you have a Domain Name Server accessible to you. You'll need to obtain the Host, Domain, and DNS Server IP Address from your system administrator.

Fig. 19.16
Enter the DNS addresses provided by your system administrator.

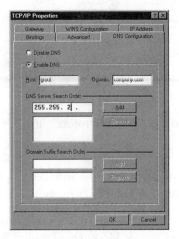

13. Enter in the DNS addresses as provided to you.

14. Click OK to save the TCP/IP configuration information.

15. Click OK on the Network dialog box to save your protocol changes and install the TCP/IP communications utilities, including the Telnet program.

16. When prompted, answer Yes to restart Windows to take advantage of the TCP/IP protocol.

> **Note**
>
> The TCP/IP protocol is outside of the scope of this book to fully discuss here. However, you should know that there are many other uses for the TCP/IP protocol, such as accessing the Internet and transferring files between Windows and UNIX systems. Your system administrator will be able to help you determine which services are available to you on your UNIX server.

> **Note**
>
> To see how you can log into your UNIX server, see the section entitled "Logging On to a UNIX Network" in chapter 20, "Using Windows with Corporate Networks."

Once you've installed the TCP/IP protocol, you can start a Telnet session from the Start menu by choosing Run, entering **TELNET** in the Open text box, and clicking OK.

You can connect to any UNIX server as long as you know its IP address and you have been given access to it via a user ID and password. One more door of the UNIX world has just been opened for you.

Artisoft LANtastic

LANtastic users have the unique distinction of being the only peer-to-peer network operating system mentioned here. The networking architecture of LANtastic is somewhat different than the other networks mentioned thus far. Since there is not a Windows 95 network client for LANtastic servers, Windows requires that the real-mode driver be used to connect into the LANtastic network. Additionally, there are some particular requirements of the real-mode LANtastic DOS drivers that preclude Windows 95 from using any protected-mode network clients.

What that means to you is that if you intend to connect to a LANtastic network, you cannot also connect into a Windows 95, NetWare, or any other network. For installations without other networks, this will not be a problem, but for installations that want to take advantage of Windows 95 file- and printer-sharing capabilities, this is a show-stopper.

In cases where your network requires the connection to another network, you may be better off upgrading your LANtastic network to Windows 95. Not only will you gain access to other networks, but you will also gain the speed and memory advantages offered by the 32-bit protected-mode networking clients native to Windows 95 file and printer sharing.

> ### Note
>
> Obviously, upgrading is an additional expense that many companies cannot afford. Remember, you do not need to change your network if you are only accessing a LANtastic server. However, you may need to make the switch to a Windows 95 network if you require access to a Novell NetWare server or other network server.

To install the LANtastic network client support for version 5.0 or later, do the following:

1. Make sure you are running the LANtastic client software before running the Windows 95 Setup application.

2. Allow Windows 95 Setup to detect your hardware in your system.

3. Verify that the driver that Windows has selected for you during the installation matches the LANtastic driver you are using (version 5.x and greater).

4. Allow Windows 95 Setup to complete the installation.

You will be able to map network drives using the Network Neighborhood or the Explorer but only by specifying the complete server and path name to your LANtastic server. LANtastic servers will not appear in the Explorer or the Network Neighborhood. You may also use the DOS commands to map network drives within a DOS window.

Banyan Vines

You can access servers running Banyan Vines v5.52(5) or greater from your Windows workstation. However, the currently available client software is a real-mode network client. This means that you will be required to use the Map Network Drive dialog box in the Explorer to access the resources on a Banyan Vines server.

To install the Banyan Vines network client, follow these steps:

1. Ensure that the Client for Microsoft Networks is installed. If you aren't sure, review the procedures described at the beginning of this chapter, "Installing the Client for Microsoft Networks."

2. Right-click the Network Neighborhood icon and select Properties from the pop-up menu. This displays the Network dialog box.

3. Select Add from the Network dialog box.

4. Select Client from the Select Network Type dialog box and click Add.

5. From the list of Manufacturers, select Banyan. From the list of Network Clients, select Banyan DOS/Windows 3.1 client.

6. Click OK to have Windows accept your choice to install a new client.

7. Click OK on the Network dialog box to save your new client configuration.

8. When prompted, answer Yes to restart Windows to let the changes take effect.

Finally, be sure your configuration files contain the entries as shown in table 19.3. If they don't, your Banyan Vines client won't work correctly.

Table 19.3   Required Entries in Configuration Files for a Banyan Vines Network Client

Configuration File	Entries
AUTOEXEC.BAT	`C:\WINDOWS\NET INITIALIZE`
	`CD \BANFILES`
	`BAN`
	`NDISBAN` ; or NDTOKBAN for token ring
	`REDIRALL`
	`C:\WINDOWS\NET START`
	`ARSWAIT`
	`Z:LOGIN`
CONFIG.SYS	`REM DEVICE=C:\BANFILES\PROTMAN.DOS / I:C:\BANFILES`
	`REM DEVICE=C:\BANFILES\NDIS2DRIVER` ;like ELNK3.DOS
PROTOCOL.INI	`[NDISBAN$]` ; NDTOKBAN$ for token ring
	`drivername=NDISBAN$` ; NDTOKBAN$ for token ring
	`bindings=ELNK3$[NWLINK$]`
	`drivername=NWLINK$`
	`frame_type=4`
	`cachesize=0`
	`bindings=ELNK3$[NETBEUI$]`
	`drivername=NETBEUI$`
	`lanabase=0`
	`sessions=10`
	`ncbs=12`

(continues)

Table 19.3 Continued	
Configuration File	**Entries**
	bindings=ELNK3$[ELNK3$]
	drivername=ELNK3$
	transceiver=external
	interrupt=2
	ioaddress=0x280
	maxtransmits=12
	datatransfer=pio_word
	xmitbufs=2[PROTMAN$]
	priority=ndishlp$
	drivername=protman$[NDISHLP$]
	drivername=ndishlp$
	bindings=ELNK3$

You now have access to Banyan Vines servers in your DOS sessions and from the Windows Explorer. Once you map a drive letter to a Banyan Vines server, you'll be able to access its resources just like any other network resource.

Troubleshooting

This section could fill an entire book; hence, the troubleshooting advice found here is not comprehensive. However, the suggestions made in this section should give you a pretty good start on the troubleshooting direction you need to take.

I can't see my network servers in the Network Neighborhood; what's wrong?

This, unfortunately, is one of the hardest questions to answer. Many problems might prevent you from seeing a server in the Network Neighborhood. One of the reasons you may not be able to see your servers, even if you have done everything right, is that some of the network clients do not interact with Network Neighborhood. That means that, although you cannot see the servers, you can still access them by using the Windows Explorer Tools menu to Map a Network Drive or right-clicking the Network Neighborhood icon. The following network clients will not show up in the Network Neighborhood. Note that all of these networks use real-mode network client software.

- Artisoft LANtastic

- Banyan Vines

- Beame and Whiteside NFS

- SunSelect PC-NFS

- TCS 10Net

My workstation is using the XYZ network server, which isn't listed in this chapter. How can I connect to it though Windows 95?

In general, you can use the real-mode DOS drivers that you currently use to connect to the server. However, you may or may not be able to use Windows 95 built-in networking along with your other network. Check to see if your network manufacturer will be providing a native Windows 95 protected-mode network client.

Why is my DOS session memory so low when I'm running a real-mode network client?

Your real-mode network clients use DOS conventional memory before Windows starts. In order to provide networking services to the command prompts and to Windows, you will not be able to regain this DOS memory. Some real-mode networking clients can take up as much as 120K of conventional memory. To avoid this RAM shortage in command prompts, try switching to a protected-mode network client if your network manufacturer supports one.

What if I need to connect to two or more networks that do not have protected-mode drivers available?

Currently, Windows does not support more than one real-mode network client. Your only choice is to get the protected-mode network client for each of your network manufacturers. If you still have more than one real-mode network client, you may not be able to run Windows and connect to all of your network servers.

Connecting to Networks

From Here...

Now that you have installed the network clients for your other networks, you will want to know how you can access these servers using Windows 95. The following chapters discuss how to connect with your corporate network servers as well as point you in the direction of some more detailed explanations for using Windows networking resources.

- Chapter 8, "Using the Network Neighborhood," explains how to view shared resources on network servers.

- Chapter 9, "Sharing Network Hardware," explores how you can set up your machine as a peer-to-peer server.

- Chapter 20, "Using Windows with Corporate Networks," discusses how you can connect to other network servers using Windows network clients.

- Appendix A, "Technical Specifications of Network Protocols," details more explicitly the various network protocols and their roles in Windows networking.

Chapter 20

Using Windows with Corporate Networks

Many companies have an existing network; therefore, you need to know how to connect to both a Windows 95 network as well as the established network server. In chapter 19, you learned the essentials of setting up a Windows 95 workstation to interoperate with such networks, and this chapter assumes that you have followed the instructions from that chapter and have already installed support for the network you are trying to attach to.

Now that you are connected, you are probably ready to dive in and start using the network. This chapter explains the process of connecting and using other networks, as well as sharing resources with other workstations on the network that might not be running Windows 95.

Specifically, this chapter covers the following:

- How to log on to many networks at the same time

- How to log on to specific networks, such as Novell NetWare

- How the Network Neighborhood can be used to simplify the connection to other network servers

- How to connect to shared resources on the network

- How to share your files, folders, and printers with non-Windows 95 workstations on the network

Logging On to the Microsoft Windows Network

As you might expect, the procedures to log on for Microsoft Windows networks are tightly integrated into the Windows operating system. The Microsoft Windows network can be made up of several different operating systems. Chapter 19 pointed out that you can use the client software to access the Windows network to connect with the computers running the following Microsoft operating systems:

- Windows 95 workstation

- Windows NT workstation

- Windows NT server

- LAN Manager server

- OS/2 LAN server

These operating systems have different features for which Windows 95 can be configured. Let's take a look at the properties that can be modified within the Control Panel of Windows.

Configuring Windows NT Validation

As you learned in chapter 9, "Sharing Network Hardware," when you share a device such as a hard disk on the network, you can select a password for that device to determine who can access it. Anyone who knows the password can access the disk. When you connect your Windows 95 computer to a network with a Windows NT computer on it, though, you have the ability to enable what is known as user-level access control. Under user-level access control, you can set up a list of users who have access to the drive. Each user can have different rights on the drive. For example, some users would have read-only access, while more trusted users might have full control. Windows NT maintains the list of users and their passwords for your Windows 95 computer. When a user tries to attach to your shared disk, the Windows NT computer validates the user or verifies that their password is correct.

The Control Panel Network dialog box enables you to manage the configuration of the networking components under Windows. To change the Windows NT validation options, you need to start the Network dialog box by using these steps:

1. Open the Start menu and choose Settings, Control Panel to open the Control Panel window.

2. Select the Network icon in Control Panel.

When the Network manager application starts, you see the Network dialog box (see fig. 20.1).

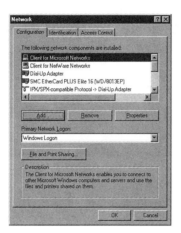

Fig. 20.1
The Network dialog box lets you manage the components of the Windows network.

To modify the Windows NT log on options, you need to bring up the Client for Microsoft Networks Properties sheet. To do this, select the Client for Microsoft Networks selection in The Following Network Components Are Installed list. Then choose the Properties button. This displays the Client for Microsoft Networks Properties sheet (see fig. 20.2).

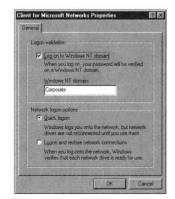

Fig. 20.2
The Client for Microsoft Networks Properties sheet is used to manage the options for connecting to Microsoft Windows networks.

VI

Connecting to Networks

Tip
If you are part of a smaller Windows NT network, your server could be running the Windows NT workstation software that enables up to 10 users to connect. In this situation, you do not need to modify the parameters in the Logon Validation section of the Client for Microsoft Networks Properties sheet.

The Logon Validation section is the place where you can change the Windows NT specific options. If you are logging on to a Windows NT server that has been configured as a domain controller, you can mark the Log On to Windows NT Domain check box. Then you can enter your domain name into the Windows NT Domain text box. This also works with Microsoft LAN Manager servers that are part of a domain. If you are unsure whether your Windows NT network is part of a domain, check with your system administrator.

> **Note**
>
> A Windows NT domain is a set of Windows NT servers that communicate with each other on the status of security and logon permissions over the network. When you log on to a Windows NT domain, your user name and password are used to validate you on all the servers that are participating in the Windows NT domain. This enables system administrators to more easily manage a group of servers.
>
> Not all Windows NT servers participate in a Windows NT domain. The reason might be that the servers are not all administered centrally. Another reason might be that all the departments or groups of users prefer to manage their server. A network might contain more than one domain and might have many nondomain servers. If you are unsure about the setup for your Windows NT network, contact your system administrator to see how you should connect to the servers.

Configuring Logon Options

The Client for Microsoft Networks Properties sheet also contains a Network Logon Options section. This section specifies how Windows reconnects your networking resources when you log on to the network.

The Quick Logon option does not try to reconnect any of your network resources when you log on. This option enables Windows to boot up faster because it does not have to find the servers and reconnect to them during boot time. This is especially useful if you are part of a WAN and you use a server that is located in a different city or even another country. The server does not reconnect these network resources. Therefore, you will probably notice some delays when you try to access information on network servers for the first time.

The Logon and Restore Network Connections option specifies that you want Windows to attach to all of the resources on the network while Windows is starting. Depending on the number of servers and printers that you are connected to, this process can be almost as fast as the Quick Logon option. Again, if you are connected to servers that are located in other cities or countries, you might experience significant delays during the logon procedure.

> **Note**
>
> Use the following guidelines to determine whether you should use the Quick Logon option:
>
> - Do you connect to less than 10 servers?
>
> - Do you only connect to servers that are located within your building?
>
> If you answered in the negative to either of these questions, you probably should use the Quick Logon option. Otherwise, you should allow Windows to reconnect your resources when you start up to ensure that they are available when you want to access them.

Logging On to a Novell NetWare Network

Novell NetWare is a network operating system that has been used for many years and is highly regarded as the leader in the industry. Because this network operating system is so popular, your company might have one or more servers running Novell NetWare. Windows 95 has support for NetWare networks built in. To configure support for your connection to a Novell NetWare server, use the Network dialog box.

To view the Client for NetWare Networks Properties sheet, follow these steps:

1. Open the Start menu and choose Settings, Control Panel.

2. Choose the Network icon in Control Panel to open the Network dialog box.

3. Choose Client for NetWare Networks in the Following Network Components Are Installed list box on the Configuration page.

4. Choose the Properties button. The Client for NetWare Networks Properties sheet appears (see fig. 20.3).

By looking at the Client for NetWare Networks Properties sheet, you notice that there are only a few options that you can configure. The Preferred Server option lets you indicate the server that you want to log on to first. Normally, you will want to set your Preferred Server to the server you do most of your work on. The Preferred Server processes your NetWare login scripts that connect you to other servers or provide you with drive letters to different areas

VI

Connecting to Networks

on the server. To set your Preferred Server, enter the name of your server into the text box provided or choose it from the drop-down menu.

Fig. 20.3

You can use the Client for NetWare Networks Properties sheet to manage the options for connecting to Novell NetWare networks.

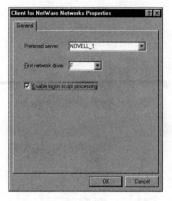

With the First Network Drive option, you can specify which drive letter the NetWare server uses to begin its letter assignments. The drive letter is typically F. However, this can vary, depending on the local drives you have on your computer. For example, if you have an internal hard disk at drive F, you wouldn't want to assign a network drive at that same letter because you would lose access to your local drive until you logged out of the network.

The Enable Logon Script Processing checkbox enables you to turn on and off the NetWare login script processing. Most system administrators have set up some sort of login script that enables the NetWare server to set up a user's environment when he or she logs on to the server. Some uses of the login scripts include:

- Mapping drive letters to server directories

- Mapping network printers to LPT ports on the local workstation

- Initiating a virus scan on the local workstation

- Taking inventory of hardware and software for the local workstation

- Displaying messages for special events or notifications of server maintenance schedules

- Loading special drivers for network databases or virus protection

> **Note**
>
> You might be able to turn off script processing if you only map drive letters and connect to network printers in your login script. These functions can be handled by Windows 95. Many other events, however, can occur in the login scripts. Therefore, you will want to check with your system administrator to determine whether or not to turn off login script processing.

Logging On to a UNIX Network

UNIX installations have two base options when it comes to logging on to the server. These options include using Network File System protocols to attach drive letters to the UNIX server or using terminal emulation to access applications on the server.

The following section briefly covers each of these techniques. However, because there are many different implementations of UNIX that use different client software, this book cannot cover them all.

Network File System

The *Network File System* (*NFS*) connection to a UNIX server is similar to a connection to a Microsoft NT or Novell NetWare server. A drive letter is typically assigned to a directory on the UNIX server on which the user has permission to work. Files can be transferred between these systems; however, it is unusual to use a UNIX server as a primary file server for a LAN.

UNIX is better suited to both local and database processing. Additionally, most UNIX implementations are very expensive. High-powered machines running expensive UNIX software to process accounting, manufacturing, or other information is rarely used to also handle file and print requests from the LAN. The reasons behind this primarily involve load balancing issues. It is far more cost effective to purchase a commodity-type LAN server and run a dedicated network operating system than to overburden a UNIX machine, which causes poor performance for both database processing and file and print servicing.

Companies who allow connection to a UNIX server through the LAN often do so to provide minimal file-sharing capabilities or to let files be created on the UNIX system for use on the Windows network.

VI

Connecting to Networks

Note

You must realize that companies can and will do whatever makes the most sense for their environment. This discussion is based on the author's experience and common practice.

Terminal Emulation

In the days before computer networking, users shared files and sent e-mail by all being attached to the same computer. They did this by using what are known as *dumb terminals*. These terminals had no processor of their own and were essentially displays for the UNIX computer they were physically attached to. Today's computers let you attach to UNIX computers in the same way by acting like or *emulating* one of those dumb terminals.

Terminal emulation is a little different than regular networking. Under terminal emulation, your local workstation is acting only as a display. The processing required to run a program is all accomplished by the remote computer. In a Windows 95, Windows NT, Novell NetWare, or UNIX NFS network, your computer is using its own processing power.

The main mechanism for terminal access is through a Telnet session to a UNIX server. Telnet is a transport mechanism over which text is sent between a server and the workstation. Both the Telnet application that is installed with Windows and the TCP/IP protocol enable your workstation to connect to a virtual terminal session on the server. (Recall that TCP/IP is the protocol that computers on the Internet use to communicate.)

The Telnet application is tucked away in your WINDOWS directory. To start a Telnet session, open the Start menu and choose Run. Enter **telnet.exe** in the Open text box and click OK. The Telnet application starts (see fig. 20.4).

To connect to your UNIX server, you need to know its network name. If you participate in the Internet, your server might have a name, such as **prod. company.com**. However, your UNIX server might not have a name, only being accessible through its network address. A TCP/IP address that consists of four numbers separated by periods might resemble something like **155.203.202.15**. Once you have obtained your UNIX server's name, you can proceed with the Telnet connection.

Fig. 20.4
The Telnet
application
connects you to a
virtual terminal
session on a UNIX
server.

To connect to a server with the name CLASS.ORG, follow these steps:

1. Select Connect from the menu bar.

2. Choose Remote System.

3. Enter the name CLASS.ORG in the dialog box, which figure 20.5 shows.

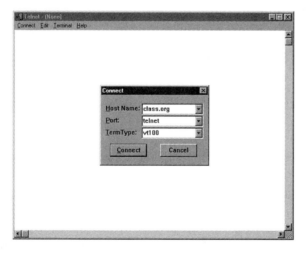

Fig. 20.5
The Telnet
accessory applica-
tion needs to
know the name of
the UNIX server to
which you will be
connecting.

VI

Connecting to Networks

4. Make sure the port is set to the default, which is Telnet.

5. Make sure the terminal type matches your UNIX server. Most servers
accept the VT100 terminal emulation default.

Your terminal session will be initiated with the UNIX host. You will most likely be presented with a login screen similar to the one shown in figure 20.6.

Fig. 20.6
Most UNIX servers prompt you for a user ID and password before you can access the server.

From this point, you need to refer to any documentation that has been provided to you by your system administrator. Most UNIX systems have a menu system to guide you to the application that you want to access.

Real-Mode Networks

Recall from chapter 19, "Connecting to Other Networks," that real-mode networks are those networks that do not have an equivalent Windows 95 client software driver. To access these servers, you need to log in to the real-mode network before Windows 95 starts. To do this, make sure that your network drivers are loaded according to your manufacturer's guidelines, and that the login commands are executed in the AUTOEXEC.BAT before Windows 95 starts. This enables any drive letter assignments or printer connections to be established for Windows to use.

> **Note**
>
> The real-mode networks will probably not show up in the Network Neighborhood or the Explorer server listings; therefore, it is important for you to establish the drive letter and printer connections before you get into Windows. It might be possible, however, to add or alter your drive letter mappings and printer connections in a DOS window within Windows 95.

Using the Network Neighborhood

The Network Neighborhood enables you to connect to other network resources through Windows 95. The Network Neighborhood displays these
servers with the same icons that show Windows 95 workstations or any Windows NT Server. This enables you to focus less on what type of server you are
accessing and more on the location of the data you need. Figure 20.7 shows a
Network Neighborhood listing of several network servers from different
vendors.

Fig. 20.7
The Network
Neighborhood
shows any type of
server on the
network.

You can determine to which type of server you have attached, as well as a
great deal of other information, by right-clicking on a server icon. You then
choose the Properties option. Figure 20.8 shows the properties of a Novell
NetWare server on the network.

Fig. 20.8
Server information
can be found by
right-clicking on
the server icon in
the Network
Neighborhood.

VI

Connecting to Networks

In addition to the server properties, right-clicking on a server icon in the
Network Neighborhood enables you to do the following:

- Log off of a server

- Determine which user name was used to validate you on a server

- Attach to a server

- Map a network drive letter to a server directory

Connecting to Other Computers

When you connect to a server using the Explorer or the Network Neighborhood, Windows sends your Windows login ID and password first. If this combination of ID and password is incorrect, Windows displays the Enter Network Password dialog box (see fig. 20.9).

Fig. 20.9
Windows asks for the user ID and password if it cannot log into a server on the network.

Once you have attached to the server with the appropriate credentials, you are able to access the directories and files to which you have been given permission. If this user ID and password combination is different from your Windows login, you can check the Remember Password check box. In this way, Windows will use these credentials when you log in next time.

Accessing Shared Directories

You can use the Network Neighborhood to find the directory on a network server you want to access. Once you have entered the directory you want, you can run programs or copy files between your computer and the server.

You might want to map a drive letter to a particular server and directory so that you can access the information easily in the future, or so that your applications are capable of using the files on that server. To map a drive letter to a directory on a server, right-click the network directory. Then choose the Map Network Drive option. This brings up a dialog box similar to the one that figure 20.10 shows.

Fig. 20.10
You can map a
network drive
letter to a server
directory. This
enables Windows
to reconnect the
drive letter the
next time you
log in.

If you intend to use this network directory frequently, you might want to
check the Reconnect at Logon checkbox. This enables Windows to maintain
the drive letter you choose as the connection to the server directory.

Accessing Shared Printers

Accessing printers on network servers can also be accomplished through the
Network Neighborhood. Simply double-click a server icon in the Network
Neighborhood to see a list of its attached printers and shared folders. Right-
clicking a printer enables you to install the printer through the Printer Installation Wizard. This installs the printer drivers for the selected network
printer, and enables you to choose a local LPT port to capture any DOS printing. Figure 20.11 shows a server sharing several network printers.

Fig. 20.11
Network printers
can be connected
through the
Network Neighbor-
hood by right-
clicking on the
printer you want
to attach.

Sharing with Others on the Network

In addition to connecting to resources on the network, you can share your
resources with those who are not using Windows 95. Chapter 9, "Sharing
Network Hardware," described how to share your directories and printers
with Windows 95 users. The following section covers sharing your directories
and files with network users who are not running Windows 95. This section
concentrates on sharing with Novell NetWare users.

VI

Connecting to Networks

Installing the Sharing Software

To share your files and folders with Novell NetWare users, you need to install the appropriate network software. This software changes your sharing capabilities so that your workstation appears as a Novell NetWare server to NetWare users on the network. To do this, though, you must have an actual Novell NetWare Server on your network.

Follow these steps to install the software on your workstation:

1. Open the Start menu and choose Settings, Control Panel.

2. Double-click the Network icon in Control Panel. The Network dialog box appears.

3. Select the File and Printer Sharing for Microsoft Networks from the list box.

4. Choose the Remove button to remove the Windows sharing software.

5. Choose the Add button. The Select Network Component Type dialog box appears.

6. Select Service. Then choose the Add button. The Select Network Service dialog box appears.

7. Choose Microsoft from the Manufacturers list box. Choose File and Printer Sharing for NetWare Networks. Click OK.

8. Select the Access Control tab in the Network dialog box.

9. Type in your Novell NetWare server name from which your users will be authenticated in the Obtain List of Users and Groups From text box. Choose OK.

10. Select the Configuration tab. Select the File and Printer Sharing for NetWare Networks item from the list box. Choose the Properties button. The File and Printer Sharing for NetWare Network Properties sheet appears.

11. Choose SAP Advertising from the Properties list. Change Value to Enabled. Click OK.

12. Reboot Windows.

You will be able, at this point, to share your resources with Novell NetWare users on the network. The following sections explain how to share your files, folders, and printers with NetWare users.

Caution

Be sure to have all your NetWare workstations configured to use a NetWare server on your network as their preferred server. If you don't specify a preferred server or a Windows 95 computer as the preferred server, you will be unable to log in to the network on that workstation.

Sharing Files and Folders

Now that you have set up your workstation to appear as a NetWare server, you need to specify which folders you want to be accessible, and who can access them. This can be accomplished through My Computer.

To set up the capability to share a directory, select the My Computer icon. Then, choose the drive that contains your directory. Right-click the directory folder. Next, choose Sharing. This displays the Properties sheet for sharing that folder. Figure 20.12 shows this Properties sheet.

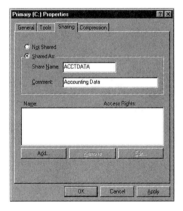

Fig. 20.12
You can find properties for sharing folders for NetWare users by right-clicking the folder you want to share.

Select the Shared As option. Then enter a short Share Name. Make sure your share name is short with no spaces, as NetWare users will have to type both the server and the volume names to connect to your shared folder.

Choose the Add button to bring up the user lists from the Novell NetWare server you have specified. Figure 20.13 shows an example of the user listing dialog box.

Fig. 20.13
Adding users
requires an actual
Novell NetWare
server to authenti-
cate the user name
and password.

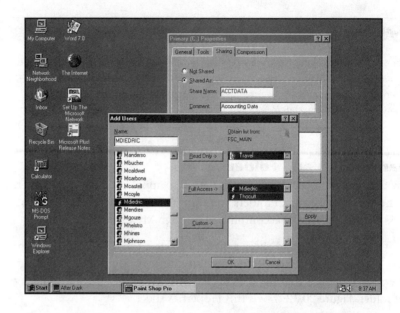

Select the users or user groups from the list. Then choose the Read Only, Full Access, or Custom buttons to determine which permissions you will be giving to particular users. Choose OK when you have finished.

NetWare users are then able to see your server when they perform an SLIST command to show all NetWare servers. They can access your workstation as if it were a Novell NetWare server.

Tip
Sharing your
printer causes an
additional load on
your machine
when someone
prints. Also, your
hard drive should
contain enough
free space to en-
able large print
jobs to be spooled
to your local hard
drive.

Sharing Printers

Printers can be shared in the same way as files. To share your local printer with NetWare users, follow these steps:

1. Open the Start menu and choose Settings, Printers.

2. Right-click the local printer that you want to share and choose Sharing from the pop-up menu. A Properties sheet for that printer appears.

3. Select the Shared As option. Then enter a short printer name.

4. Add users as mentioned in the file sharing section. Then choose OK.

From Here...

Now that you are able to share network resources with other servers on your network, you might want to review these chapters:

- Chapter 16, "Introduction to the Internet," explains what the Internet is, and how you can use it.

- Chapter 17, "Connecting to the Internet," details how to connect to the Internet through Windows 95.

- Chapter 18, "Using Internet Services in Windows," shows how to use the Internet to download files and search for information.

Chapter 21

Using the Built-In Network Tools

Windows comes with a variety of tools to help you manage the day-to-day operations of your network. These programs enable you to gather information about your network, such as information about which users are connected and which devices are being shared. They also enable you to gather statistics about network traffic and display them in a graphical, easy-to-understand format.

This chapter covers the following:

- Finding out who is connected to your computer
- How to disconnect users manually
- Gathering system statistics by using System Monitor
- Using Ping to see if another workstation is on the network
- How to set up remote administration

Network Administration in Windows

Network administration is the set of tasks that you, as the person who keeps the network running, perform on a regular basis to keep things functioning smoothly. It includes diagnosing problems and fixing them when the network suddenly stops working; setting up new machines so that they can use the network; and keeping track of system usage to determine whether an individual computer is being overloaded by network users. Network administration also includes simple tasks, such as checking which users are connected to a given machine and disconnecting them manually if necessary.

Administrating your network is not necessarily a difficult task. In fact, in many cases it is no more than a series of very short tasks. Fortunately, Windows comes with some tools to make your job even easier.

Setting Up and Starting NetWatcher

Figure 21.1 shows NetWatcher, which enables you to view and manage the network connections and shares on your network. NetWatcher lets you monitor the activity on your local machine and also on remote machines. NetWatcher lets you see what computer is attached to a given machine, what users are logged on, how long they have been attached, and what files they have open. You can add and remove shared disks and folders. You can even disconnect another user that is attached.

Fig. 21.1
NetWatcher enables you to view and manage the connections to your computer.

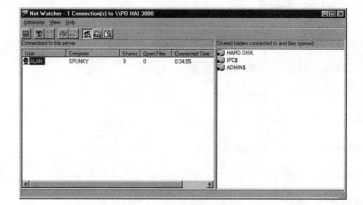

Installing NetWatcher

NetWatcher is not a part of the standard Windows installation; therefore, you have to add it by going to the Add/Remove Programs icon in Control Panel. To do this, follow these steps:

1. Open the Start menu, choose Settings, Control Panel. This opens the Control Panel window, which contains various icons.

2. Double-click the Add/Remove Programs icon. The Add/Remove Programs Properties sheet allows you to easily add and remove programs (see fig. 21.2).

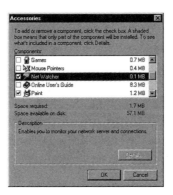

Fig. 21.2
To install
NetWatcher, open
the Add/Remove
Programs Proper-
ties sheet.

3. Click the Windows Setup tab in the Add/Remove Programs Properties sheet, which displays a Setup page similar to the one you used when you first installed Windows 95. From here, you can install and remove Windows components.

4. Highlight Accessories in the Components list box, and click the Details button to display the Accessories dialog box, from which you choose which accessories you want installed. You can also double-click the Accessories icon in the Components list box.

5. Find the NetWatcher icon in the Components list box in the Accessories dialog box. Mark the checkbox next to the NetWatcher icon to choose it for installation.

6. Click OK to close the Accessories dialog box, which brings you back to the Add/Remove Programs Properties sheet.

7. Click OK in the Add/Remove Programs Properties sheet. This starts the installation of NetWatcher.

8. You are prompted for a Windows 95 installation disk or CD-ROM. Insert the disk or CD-ROM and click OK.

Windows will copy the files necessary to install NetWatcher. The NetWatcher icon is installed in the System Tools group. To get to the System Tools group, open the Start menu and choose Programs, Accessories, System Tools.

Setting Up NetWatcher for Remote Administration

To monitor the activity on your own computer, all you need to do is install and launch NetWatcher as described above. NetWatcher also provides the ability to view network activity on remote computers.

VI

Connecting to Networks

As the administrator of a network, you need to know what's going on with both your local machine and all other machines on your network. For example, you need to make some changes to a spreadsheet on a co-worker's hard disk (over the network, of course—no need to go sit at his computer now that you have a Windows 95 network). Before you go making changes, though, you need to know if someone else is already accessing the file. Using NetWatcher to monitor the remote machine, you can tell who, if anyone, is attached to the machine, and which files that person has open. First, though, you will need to configure the remote machine you want to access for remote administration.

To configure a machine for remote administration, open the Start menu, choose Settings, Control Panel, and double-click the Passwords icon. This opens the Passwords Properties sheet (see fig. 21.3). To use NetWatcher on a remote machine, remote administration must be turned on for the machine that you want to monitor. To do this, mark the Enable Remote Administration of This Server checkbox. Then type a password for the server in the Password text box, enter the same password again in the Confirm Password text box (to verify you typed what you think you did in the password box), and click the OK button.

Fig. 21.3
You must enable remote administration from the Passwords Properties sheet to use NetWatcher.

Starting NetWatcher

To start NetWatcher, open the Start menu and choose Programs, Accessories, System Tools, NetWatcher. This displays the NetWatcher window. From here, you can get information about the connections to your local machine.

If you want to get information about another machine on your network, choose Administer, Select Server from the NetWatcher window. This displays the Select Server dialog box. Type the name of the computer you want to monitor into the Name text box. Then click OK. If you cannot remember the exact name of the computer, select Browse. This displays a browse window, similar to a Network Neighborhood window. From here, you can select the machine you want to connect to by double-clicking its icon.

After you click OK, the Enter Network Password dialog box appears and prompts you for the remote administration password for that machine (see fig. 21.4). Enter the password in the box. Then click OK. If you mark the Save This Password in Your Password List checkbox, you can bypass this step the next time you use NetWatcher to connect to this machine. You are now connected to the remote machine.

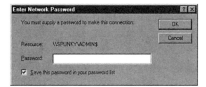

Fig. 21.4
When you use NetWatcher to connect to a remote computer, you must enter the password of that remote computer.

Launching NetWatcher from the Network Neighborhood

If you want to use NetWatcher to monitor a remote computer, it's often easier to launch NetWatcher while you are browsing the Network Neighborhood. Windows makes this process easy. From the Network Neighborhood, right-click the computer you want to monitor. Then choose Properties in the pop-up menu. From the Properties sheet for the computer, click the Tools tab. Next click NetWatcher (see fig. 21.5). You are presented with the NetWatcher window with the remote computer's information. You might need to enter the remote administration password for the machine first if you have not used NetWatcher for this machine before. You might also have to enter this password if you did not save the remote administration password in your password list the last time you connected to that machine.

Fig. 21.5
Select NetWatcher from the Properties sheet for a remote computer in the Network Neighborhood.

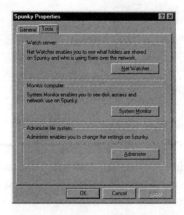

Using NetWatcher

Using NetWatcher, you can get information about who is connected to various computers on the network. You can obtain information about the shared folders on a computer as well as add, delete, and change shared folders. You can also look at which files remote users have opened.

Viewing Connections

Figure 21.6 shows the connections to the computer named Spunky. When you first open NetWatcher, it is in *View by Connections* mode, which means that it is ready to display information about who is connected to the computer. The other modes it may run in are *View by Shared Folders*, which displays which folders on the machine are being shared, and *View by Open Files*, which shows which files on the machine are currently in use by remote users. To change the viewing mode, select View, and then the mode you want: by Connections, by Shared Folders or by Open Files. Alternatively, you can select the appropriate icon from the toolbar.

Figure 21.6 shows NetWatcher being used to manage a remote computer named Spunky. As you can see in the title bar for the NetWatcher window, there is currently one machine attached to Spunky. Looking in the open window on the left, you see that the user's name is Rob, and he is connected from a computer named Po Hai 3000. He is also connected to four shared folders, has no open files, and has been connected to Spunky for one hour, 49 minutes, and 41 seconds. In the box on the right, you can see the names of the folders to which Rob is connected.

View by   View by   View by
Connections   Shared Folders   Open Files

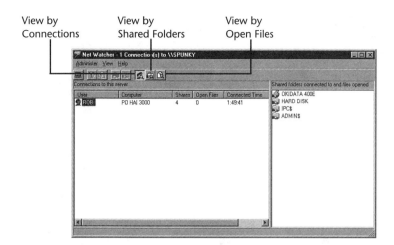

Fig. 21.6
NetWatcher
enables you to
find out which
users are con-
nected to a
computer and
what resources
they are sharing.

If you need to shut down Spunky, you must first disconnect all network users before doing so. Choose <u>A</u>dminister, <u>D</u>isconnect User. You are prompted to make sure you really want to disconnect the user. Choose <u>Y</u>es to disconnect the user or <u>N</u>o to cancel the disconnection.

Tip
You can only
disconnect users
from your local
machine. If you
are using
NetWatcher to
manage a remote
machine, you
cannot disconnect
users.

> **Caution**
>
> If you disconnect users who have an open file on your machine, they lose any un-
> saved data in the file that they were working on. You can use NetWatcher to deter-
> mine if remote users have files open. See the section "Viewing Open Files" later in
> this chapter.

Viewing Shared Folders

Figure 21.7 shows NetWatcher in the View by Shared Folders mode. You can switch NetWatcher to this mode by choosing the <u>V</u>iew, by <u>S</u>hared Folders, or clicking the View by Shared Folders icon from the NetWatcher toolbar.

In Figure 21.7 you can see in the open window on the left that there are three shared devices on Spunky, A:, C:, and an Okidata Laser Printer. These devices are shared under the names Floppy Disk, Hard Disk, and Okidata 400E, respectively. The access on all three devices is set to full. In the box on the right, you can see the computer that is connected to the shared device Hard Drive.

Fig. 21.7
You can view
NetWatcher
connections in
View by Shared
Folder mode.

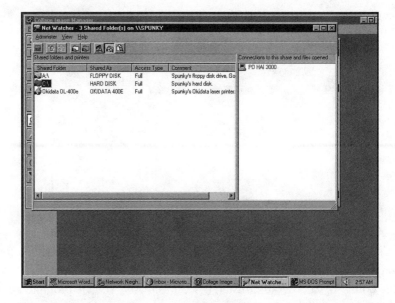

Adding, Changing, and Deleting Shared Folders

The ability to change the folders that are shared is another feature of
NetWatcher. To make changes to shared folders, you must first be in the View
by Shared Folders mode.

To add a shared folder, choose Administer, Add Shared Folder. You should see
a dialog box that prompts you for the path of the folder you want to share.
Type the path in the box and click the OK button. Alternatively, you can
click Browse and select the folder from the Browse for Folder window, which
works the same way as the Explorer. After you select the folder you want to
share, you are presented with a familiar Sharing properties sheet, which allows you to enter the Share Name, Comment, Access Type, and Password for
the shared folder. Enter the options you want, and click OK when you are
finished. Your newly shared folder appears in the NetWatcher window. (For
a refresher on how to share folders, see chapter 9, "Sharing Network Hardware.")

NetWatcher also allows you to stop sharing folders you have already shared.
To stop sharing a folder, first highlight the folder in the NetWatcher window
by clicking it. Next, choose Administer, Stop Sharing Folder. This displays a
NetWatcher dialog box that asks if you are sure you want to stop sharing the
folder in question. If you are, select Yes and the folder is no longer shared
and is no longer seen in the NetWatcher window.

In addition to adding and deleting shared folders, NetWatcher provides a shortcut for you to make changes to folders you have already shared. To make changes to the share name, comment, access type and password of a shared folder, you once again need to go to the Administer menu. From there, choose Shared Folder Properties to display the shared folder's Properties sheet. Make the changes you require and click OK. The changes take effect immediately. (For a refresher on shared folder Properties sheet, see chapter 9, "Sharing Network Hardware.")

Viewing Open Files

Figure 21.8 shows NetWatcher in View by Open Files mode. To put NetWatcher in this state, choose View, by Open Files. Or you can click the View by Open Files button on the toolbar.

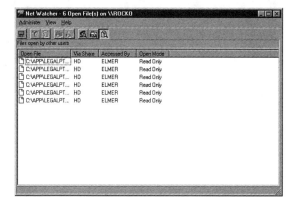

Fig. 21.8

You can use NetWatcher to view which files on your machine are being accessed by users on the network.

From here, you can see the files on your computer that are being accessed. The NetWatcher window contains information about the file name, the share name of the device the user is using, the name of the computer accessing the file, and the mode the file is open in, such as Read-Only or Read/Write.

NetWatcher enables you to manually close a file that other users on the network have open. For example, a user on your network opens a spreadsheet file on your computer and then goes home for the day. Later in the day, you also need to work on that spreadsheet but are unable to make changes to it because your co-worker already has it open. Using NetWatcher, you can free the file for your personal use.

To do this, highlight the file you want to close in the NetWatcher window. Then select Administer, Close File. You can also use the Close File icon from the toolbar.

VI

Connecting to Networks

Troubleshooting

I want to disconnect a user from my machine by using NetWatcher, but when I go to the Administer menu, the Disconnect User option is grayed out.

Remember that you can only disconnect users from your local machine. If you are managing a remote computer with NetWatcher, you cannot disconnect users.

Another possibility is that you have not selected the user you want to disconnect. This can easily happen if there is only one user connected to your machine. To be able to disconnect users, they must be highlighted. When you highlight the user, the option to disconnect should become available.

Using System Monitor To Check Network and System Use

The System Monitor enables you to gather information about your network. This includes information about the computers on your network and the traffic among computers on your network. Want to know what the size of the swap file is on a computer? System Monitor can provide you with the answer. Need to find out how many packets you are sending on the network per second? System Monitor can tell you.

System Monitor allows you to select the items you want to track for a given computer, such as its disk-cache size, percentage of processor usage, or number of times per second the hard disk is getting a request to read data. For each item you want to track, it displays a graph which gets updated periodically.

Installing System Monitor

If you have not already installed System Monitor, you can add it from the Add/Remove Programs Properties sheet. To do this, follow these steps:

1. Open the Start menu, choose Settings, Control Panel. This opens the Control Panel window, which contains various icons.

2. Double-click the Add/Remove Programs icon. The Add/Remove Programs Properties sheet appears and lets you add and remove programs.

3. Click the Windows Setup tab in the Add/Remove Programs Properties sheet, which displays the Setup page similar to the one you used when you first installed Windows 95. From here, you can install and remove Windows components.

4. Highlight Accessories in the Components list box, and click the Details button to display the Accessories dialog box, from which you choose which accessories you want installed. Alternatively, you can double-click on the Accessories icon in the Components list box.

5. Find the System Monitor icon in the Components list box in the Accessories dialog box. Mark the checkbox next to the System Monitor icon to choose it for installation.

6. Click OK to close the Accessories dialog box, which takes you back to the Add/Remove Programs Properties sheet.

7. Click OK in the Add/Remove Programs Properties sheet. This starts the installation of System Monitor.

8. You are prompted for a Windows 95 installation disk or CD-ROM. Insert the disk or CD-ROM and click OK.

Windows copies the files necessary to install System Monitor. The System Monitor icon is installed in the System Tools group. To get to the System Tools group, open the Start menu and choose Programs, Accessories, System Tools.

Using System Monitor To Access a Remote Computer

After you install System Monitor on your local computer, you can launch it and begin gathering information about your system. In many cases, though, you will also want to gather information about the other computers on your network. System Monitor can help you do this, but first you need to set up the remote computers so System Monitor can access them.

First, user-level access control must be enabled, which means you must have a NetWare or Windows NT Server on the network to do the user authentication. If you have an authentication server, you can turn on user-level access control from the Network dialog box. To do this, open the Start menu, choose Settings, Control Panel, and double-click the Network icon. The Network dialog box appears. Choose the Access Control tab. Then mark the User-Level Access Control checkbox. Next, enter the name of the Windows NT or NetWare server that will be doing authentication for you in the Obtain List of Users and Groups From text box. Then click OK.

You must also have the remote Registry service loaded on both machines. The Remote Registry Service, REGSERV.EXE, is hidden on your Windows installation CD-ROM. In the \ADMIN\NETTOOLS directory on your

VI

Connecting to Networks

CD-ROM, there is a subdirectory called REMOTREG, which contains three files, REGSERV.EXE, WINREG.DLL, and REGSRV.INF. To install these files, you need to run the Add/Remove Programs utility:

1. Open the Start menu, choose Settings, Control Panel. This opens the Control Panel window, which contains various icons.

2. Double-click the Add/Remove Programs icon. The Add/Remove Programs Properties sheet appears and lets you add and remove programs.

3. Click the Install button in the Add/Remove Programs Properties sheet, which displays the Install Program from Floppy Disk or CD-ROM Wizard. From here, you can install and remove Windows programs. Click Next to continue.

4. Enter the path to the Remote Registry service in the Command Line for Installation Program text box. The program name is REGSERV.EXE and it is in \ADMIN\NETTOOLS\REMOTREG on the installation CD-ROM. Click Finish and the software is installed.

For more information about the Registry, see appendix B, "Registry Entries for Networking."

To configure a machine for remote administration, open the Start menu, choose Settings, Control Panel, and double-click the Passwords icon. This opens the Passwords Properties sheet (refer to fig. 21.3). To use NetWatcher on a remote machine, remote administration must be turned on for the machine that you want to monitor. To do this, check the Enable Remote Administration of This Server checkbox. Then type a password for the server in the Password text box, type the same password again in the Confirm Password box (to verify you typed what you think you did in the password box), and click the OK button.

Once you have set up the remote computer for System Monitor, you can connect to it in one of two ways. Your first option is to start the System Monitor. Then you choose File, Connect. Next, you enter the name of the computer you want to monitor and click OK.

The easier method is to launch System Monitor from the Network Neighborhood. This is handy if you can't remember the exact name of the computer you want to monitor. (Because System Monitor provides no way for you to browse the network, you have to remember the exact name of the computer you want to monitor.) Right-click the icon for the computer that you want to run System Monitor on. Choose Properties from the pop-up menu. Click the Tools tab and choose System Monitor.

Changing the Format of System Monitor Charts

System Monitor, shown in figure 21.9, can display its charts in three different formats. Depending on how you prefer to view your information, you can choose Line Charts, Bar Charts, or Numeric Charts. To select a chart format, select Line Charts, Bar Charts, or Numeric Charts from the View menu. Alternatively, you can select the corresponding button on the toolbar.

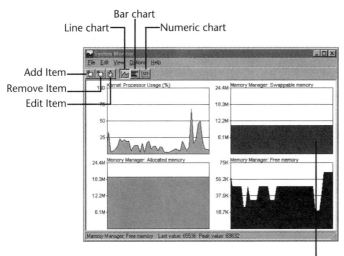

Fig. 21.9

System Monitor provides statistics about the computers on your network in easy-to-read graphs.

Individual charts provide you with information about your computer

Clearing Chart Windows

After you have been viewing system statistics for a while, your chart windows may become cluttered. You might want to clear the chart windows you have open and start fresh by erasing the graphs that they contain. To do this, choose Edit, Clear Window.

Changing the Scale and Color of a Chart

System Monitor gives you the option to change the appearance of your chart windows. Specifically, you can change the scale and color of the charts by using the Chart Options window. You can bring up the Chart Options window for the chart you want to modify by selecting the item you want to edit and choosing Edit, Edit Item. Then highlight the item you want to edit in the list box and click OK. Alternatively, you can select the Edit Item button from the toolbar. Next, select the name of the chart you want to edit from the list. Click OK.

VI

Connecting to Networks

Tip

A faster way to bring up the Chart Options window is to double-click the chart you want to modify.

From here, to change the color of the chart, click the Change button, which will display the Color dialog box. Next, choose the color you want to make the graph and click OK. Click OK from the Chart Options window to make the changes take effect.

The second chart property you can change from the Chart Options window is scale. The scale of the graph can be set to either Automatic or Fixed. If you set the scale to Automatic, the System Monitor selects a maximum chart value based on the peak value that the given chart has had so far. If you set the scale to Fixed, you must supply the maximum value for the chart in the Value box. Select the type of scale by selecting the option button corresponding to the scale type you want. Click OK when you are finished so that the system makes the changes.

Modifying the Update Interval

The update interval is the period of time it takes for the System Monitor to display another reading in each of the chart windows. You can have System Monitor make the changes anywhere from every second to every one hour. To do this, choose Options, Chart, which displays the Options dialog box. Then use the slider to select the update interval you want. When you are finished, click OK.

Adding and Removing Charts

If you no longer need to monitor a chart, you can remove it by selecting Edit, Remove Item, which opens the Remove Item dialog box. Choose the name of the chart you no longer want to track and click OK. The chart is removed from your display. You can also select the Remove Item icon on the toolbar.

If you want to add a chart to the list you are keeping track of, choose Edit, Add Item. This displays the Add Item dialog box, which has two list boxes, Category and Item. Clicking a category in the Category list box displays a corresponding list in the items list box. To add a chart, highlight the name of the item you want to add. Then click OK. The chart appears in the System Monitor window.

If you want to find out what the chart item means, the Add Item dialog box can give you an explanation. Click the category in the Category list box and click the item in the Item list box. Then click Explanation to find out more on that item.

> **Troubleshooting**
>
> *When I try to run the System Monitor for a remote computer, I get a message that indicates that Windows cannot connect.*
>
> To use System Monitor, you must have user-level access turned on. For help selecting user-level access, see the section on "Using System Monitor To Access a Remote Computer" earlier in this chapter.

Using Ping To Locate Other Network Systems

Ping is a DOS-based program that tests to see whether another computer is on the network. It is a quick test that asks the other computer if it is there. If the other computer is attached to the network and set up properly, it responds to Ping, letting you know that everything is okay.

Setting Up Ping

Ping is a TCP/IP-based program. This means that to use it you need to have TCP/IP installed, which you can do from the Network dialog box. For detailed information on how to do this, see chapter 19, "Connecting to Other Networks." Once TCP/IP is installed and configured, all you need to do is open a DOS window.

Basically, Ping sends 32 bytes of data to another machine on the network. If the other machine is connected to the network and has TCP/IP installed, it sends the same 32 bytes back to the computer that sent it. Once your computer gets the data back, it knows that the other machine is responding on the network.

Using the PING Command

Ping is located in the WINDOWS directory, which should be in your DOS path. All you need to do is type the name of the program.

The format of the PING command is

    ping *ip_address*

or

    ping *computer_name*

Tip
Some versions of the Ping program exist that have been written to use the Windows interface instead of a DOS window. One is the WS_PING program, which is freely available on the Internet.

VI

Connecting to Networks

ip_address is the Internet Protocol address of the machine. If the machine you are trying to ping is a Windows 95 machine on your network, you can determine its number by checking the Network dialog box. The IP address is under the properties for the TCP/IP protocol.

computer_name is the name of the computer you want to check, as specified in your hosts file or the domain name server. Typing a computer name is basically the same as typing an IP address. When you enter **ping computer_name**, your system checks the hosts file in your WINDOWS directory to determine the IP address of the system. It then pings that address.

For more information on setting up TCP/IP, your hosts file, and the domain name server, see chapter 19, "Connecting to Other Networks."

The Ping program that comes with Windows tests the target computer four times and then exits. As you can see in figure 21.10, if the other computer responds, you get the Reply from message. This message tells you that the computer responded. It also diplays the IP address of the responding computer, the number of bytes it returned, and the amount of time that it took to return them.

Fig. 21.10
Use Ping to check whether another workstation can be reached on the network.

If there is a problem with the other computer, it cannot respond to your Ping. If this happens, you get a result similar to the one that figure 21.11 shows. After your computer sends the Ping message, it waits for the response. If the reponse doesn't come back in a certain amount of time, you get the message Request timed out.

Fig. 21.11
A failed Ping
shows that the
remote computer
is unreachable on
the network.

Troubleshooting

When I Ping a computer on my network, I get a Bad IP Address message.

The Bad IP Address message appears when you are pinging a remote computer using a name instead of a numeric address and you have typed a name that does not appear in your hosts file. Check the name and try again.

When I Ping a computer on my network, I get a Destination host unreachable message.

You have probably mistyped the IP address of the destination machine. The Destination host unreachable message means that you are trying to Ping a machine on another network. However, your computer was unable to get a Ping to that other network. If you are trying to Ping a computer on your local network, check the IP address and try again. If you are, in fact, trying to Ping a computer on a foreign network, check your network connection to the foreign network. Also, check that you have set up your default gateway to the proper IP address. For information on setting up the default gateway, see chapter 19, "Connecting to Other Networks."

From Here...

This chapter gave you an introduction to network administration, including some of the tools that come with Windows to make administrating your network easier. You can use NetWatcher to get information on shared folders and network connections and System Monitor to get statistics about the network itself. You also learned how to use Ping as a quick test to see whether another computer is on the network.

For more information on the items that this chapter covers, review the following:

- Chapter 19, "Connecting to Other Networks," tells you how to set up TCP/IP so that you can use the Ping utility discussed in this chapter.

- Appendix B, "Registry Entries for Networking," introduces you to another powerful network administration tool, the remote Registry.

Part VII

Appendixes

Files
now
alan

Power status
Battery level: low
14% remaining

OK

Print

☑ Enable low battery warning

agic
Gipres
ken

ent
Resume
rob
Shortcut to
Gamagic

Netscape - [Welcome to Netscape]
File Edit View Go Bookmarks Options Directory

Back Forward Home   Reload Images Open Print Find

Netsite: http://home.netscape.com/

What's New! What's Cool! Handbook Net Search Net Directory Newsgroups

N   WELCOME   TO   NETSC

GENERAL

EXPLORING   COMPANY &   NETSCAPE   NEWS &   ASSISTAN
THE NET   PRODUCTS   STORE   REFERENCE

+ NETSCAPE SERVER GALLERIA

NETSCAPE AT WORK
See how companies are using Netscape Server software to create business app
employees to information on internal web sites.

OPEN WINDOWS TO THE INTERNET
Netscape announces Netscape Navigator 1.2 LAN and Personal Edition, provi
and features for Windows users. Get up-to-date information on using Navigator
Download 1.2 with Netscape Now!

Global Image
SurfStation

4.61MB

Document: Done

ew
Hardware
Programs

Internet
Joystick
Keyboard

Multimedia
Network
ODBC

Printers
Regional
Settings
Sounds

icrosoft Exchange
Tools Compose Help

B Z U

ogos currently available as scanned images

ALCO
Alco

Configures network hardware and software.

Fsc_main
File Edit View Help

Fsc_main

fsc_admin
fsc_color_dy... f

fsc_dev-wsv
fsc_ds

fsc_mac
fsc_mktg

Appendix A

Technical Specifications of Network Protocols

This appendix will give you a technical overview of several of the most popular network protocols and their uses. Typically, specific network services require specific protocols to access them. A protocol is a way for your networked workstation to communicate with a server on the network. Since each server may be offering different services, such as customer databases, e-mail, file and printer sharing, or Internet access, many different protocols have emerged to facilitate these network services.

This appendix outlines the basics of a protocol and describes what each of the functions of a protocol does and where it's used. Specifically, you learn about the following protocols:

- OSI networking model

- Ethernet

- Token ring

- TCP/IP

- IPX/SPX

- NetBIOS

OSI Networking Model

The *Open Systems Interconnect* (OSI) networking model is a standard method for understanding the various levels of communications on a network. These generic labels give the capability to focus on the function that is being served by a particular networking component to aid in designing more efficient communications between network clients and the services that they are trying to access.

The OSI model is divided into seven layers, as illustrated in figure A.1. These layers are typically shown stacked vertically as an indication of each layer's dependence on the prior layers for communication with another device. Discussion of these layers usually starts at the bottom of the stack where the most elemental communications occur.

Fig. A.1
The OSI networking model has seven layers.

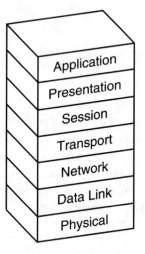

Physical Layer

This is where the most basic level of connectivity takes place. If your PC is connected to a local area network, you have some sort of network interface card that plugs into your PC and provides the capability to send electronic pulses up and down a wire to communicate with other computers.

As shown in figure A.2, the *physical layer* does not need to be a wire, however. Wireless spread-spectrum and microwave radio signals or satellite transmissions can be used to propagate the signal between computers. Light pulses can also be used to transfer information across a fiber-optic cable or through the air with a laser-beam. The main concept of the physical layer is that it is the signaling means between the hosts.

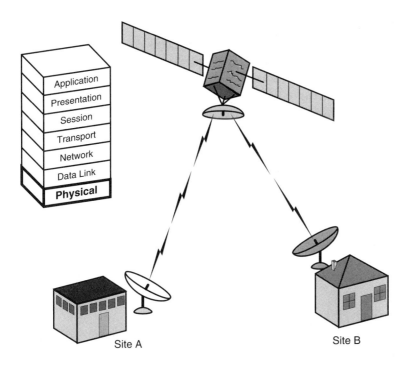

Fig. A.2
The physical layer
doesn't have to be
a wire.

Data Link Layer

Once a physical network has been established, there needs to be rules governing how the physical layer is used so all of the participants can communicate.
If a wire represents the physical layer, what voltages will be used? How will
the binary zeros and ones be defined? What is the rate at which these binary
states can change? As shown in figure A.3, the *data link layer* provides the
facility to interpret these types of issues and provide the network connection.

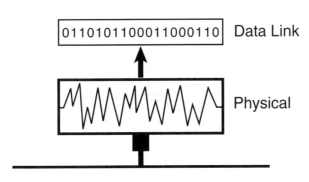

Fig. A.3
The data link layer
interprets physical
links to make the
connection.

Network Layer

The *network layer* allows the devices on the network to tell the difference between one another. Unlike your electrical wiring in your house where your toaster doesn't care if your hair-dryer is plugged in, every device that plugs into a network needs to have an address associated with it to allow proper communications with other devices. Addressing and basic communications flow is handled by the network layer (see fig. A.4). This layer also sets up rules for the size of the packets and possibly for error correction.

Fig. A.4
The network layer helps connected devices with addressing.

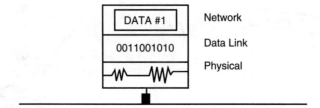

Transport Layer

The packets flowing from one computer to another may not arrive as they were sent. For a variety of reasons, such as routing or network errors, information from a computer may not arrive at the destination in the same order that it was sent. The *transport layer* helps to reorder the packets (see fig. A.5) into the correct sequence and typically uses some sort of checking mechanism to determine if the packet arrived looking the same way that it was sent.

The transport layer can request the originating host to resend a packet that was either garbled or lost during transmission. This allows the network connections to be more reliable under many different circumstances.

Fig. A.5
The transport layer can reorder packets that are out of sequence.

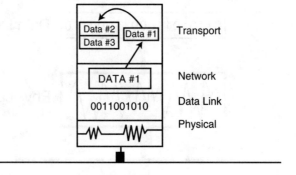

Session Layer

After the packets have arrived at the destination and have been placed in the correct order, they are delivered to the *session layer*. The session layer allows the computer to be able to communicate with many other computers simultaneously by assigning each connection its own session. The packets that arrive at the session layer are then sorted out to the correct computer communication association. Figure A.6 illustrates how the session layer handles multiple connections.

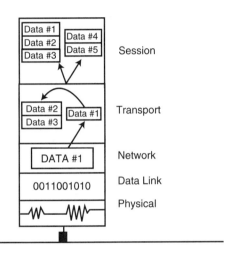

Fig. A.6
The session layer sorts packets to allow for multiple connections.

Presentation Layer

Packets that arrive into the *presentation layer* are in the correct order from the particular connection that has been established. To be used by a program, the packets must be stripped of their network "packaging." This means that instead of having 10 correctly ordered packets for the program to interpret, the presentation layer reassembles the original message in its entirety. As illustrated in figure A.7, the original message that was chopped up for sending over the network is now put back together.

Application Layer

After the message finally reaches its destination, the program that receives it has to know what to do with it. The messages between the applications allow for interactions between hosts for various tasks, such as file transfer, user authentication, and database queries.

Fig. A.7
The presentation
layer reassembles
the message from
the individual
packet fragments.

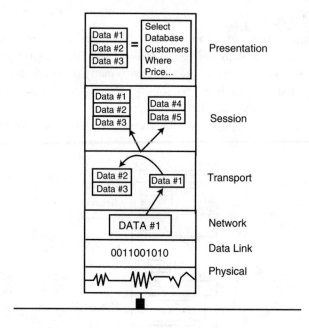

The *application layer* includes any program that communicates with a server over the network (see fig. A.8). Some programs will not know that they are using the application layer of the networking model because Windows provides an interface that makes the network appear as a drive letter or as a printer. Other applications are written specifically to talk with servers on the network. Some of these applications would include client/server database applications; Internet programs, such as Telnet, Gopher, and World Wide Web browsers; and workgroup applications like Lotus Notes.

Now that you have seen the networking model, let's look at some specific uses of the various layers as they relate to different protocols.

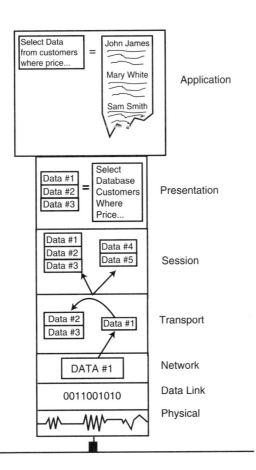

Fig. A.8
The application layer is where programs can offer and request services on a network.

Ethernet Network Communication

Ethernet specifies the way computers communicate at the bottom two layers of the OSI networking model (see fig. A.9). The upper layers are handled by higher-level protocols, such as IPX, TCP/IP, and NetBIOS, which will be discussed later in this appendix.

This protocol uses the CSMA/CD (Carrier Sense Multiple Access/Carrier Detect) method of determining when to send data on the network. That means that any time a computer wants to transmit information on the network, it first listens to see if any other computer is transmitting data. If the wire is available, it will begin sending the data on the network. If the wire is busy, it will wait a short time and try it sending again.

Fig. A.9
The physical and data link layers are managed by the Ethernet protocol.

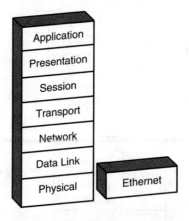

When a computer sends data on an Ethernet network, it does not send the packets to a particular computer. Since Ethernet works on a linear-bus topology, meaning every device connected to the network "hears" every other device's conversation, all computers attached to the network will receive the packets at the same time. Since the Ethernet data link layer is handling the addressing, only the computer to which the data is addressed will actually get the information passed along to a higher-level protocol. The other workstations on the network simply ignore the data that is not addressed to them.

Of course there are situations and circumstances where this basic operation varies, such as broadcast packets, but the general operation of Ethernet follows these rules.

Token Ring

Token ring also specifies the lower levels of the OSI networking model; however, it specifies portions of the network and transport layers also (see fig. A.10). Like Ethernet, token ring lets higher-level protocols handle the upper layers of the OSI networking model.

Token ring uses a different access mechanism than Ethernet. A special data packet called a token (hence the name) is passed along the wire that connects computers together. As figure A.11 shows, each computer circulates the token to determine which computer can send data. The data is then passed around the ring until the workstation to which the data is addressed receives it. When the sending computer is finished or a certain time limit is reached, the token is passed to the next computer.

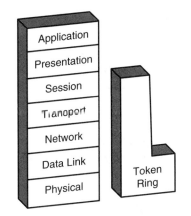

Fig. A.10
Token ring specifies the operation up to portions of the network and transport layers.

Fig. A.11
Each computer on a token-ring network waits its turn for the token to send data on the network.

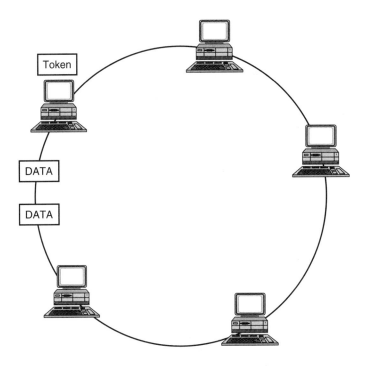

TCP/IP

TCP/IP stands for Transmission Control Protocol/Internet Protocol. This is a low-level language that lets the computers understand where messages should be sent. A network protocol like TCP/IP has often been compared to sending a letter to a friend. After you write a letter, you place it into an envelope and print the name and address of your friend on the outside.

The address tells the postal service where to deliver your mail. Your letter gets placed into a local mailbox, then gets transported to your friend using the postal service protocol. Even though your letter got mixed in with millions of other letters, it eventually reached your friend's house. This is quite similar to the way TCP/IP works with its protocol system.

Network Addressing

With TCP/IP each network and each host are given a specific address. This address is composed of a 32-bit string of four octets that is expressed as four numbers separated by periods (see fig. A.12).

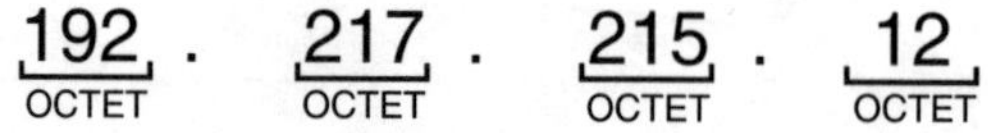

Fig. A.12
A TCP/IP address consists of four octets.

$$\underset{\text{OCTET}}{192} \cdot \underset{\text{OCTET}}{217} \cdot \underset{\text{OCTET}}{215} \cdot \underset{\text{OCTET}}{12}$$

The numbering system allows for a hierarchical system of networking. The address is separated into two parts depending on the level of the hierarchy. The InterNIC organization, which is the official address assignment agency for the Internet, has assigned class definitions to each of the levels. For Class A network addresses, the number of potential hosts on the network is over 16 million. For a Class B network address, over 65 thousand hosts can be addressed. For a Class C network, only 252 hosts can be attached.

If you happened to notice that the Class C network of 252 hosts should be 255 (since there are eight bits to use), you are right and you are wrong. The TCP/IP protocol uses several addresses in a special way. First, the zero and 255 values are used for the network address and for the broadcast to the network, respectively. That leaves 253, but the routing host interface also requires its own address—leaving 252 for the rest of the hosts.

Names and Addresses

The essential computer workings use electrical signals—represented by zeros and ones—to function. However, people have a more difficult time doing that. To make the TCP/IP addressing somewhat easier to use, a naming convention was devised called the *Domain Name System* (DNS). A domain is a group of hosts that ultimately have host names associated with them.

To illustrate this point, let's assume a company has a connection to the Internet. This company may have the domain name **bigcorp.com**, which means that any host under that name will have the domain name appended to it. The mail server could be called **mail.bigcorp.com**, while the accounting server could be **ledger.bigcorp.com**. Access to the accounting server could be done either by using the TCP/IP address or by using the DNS name. Obviously, it would be easier to remember the names of the hosts rather than the individual addresses.

If you noticed, the naming scheme is hierarchical like the addressing scheme. However, there is not necessarily a one-to-one relationship between the levels of an address and the levels of a name. A fully qualified domain name includes the host name followed by the domain name separated by periods. There are 26 major top-level domains that every registered DNS name must fall under. Table A.1 has the list of top-level domain names.

Table A.1   Top-Level Domain Names

Domain Name	Description
com	Commercial organizations
org	Non-Profit organizations
net	Network service providers
gov	United States Government organizations
mil	United States Military organizations
edu	Educational institutions
int	International organizations
au	Australian hosts
at	Austrian hosts
ca	Canadian hosts
cl	Chilean hosts
dk	Dutch hosts
ec	Ecuadorian hosts
fi	Finnish hosts
fr	French hosts
de	German hosts
is	Icelandic hosts
it	Italian hosts

(continues)

Table A.1 Continued	
Domain Name	**Description**
jp	Japanese hosts
kr	Korean hosts
nz	New Zealand hosts
es	Spanish hosts
se	Swedish hosts
tw	Taiwanese hosts
uk	British and Irish hosts
us	United States hosts

Note

Domain Name System addressing always ends in a top-level domain. Some domains may have similar domain addresses, such as **host1.ca** and **host1.ca.us**. The first address points to a host in Canada while the second points to a host in California.

An additional benefit for using DNS naming rather than TCP/IP addresses to access hosts is the ability to change the underlying TCP/IP address for a host that has a name. For example, if the Nuts-N-Bolts company began to do more business than they could handle in their current location, they might move to a larger facility in another state. It is likely that the move would require them to change TCP/IP addresses for their hosts. If access to the hosts was done with the DNS names, then when the DNS pointers were changed from the old addresses to the new ones, the end user would not notice any difference since the DNS name got access to the host as expected.

IPX/SPX

The *IPX/SPX* protocol was developed by Novell for their NetWare servers. IPX (Internetwork Packet Exchange) is a *connectionless protocol*, which means that any verification of successful data delivery is left up to the transport layer and higher layers to handle. SPX (Sequenced Packet Exchange), on the other hand, does verify packet delivery yet is somewhat slower than IPX. Typically, Novell has chosen to use IPX for everything except its database servers.

IPX on an Ethernet network can use one of two Ethernet packet types. The Ethernet 802.3 packet is considered to be "raw" Ethernet. An Ethernet 802.2 packet uses a field in the Ethernet header that is ignored under the Ethernet 802.3 packet. The reason that this is significant is that Novell had chosen the Ethernet 802.3 packet as the default installation for its servers until Novell released its most current versions of NetWare 4.x, and NetWare 3.12. Then Novell switched to the Ethernet 802.2 packet type to use the special header field to send packet IDs that protected against intruders.

IPX uses the Ethernet network card ID along with a server-assigned network number to determine a computer's address on the network. This allows work-stations on a Novell NetWare network running IPX to run without pre-configuring a network address.

NetBIOS

The *NetBIOS* protocol is a low-overhead protocol that is used to connect computers together on a local area network. Because of the addressing scheme of NetBIOS, only 255 computers can participate on the network. Also, NetBIOS has no network numbering scheme (it assumes only one network), so if a company has many servers that are connected to many other networks, the computers on one network cannot talk to the computers on another network using NetBIOS.

Microsoft and IBM have long used NetBIOS as the foundation of their communications protocols. But now Microsoft is moving away from NetBIOS towards IPX/SPX. NetBIOS will still remain an effective protocol for small networks since it has very little header information and no routing information to process.

Appendix B

Registry Entries for Networking

The Registry is the database where Windows stores its configuration information. It contains all of the setup information about the hardware in the computer, the user's configuration, and the network configuration. For example, all of the specifics as to the layout of the desktop, the resolution of the display, the network workgroup the computer is in, and the toolbar configuration are all stored in the Registry.

The Registry is the replacement for the INI files of Windows 3.x, but the Registry also contains information that once was in DOS's CONFIG.SYS and AUTOEXEC.BAT files. Not only does Windows 95 store its information in the Registry, but applications do too. So the only time you see INI files created is when you install a Windows 3.1 16-bit application.

Working with the Registry—REGEDIT

REGEDIT is a program designed to allow you to make changes to the Registry by hand. The Registry is stored in two hidden files in the WINDOWS directory. They are USER.DAT, which stores user specific information such as your default desktop font and background, and SYSTEM.DAT, which contains the hardware information for your computer such as the sound card you have installed and what video adapter your computer has.

Normally, the way you interact with these files is through the Windows Properties sheets. As you make changes to your settings in the Properties sheets, Windows makes the corresponding changes to the Registry for you. Occasionally, though, you may run into a situation where you need to tweak the Registry entries by hand—you do that using REGEDIT.

Note

Windows 95 automatically keeps a backup copy of the Registry for you in case of an emergency. If your Registry gets corrupted and Windows 95 will not boot, you can restore the Registry to the state it was in at the time of the last known good boot. To do so,

1. Restart the computer in DOS mode by selecting F8 as the computer is booting and choosing DOS mode from the list of available boot options.

2. Change to the WINDOWS directory.

3. Unhide the Registry files and backups and make them writable by using the following commands (press Enter after each command).

   attrib -h -r -s system.dat

   attrib -h -r -s system.da0

   attrib -h -r -s user.dat

   attrib -h -r -s user.da0

4. Copy the backups over the existing Registry files with the following commands.

   copy system.da0 system.dat

   copy user.da0 user.dat

5. Reboot your computer. It will start Windows 95 using the newly restored Registry.

Caution

If you make a mistake when you are making manual changes to the Registry, your computer might not start properly. We do not recommend that you manually edit the Registry except under extreme circumstances. Use the Properties sheets from the Control Panel window instead.

The REGEDIT.EXE file is tucked away in your WINDOWS directory. After you launch it, you should see something similar to figure B.1.

The Registry looks similar to the Explorer, which you are already familiar with. There is a tree in the left-hand box (the key box), which you can expand by clicking the plus boxes just as in the Explorer. The entries in the left-hand box are *keys*, which represent the attributes of your computer. The box on the right is called the *values box*. It contains the value names and data for the highlighted attribute on the left.

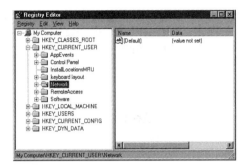

Fig. B.1
Use REGEDIT, the Registry Editor, to make changes to the Registry.

Adding or Editing the Registry Keys

Chances are, you would never want to add or rename a Registry key unless you are a software developer. Still, the Registry Editor enables you to make changes should the need arise. To make a change to an entry in the key box of the Registry, simply right-click the key you want to change. This displays a pop-up menu with options to add a new key or rename or delete the selected key. To add another key, right-click the selected item and choose New, Key. The new key appears in the tree one level below the currently selected key. Its default name will be New Key #1. Change the name of the key to the desired name.

To rename a key, right-click the key you want to rename and select Rename. Then enter the new name. To delete a key, right-click it and select Delete. Alternatively, you can select the key you want to delete and press the Delete key on your keyboard.

Adding and Editing the Registry Values

Adding and editing Registry values is far more common than changing or adding entire keys. To add a new value to the values box for a key, right-click the key and select New. Then choose the type of value you want to add: String, Binary, or DWORD. Then enter the name of the value.

To change the value's data, right-click the value name in the value box, and select Modify. This displays the edit window for the type of data you are entering. For example, if you are making changes to a binary value, you see the Edit Binary Value window. If you are changing a string, you see the Edit String window. Once the edit window is open, enter the value you want in the Value Data text box.

Using the Remote Registry

In addition to providing a means for you to manage the Registry on your local computer, REGEDIT can also be used to manage the Registries on remote computers on your network without leaving your desk. For example, you can change the default workgroup for another workstation or select a new default desktop font. This feature makes it much easier to manage a network of Windows computers.

Setting Up the Remote Registry

In order to use the features of the Remote Registry, you must first get it installed and configured. This consists of three steps. First, you must make sure that the remote computer is configured for user-level access control. Secondly, you must make sure that remote administration is enabled on the remote computer. And finally, the Remote Registry Service must be running on both the remote and local computers.

Setting Up User-Level Access Control

To specify user-level access control, you need to use the Network dialog box. (Note that to use user-level access control you must be on a network with either a Novell NetWare or a Windows NT Server.) Open the Start menu and choose Settings, Control Panel. Double-click the Network icon to view the Network dialog box. Click the Access Control tab to display the Access Control page.

From the Access Control page, select User-Level Access Control. Then enter the name of the NetWare or Windows NT Server you want to use for user authentication. Click OK and restart your computer to make the changes take effect.

Enabling Remote Administration

You enable remote administration from the Passwords Properties sheet. To open the Password Properties sheet, open the Start menu and choose Settings, Control Panel. Double-click the Passwords icon to launch the Passwords Properties sheet. From here, mark the Enable Remote Administration of This Server Mark checkbox.

The Administrators list box contains the list of users who are allowed to connect to this computer and perform administration. By default, the only user in this box is the supervisor if you are using a NetWare network or administrator if you are using a Windows NT network. If you want to add another user, simply click the Add button and select the user's ID from the list.

Starting the Remote Registry Service

The Remote Registry Service, REGSERV.EXE, is hidden on your Windows installation CD-ROM. In the \ADMIN\NETTOOLS directory on your CD-ROM, there is a subdirectory called REMOTREG, which contains three files, REGSERV.EXE, WINREG.DLL, and REGSRV.INF. To install these files, you will need to run the Add/Remove Programs utility in the Control Panel window:

1. Open the Start menu and choose Settings, Control Panel. This will open the Control Panel window, which contains the various Control Panel icons.

2. Double-click the Add/Remove Programs icon. The Add/Remove Programs Properties sheet allows you to easily add and remove programs.

3. Click the Install button in the Add/Remove Programs Properties sheet, which displays the Install Program from Floppy Disk or CD-ROM Wizard. From here, you can install and remove Windows programs. Click Next to continue.

4. Enter the path to the Remote Registry service in the Command Line for Installation Program text box. The program name is REGSERV.EXE and it is in \ADMIN\NETTOOLS\REMOTREG on the installation CD-ROM. Click Finish and the software is installed.

Connecting to Another Computer's Registry

After both the local and remote computers are configured properly, connecting to the remote computer's Registry is easy. Start REGEDIT, just as you normally would to edit your local Registry. Choose Registry, Connect Network Registry. Type the name of the computer, or click Browse and select the computer name from the list. Click OK when you are finished. You are then able to edit the Remote Registry from within REGEDIT, just as you do with the local Registry.

For example, you have a user who wants to turn off his screen saver, but doesn't know how to get it done. You can make the necessary changes to his machine for him by using the remote Registry. To turn off the screen saver on the remote computer, follow these steps:

1. Launch REGEDIT by opening the Start menu and choosing Run. Enter **regedit.exe** in the Open text box.

2. From the Registry Editor window, choose Registry, Connect Network Registry. This opens the Registry for the remote machine in the Registry Editor window.

3. In the Registry tree, choose HKEY_CURRENT_USER, Control Panel, Desktop by double-clicking on each icon in the tree. This displays a list of values for the Display key.

4. Edit the ScreenSaveActive value by double-clicking it. This displays the Edit String window. With ScreenSaveActive displayed as the Value Name and 1 displayed as the Value data.

5. To disable the Screen Saver, enter a **0** in the Value Data text box and click OK. When the remote machine reboots, the screen saver is disabled.

Appendix C

Glossary of Networking Terms

802.2   The IEEE standard for Logical Link Control, or LLC. LLC is that layer of the network model that ensures error-free transmission to the network layer and is actually a portion of the Data Link Layer of the OSI model. See *OSI Model*.

802.3   802.3 is the IEEE standard for Carrier Sense Multiple Access with Collision Detection (CSMA/CD) on a bus topology. This standard was modelled after the original specifications for Ethernet.

802.5   The physical standard for a LAN in a ring topology that passes tokens of data over STP wire. Normal data speeds for this type of network are 4 or 16 Mbps. This specification is used by IBM's token ring.

10Base2   IEEE name for Ethernet over thin coaxial cable (RG58 A/U) at 10 Mbps. 10Base2 uses baseband signaling and has a maximum unrepeated segment length of 185 meters. Also known as *thinnet* or *cheapnet*. See *Baseband* and *Ethernet*.

10Base5   IEEE name for Ethernet over a thick coaxial cable (RG8 or RG11). 10Base5 uses baseband signaling and has a maximum segment length of 500 meters. Also known as *thicknet* or *thick Ethernet*. See *Baseband* and *Ethernet*.

10BaseT   IEEE name for Ethernet over unshielded twisted-pair wiring similar to that used by many phone systems. 10BaseT uses baseband signaling and has a maximum cable segment of 100 meters. See *Ethernet*.

Access Method   The set of rules or algorithms that describes how to access a LAN. The access method defines how data is transmitted and received across the wire.

Address   A number that identifies each station on a network. This number must be unique for each device on the network and, in the case of IEEE physical addresses, is actually unique worldwide. See *Physical Address* and *Network Address*.

ANSI   The American National Standards Institute is the United States representative to the International Standards Organization (ISO).

Application Layer   The highest layer in the OSI model. This layer contains applications designed to work over a network, such as remote terminal programs, e-mail packages, and file transfer applications.

ASCII   The American Standard Code for Information Interchange is the standard for representing plain text in computer format.

AUI   Attachment Unit Interface. This normally refers to the 15-pin d-shell connector that connects an Ethernet adapter card to a transceiver. See *Ethernet*.

AWG   American Wire Gauge. Gauge is a measure of the thickness of a cable. The higher the AWG number, the thinner the cable. For example, industrial wiring is gauge 2, but the twisted pair used in 10BaseT networks is gauge 24.

Baseband   Baseband refers to a signalling scheme in which only one device may transmit on the cable at a time. The transmitting device (usually a NIC) is able to use the entire available bandwidth of the cable.

BNC Connector   The connector used in a 10Base2 cable. These connectors are used to attach cable segments to T connectors and terminators.

Bridge   A device that connects two network segments and forwards packets from one segment to the other if the packet has a destination address on a different segment than the sending station. Bridges operate at the data link layer of the OSI model and have two advantages. First, they allow traffic to be controlled by dividing the network into two separate parts. This doubles the theoretical maximum network throughput. Second, dividing the network into two segments allows the total network to be longer and have more stations because the limitations are for each individual segment. See also *Repeater* and *Router*.

Bus   A network topology often used in Ethernet networks in which all stations are attached to a single cable. This cable is terminated at its ends.

Carrier Sense Multiple Access with Collision Detection   See *CSMA/CD*.

Category 3   Unshielded twisted-pair wire that is certified by the Electronic Industries Association for use in LANs up to 10 Mbps. Category 3 cable consists of eight strands of wire in four pairs. It is commonly used in 10BaseT Ethernet networks. See *Category 5* and *UTP*.

Category 5   High-quality unshielded twisted-pair wire that has been tested up to 100 Mbps by the Electronic Industries Association. Category 5 cable consists of eight strands of wire in four twisted pairs, but it is able to handle higher transmission rates than Category 3 UTP because it has more twists per linear inch. See *Category 3* and *UTP*.

Client   A network client is any computer that is using a resource on the network. If you are using a hard disk on another computer on the LAN, then you are a client and the machine whose hard disk you are using is a server. See *Server*.

Coaxial Cable   A cable consisting of a center conductor surrounded by a layer of braided mesh. The braid, or the shield, serves to protect the center conducting wire from electromagnetic interference. Coaxial cable is used in Ethernet 10Base2 networks and by your local cable television company to carry television signals.

Collision   A collision occurs when two devices on an Ethernet network begin sending data simultaneously. Since only one device can transmit at any given time, both devices back off for some random period of time and then try to send again.

Concentrator   This device is the central point in a star network and is sometimes referred to as a hub because it is the central point that connects all the cable runs. Each computer is connected to the concentrator, and data that comes to the concentrator from one station is then sent out to all other stations.

CSMA/CD   Carrier Sense Multiple Access with Collision Detection. These are the rules by which an Ethernet network determines which stations can transmit data.

Data Link Layer   The second layer in the OSI model. This layer takes care of putting the data into an appropriate form for transmission over the network, adding error-correction information and the address of the machine that the data is to be sent to. The data link layer then hands the data over to the physical layer for actual transmission. The data link layer has been divided into two separate pieces by the IEEE 802.2 specification, Logical Link Control (LLC), and Media Access Control (MAC). See *LLC* and *MAC*.

Electronic Mail   Electronic mail or e-mail commonly refers to sending text messages over the network from one user to another. In addition to regular ASCII text, many e-mail packages also allow you to send a variety of other data, such as spreadsheets and graphics.

EMI   ElectroMagnetic Interference. Distortions and interference in the signal being transmitted on a LAN cable caused by electrical devices such as air conditioners and fluorescent lighting. See *RFI*.

Ethernet   A LAN access method that is based on CSMA/CD and operates at 10 Mbps. Ethernet was invented by Xerox in 1973 but wasn't introduced as a standardized network until 1980. Ethernet networks are commonly found in a bus topology but may also run in a star topology. Ethernet runs over coaxial cable in its bus topology and over UTP in its star topology.

FDDI   Fiber Distributed Data Interface. FDDI has a ring topology. FDDI is commonly run over fiber-optic cable, but it is also approved for use over category 5 UTP. When FDDI is run over copper UTP cable, it is called Copper Distributed Data Interface (CDDI). FDDI operates at 100 Mbps.

Fiber-Optic Cable   At the center of a fiber-optic cable is a thin cylinder of glass or plastic. Light generated by a laser or a light emitting diode (LED) is passed through the cable to transmit data. Fiber-optic cable comes in two varieties: multi mode and single mode. Single mode is used to traverse longer distances. Multi mode cable is able to handle many light rays at once. Multi mode fiber normally uses LEDs for the light source, which are less powerful than lasers. Multi mode may be used to attach stations that are $1^1/_4$ mile apart. Single mode fiber, on the other hand, is able to handle only one light ray at a time. It uses lasers as a light source and may be used to connect stations that are $12^1/_2$ miles apart.

Frame   See *Packet*.

Hardware Address   See *Physical Address*.

Hub   See *Concentrator*.

IEEE   The Institute of Electrical and Electronics Engineers has developed a group of standards that governs how networks work. The IEEE invented the 802 series standards for LANs. See *802.2*, *802.3*, and *802.5*.

Intelligent Concentrator   A concentrator that contains a CPU and has the ability to manage some of its functions via software. Intelligent concentrators often have the ability to be managed remotely over the network.

Interference   In networking, a disruption of the data signal on a LAN cable from some outside source. See *EMI* and *RFI*.

Internet   An internetwork collection of different networks that function as one through the use of bridges and routers.

The Internet   A worldwide internetwork that connects many government, commercial, and educational institutions. The Internet communicates via the TCP/IP protocol.

IPX   Internet Packet eXchange. This is the protocol that Novell NetWare uses to transmit data from one station to another.

ISO   The International Standards Organization. This organization, based in Switzerland, has developed a variety of standards regarding computer networking, including the Open Systems Interconnection model (OSI).

LAN   Local Area Network. A network that geographically covers only a small area, typically no more than a few rooms or a single building.

LAN Manager   A server-based networking solution from Microsoft Corporation based on NetBIOS for LAN communication. LAN Manager has largely been replaced by Windows NT Server as Microsoft's LAN package.

LAN Server   An OS/2 server-based networking package from IBM. LAN Server was originally developed in cooperation with Microsoft and operates using NetBIOS, as does LAN Manager.

LLC   Logical Link Control. The IEEE 802.2 standard subdivided the data link layer of the OSI model into two sublayers, LLC and MAC. The uppermost sublayer is LLC. LLC is responsible for breaking the data into packets so it can be sent across the wire, addressing the packet with the address of the station it is going to, and applying error correction. See *MAC* and *Data Link Layer*.

MAC   Media Access Control. The lower sublayer of the data link layer of the OSI model. MAC is responsible for actually handing the packetized data to the physical layer. On Ethernet networks it implements the CSMA/CD access method to get the data transmitted. On token-ring networks, it uses the token-ring access method.

MAN   Metropolitan Area Network. A network that covers a geographical area of a city. An example is a company that networks three different buildings across town.

MAU   Multistation Access Unit. This is a concentrator for token-ring networks. It provides ports for the connection of both stations and other MAUs. See *Concentrator*.

NDIS   Network Driver Interface Specification. NDIS is a standard written by Microsoft and 3Com that provides a common interface to the NIC. If network protocols are written to the NDIS interface, then the NIC in the machine becomes irrelevant. Just add any card and its appropriate NDIS driver and the protocols work. NDIS also provides the ability to multitask network protocols. In other words, it allows more than one protocol to access the NIC at the same time. NDIS is similar to the Open Data Link Interface (ODI) developed by Novell and Apple. See *ODI.*

NetBEUI   NetBIOS Extended User Interface. NetBEUI, pronounced *net-booey*, provides transport layer services for networks such as Microsoft LAN Manager, Windows NT Server, Windows for Workgroups, and Windows. See *Transport Layer.*

NetBIOS   Network Basic Input/Output System. NetBIOS is a protocol that provides transport and session layer services. It was first designed for use in IBM's PC Network. NetBIOS's successor is NetBEUI.

NetWare   A server-based network operating system from Novell. NetWare is the most widely used LAN package in the world and is based on the IPX network protocol.

Network   A collection of computers and related peripherals that are all connected and are able to communicate with one another.

Network Address   Network addresses are a way of grouping physical addresses together. They do not become important, really, until the network grows large enough so that there is more than one network segment. Each network segment gets its own network address. Stations connected to a certain segment can then be identified by both network and physical addresses. This can greatly simplify matters in large networks. The devices that connect these network segments are called bridges and routers. See *Bridge* and *Router.*

Network Layer   Layer three of the OSI model. The network layer examines network addresses and performs routing. See *Network Address* and *Router.*

NFS   Network File System. This is one of the many protocols that allows files and peripherals on one system to be used by a remote system over the network. NFS is the *de facto* network standard for the UNIX operating system.

NIC   Network Interface Card. This is the card in your computer that connects to the LAN cabling.

Node   Another word for a device on a network.

ODI   Open Data Link Interface. ODI provides a common hardware-independent interface to the network adapter and provides protocol multitasking, which is the ability to run more than one protocol at the same time. ODI was developed by Novell and Apple and is similar to NDIS. See *NDIS*.

OSI Model   Open Systems Interconnection. A standard for data communications set by the ISO. The OSI model defines network protocols in seven layers: the Application Layer, the Presentation Layer, the Session Layer, the Transport Layer, the Network Layer, the Data Link Layer, and the Physical Layer.

Packet   A small package of data that can be transmitted over a network. Before data can be sent over a LAN, it must be formatted in such a way that the receiving station understands the data when the station receives the data. Packets consist of three main parts. At the beginning of the packet is the transmission information, which includes the address of the machine that sent the packet, the address of the destination machine, and the network type of the packet. Next comes the actual data that is being transmitted. At the end of the packet are some fields that can help determine if there was an error in the transmission of the packet and, if so, correct that error.

Peer-To-Peer Network   A network in which all stations on the network can use the resources of every other station on the network. Contrast this with a server-based network, in which only the resources of the server machines may be shared.

Physical Address   A unique number (usually six bytes long) that is used to identify the different stations on a network. Each NIC has a unique number that has been assigned by the IEEE to prevent duplication.

Physical Layer   Layer one of the OSI model, which is the lowest layer. This layer includes the actual hardware that forms the network, including network cards and cabling. Standards at the physical layer include the type of connectors to be used in a LAN and the electrical characteristics of the cabling. See *OSI Model*.

Presentation Layer   Layer six of the OSI model. The presentation layer translates the data into a format that both computers can understand and use. Data encryption and compression are also implemented at this layer if necessary. See *OSI Model*.

Protocol   A set of rules that defines how computers talk to each other over a network. As long as both computers conform to the protocol standard, they can communicate. A protocol is similar to a language. If two people both understand English, then as long as one of them is speaking English words to the other that person can understand them.

Repeater   A device that connects two LAN cable segments together. Repeaters work at the physical layer of the OSI model and simply resend all electrical signals from one wire segment to the other. See also *Bridge* and *Router*.

RFI   Radio Frequency Interference. RFI is sometimes mistakenly called EMI, or electromagnetic interference. RFI occurs at the higher frequencies usually associated with radio waves, while EMI usually refers to lower frequency waves.

Ring   A network topology in which the two ends of the cable are connected to each other. The wire forms a circle. Ring networks can be difficult to physically implement.

RJ45   A larger version of the standard phone wire connector that holds eight wires instead of four. The RJ45 is the connector used on the unshielded twisted-pair wire in 10BaseT Ethernet networks. See *10BaseT*.

Router   A device that allows the interconnection of multiple cable segments. These cable segments may be of different types. Routers operate at the network layer of the OSI model and forward packets of data from one segment to another based on the network information contained in the packet.

Server   A computer that provides a service to LAN users, such as shared access to disks, files, a printer, or an electronic mail system. Usually, a server is a combination of hardware and software.

Server-Based Network   A network in which only the resources of a specialized machine may be shared by other machines on the LAN. Servers are generally dedicated computers—that is, they may not be used for anything other than sharing.

Session Layer   Layer five of the OSI model. The session layer creates and manages network connections from one computer to another on the network.

Sharing   Allowing other users on the network to have access to the resources on your computer.

SNMP   Simple Network Management Protocol. SNMP provides the ability to monitor and manage the network. It provides network statistics such as utilization and allows for the management of remote devices over the network.

SPX   Sequenced Packet eXchange. SPX is a protocol that works in tandem with the IPX protocol. IPX provides transport for the data on the network. SPX, on the other hand, ensures that the data actually arrives at the destination computer and that it is received properly.

Star   A network topology in which all stations are connected to one central point.

STP   Shielded Twisted Pair. A type of cabling often found in token-ring LANs. STP consists of two pairs of wire that are wound around each other. To help reduce electromagnetic interference, the cable has been shielded. The shielding consists of foil wrapped around each pair of wires and a braided wire mesh surrounding the entire cable. All this is then enclosed in a jacket of Teflon or PVC (polyvinyl chloride). See *UTP*.

T Connector   A T-shaped device that connects an Ethernet adapter to the network cabling in a 10Base2 network. A T-connector consists of two female ends and a male end. The male end connects to the NIC, and the two female ends attach to the ends of the two cables.

TCP/IP   Transport Control Protocol/Internet Protocol. TCP/IP is a set of protocols used to transmit data on the Internet. The Internet Protocol operates at the network layer of the OSI model, and the Transport Control Protocol provides transport layer services. TCP/IP is a another *de facto* standard in the UNIX environment. See *NFS*.

TCP/IP Address   A number that uniquely defines a machine on a TCP/IP network.

Terminator   A device placed at the extreme ends of a bus topology network, such as 10Base2 Ethernet. The terminator provides an impedance to the wire (50 ohms) and prevents the signal from being reflected off the end of the cable, which would interfere with subsequent signals on the network.

Thicknet   See *10Base5*.

Thinnet   See *10Base2*.

Token   A special 24-bit pattern used in token-ring networks. When a station receives the token, that means it is allowed to transmit data.

Token Ring An access method developed by IBM that operates over UTP at either 4 or 16 Mbps. Token ring relies on a special 24-bit pattern called a token to determine which station may send data. No station may begin transmitting data until it receives the token, and only one station at a time may have the token. Once the station receives the token, the station is allowed to hold it for exactly .01 milliseconds before it must give the token up. The token is then passed to the next machine in the ring. The first computer does not have the opportunity to transmit again until all the other stations have had a chance.

Topology The geometric shape that a network has, or how the network is laid out. Some common topologies are bus, star, and ring.

Transceiver Transmitter/Receiver. A device on an Ethernet network that actually sends and receives the signals across the wire.

Transport Layer Layer four of the OSI model. The transport layer makes sure that the data that was sent from the source computer arrives and is received properly by the destination computer.

Type 1 A type of shielded twisted-pair cable defined by IBM for use in token-ring networks. It contains two twisted pairs of 22 AWG (American Wire Gauge) wire. See *AWG*.

Type 2 A type of shielded twisted-pair cable defined by IBM for use in token-ring networks. It contains four twisted pairs of 26 AWG (American Wire Gauge) wire, which is thin and ideal for voice communications. Type 2 cable allows telephone and computer communications over the same wire. See *AWG* and *Type 1*.

Type 3 Type 3 is unshielded twisted-pair cable that is used for token rings at 4 Mbps. It is identical to category 3 Ethernet cable, except the pin-outs on the connectors are different. See *Category 3*.

Type 5 Fiber-optic cable for token-ring networks. Used for connections between MAUs. See *MAU*.

Type 6 Shielded twisted-pair cable used as patch cables to connect to ports on the MAU. It consists of two pairs of 26 AWG (American Wire Gauge) wire.

Type 8 Type 8 is a flat cable with no twists that is meant for running under carpeting.

Type 9   Shielded twisted-pair cable is meant for use in building plenums without a metal conduit. (The plenum is the area between a drop ceiling and the floor of the level above in a building.) Type 9 cable has a Teflon coating, which is superior to PVC (polyvinyl chloride, the coating found on Type 1 and UTP cable) because it does not give off toxic fumes if it burns in a building fire.

UTP   A type of network cabling that consists of four pairs of wire. Each wire in a pair is wrapped around the other. The four pairs are then covered in a PVC (polyvinyl chloride) coating. UTP cabling is used in both Ethernet and token-ring networks. It is also used as phone wiring. Contrast UTP with shielded twisted pair, which has a thin wire braid enclosing its internal wiring. The shield helps reduce the effect of electromagnetic interference. The quality of UTP cable depends on the number of twists per linear inch and is rated according to the Electronic Industries Association's category rating system. See *Category 3*, *Category 5*, and *EMI*.

UNIX   A powerful, text-based, multiuser operating system often found in high-end workstations and minicomputers.

WAN   Wide Area Network. A computer network that covers a very large geographical area, such as a state or country. Some companies even have worldwide WANs. An example of a WAN would be a network that included machines in an office in Columbia, Missouri, and an office in Berlin, Germany.

Appendix D

Internet Access Providers

To connect your Windows 95 network to the global network, you need an Internet connection. Connections have to come from somewhere; here is a list of Internet access providers in the United States and around the world.

This list is not complete. It can't be. There are new access providers entering the market every day. These are some of the better-known providers today.

The list is divided into two groups: providers in the U.S. and providers around the rest of the world.

United States

Nationwide

Cyberspace
300 Queen Anne Avenue N #396
Seattle, WA 98109-4599
(206) 505-5516
info@cyberspace.com

Advanced Networks & Services, Inc.
100 Clearbrook Road
Elmsford, NY 10523
(703) 758-7700
info@ans.net

NETCOM On-Line Communications Services
3031 Tisch Way, Mezzanine
San Jose, CA 95128
(408) 554-8649
info@netcom.com

Performance Systems International
510 Huntmar Park Drive
Herndon, VA 22070
(800) 827-7482
all-info@psi.com

By State

Alabama
Community Internet Connect, Inc.
120 Suffolk Drive
Madison, AL 35758
(205) 722-0199
info@cici.com

Alaska
Alaska Virtual Online
P.O. Box 221845
Anchorage, AK 99522-2218
(907) 522-2347
viper@avo.com

Arizona
Opus One
1404 East Lind Road
Tucson, AZ 85719
(602) 324-0494
sales@opus1.com

Internet Direct, Inc.
1366 East Thomas Road, Suite 210
Phoenix, AZ 85014-5741
(602) 274-0100
info@indirect.com

Crossroads Communications
955 East Javelina
Mesa, AZ 85204
(602) 813-9040
crossroads@xroads.com

Arkansas

Cloverleaf Technologies
25 Elmwood
Texarkana, TX 75501
(501) 772-9955
helpdesk@clover.cleaf.com

Arkansas River Valley Online Services, Inc.
136 Vance Lane
Russellville, AR 72801-0000
(501) 968-1506
info@arvos.com

California

ElectriCiti, Inc.
2171 India Street, Suite C
San Diego, CA 92101
(619) 338-9000
info@powergrid.electriciti.com

Delta Internet Services, Inc.
731 East Ball Road, Suite
Anaheim, CA 92805
(714) 778-0370
info@deltanet.com

DigiLink.Net
4429 West 169th
Lawndale, CA 90260-3252
(310) 542-7421
info@digilink.net

Whole Earth 'Lectronic Link
1750 Bridgeway Suite A200
Sausalito, CA 94965-1900
(415) 332-4335
info@well.com

InterNex Information Services
Chestnut Street Suite 202
Menlo Park, CA 94025
(415) 473-3060
info@internex.net

RAIN Network
P.O. Box 2683
Santa Barbara, CA 93120-2683
(805) 967-7246
info@rain.org

Lightside, Inc.
101 North Citrus, #4A
Covina, CA 91723
(818) 858-9261
info@lightside.com

Colorado

Rocky Mountain Internet, Inc.
2860 South Circle Drive, Suite 2202
Colorado Springs, CO 80906
(800) 900-7644
info@rmii.com

Old Colorado City Communications
West Colorado Avenue #203
Colorado Springs, CO 80904
(719) 528-5849
dave@oldcolo.com

Connecticut

Caravela Software
6 Way Road, Suite #33
Middlefield, CT 06455
(203) 349-7059
info@connix.com

Futuris Networks, Inc.
500 Summer Street, Suite 303
Stamford, CT 06901
(203) 359-8868
info@futuris.net

Delaware

SSNet, Inc.
1254 Lorewood Grove
Middletown, DE 19709
(302) 378-1386
info@ssnet.com

Delaware Common Access Network
1204 West Street
Wilmington, DE 19801
(302) 654-1019
awhite@global.dca.net

District of Columbia

DC Information Exchange
3110 Mount Vernon Avenue, Suite 1408
Alexandria, VA 22305-2658
(703) 836-1944

Florida

CyberGate, Inc.
662 South Military Trail
Deerfield Beach, FL 33442
(305) 428-4283
info@gate.net

SymNet
P.O. Box 20074
Tallahassee, FL 32316-0074
(904) 385-1061
info@symnet.net

Digital Decisions, Inc.
3815 North U.S. 1
Cocoa, FL 32926
(407) 635-8888
info@digital.net

Packetworks, Inc.
1100 Cleveland Street
Clearwater, FL 34615
(813) 446-8826
info@packet.net

Georgia

Network Atlanta
340 Knoll Ridge Court
Alpharetta, GA 30202-5039
(404) 410-9000
info@atlanta.com

MindSpring Enterprises, Inc.
200 Montgomery Ferry Drive, #36
Atlanta, GA 30309
(404) 888-0725
info@mindspring.com

Atlanta Internet Services, Inc.
1811 Bering, Suite 100
Houston, TX 77057
(713) 917-5000
info@sccsi.com

Hawaii

Hawaii Online, Network Services
737 Bishop Street, Suite 2305
Honolulu, HI 96813
(808) 533-6981
info@aloha.net

LavaNet, Inc.
Grosvenor Center
Makai Tower, Suite 1590
733 Bishop Street
Honolulu, HI 96813
(808) 545-5282
info@lava.net

Idaho

NICOH Net
200 South Main, Suite O
Pocatello, ID 83204
(208) 233-5802
info@nicoh.com

Illinois

Inter Access Company
9400 West Foster Avenue, Suite 111
Chicago, IL 60656
(800) 967-1580
info@interaccess.com

Computing Engineers, Inc.
P.O. Box 285
Vernon Hills, IL 60061-3258
(708) 367-1870
info@wwa.com

Macro Computer Solutions, Inc.
1300 West Belmont
Chicago, IL 60657
(312) 248-8649
info@mcs.net

Indiana

IQuest Network Services (IQUEST2-DOM)
2035 East 46th Street
Indianapolis, IN 46205
(317) 259-5050
info@iquest.net

INTERNET Indiana
8227 Northwest Boulevard, Suite 100
Indianapolis, IN 46278
(317) 876-5638
info@in.net

Iowa

Iowa Communications Network
Department of General Services
Hoover Building, Level A
Des Moines, IA 53019
(515) 281-7986

VI

Appendixes

Kansas

Southwind Internet Access, Inc.
120 South Market, Suite 330
Wichita, KS 67202
(316) 263-7963
info@southwind.net

Kentucky

IgLou Internet Services
3315 Gilmore Industrial Boulevard
Louisville, KY 40213
(800) 436-4456
info@iglou.com

Lousiana

Communique Computer
1515 Poydras Street, Suite 1305
New Orleans, LA 70112
(504) 527-6200
info@communique.net

Maine

netMAINE
P.O. Box 8258
Portland, ME 04104-8258
(207) 780-6381
atr@maine.net

Maryland

Charm Net (CHARM-DOM)
2228 East Lombard Street
Baltimore, MD 21231
(410) 558-3900
info@charm.net

Clark Internet Services
10600 Route 108
Ellicott City, MD 21042
(410) 995-0691
info@clark.net

Digital Express Group, Inc.
6006 Greenbelt Road, #228
Greenbelt, MD 20770
(301) 220-2020
info@digex.net

Massachusetts

Eco Software, Inc.
145 Munroe Street, Suite 405
Lynn, MA 01901-1222
(617) 593-3110
info@shore.net

intuitive information, inc.
1 Oak Hill Road
Fitchburg, MA 01420
(508) 341-1100
info@iii.net

The Internet Access Company
7 Railroad Avenue, Suite G
Bedford, MA 01730
(617) 276-7200
info@tiac.net

Michigan

Branch Information Services
2901 Hubbard
Ann Arbor, MI 48105
(313) 741-4442
branch-info@branch.com

Msen, Inc.
628 Brooks
Ann Arbor, MI 48103
(313) 998-4562
info@msen.com

CICNet, Inc.
ITI Building, Pod G
2901 Hubbard
Ann Arbor, MI 48105
(313) 998-6103
info@cic.net

Innovative Concepts
2662 Valley Drive
Ann Arbor, MI 48103
(313) 998-0090
info@ic.net

Minnesota

Millenium Communications
1300 Niccolett Mall, Suite 5083
Minneapolis, MN 55403
(612) 338-5509
info@millcomm.com

Minnesota Regional Network
511 11th Avenue South, Box 212
Minneapolis, MN 55415
(612) 342-2570
info@mr.net

Missouri

Socket Internet Services
607 East Jackson Street
Columbia, MO 65203
(314) 499-9807
info@socketis.net

ThoughtPort Networking Services
P.O. Box 242 2000 East Broadway
Columbia, MO 65201
(314) 474-6870
omar@thoughtport.com

Missouri Research and Education Network
University of Missouri-Columbia
200 Heinkel Building
Columbia, MO 65211
(314) 882-2121
ben@more.net

Montana

Montana Online
1801 South 3rd West
Missoula, MT 59801
(406) 721-4952
info@montana.com

Nebraska

Internet Nebraska
1719 North Cotner, Suite B
P.O. Box 5301
Lincoln, NE 68505-5301
(402) 434-8680
info@inetnebr.com

Omaha Free-Net
KVNO, Eng 200
University of Nebraska at Omaha
60th and Dodge Street
Omaha, NE 68182
(402) 554-2516
lowe@unomaha.edu

Nevada

TECH COM USA
3355 Spring Mountain Road, Suite 267
Las Vegas, NV 89102
(702) 871-4461
info@wizard.com

BK Systems, Inc.
dba Sierra-Net
P.O. Box 3709
Incline Village, NV 89450
(702) 831-3353
giles@sierra.net

Great Basin Internet Services
5301 Longley Lane, Suite D-144
Reno, NV 89511
(702) 829-2244
info@greatbasin.com

VI

Appendixes

New Hampshire

The Destek Group, Limited
21 Hinds Lane
Pelham, NH 03076-3013
(603) 635-3857
inquire@destek.net

MV Communications, Inc.
P.O. Box 4963
Manchester, NH 03108
(603) 429-2223
info@mv.mv.com

New Jersey

INTAC Access Corporation
256 Broad Avenue
Palisades Park, NJ 07650
(800) 504-6822
info@intac.com

NIC
637 Wyckoff Avenue, Box 294
Wyckoff, NJ 07481
(201) 934-1445
info@nic.com

Internet Online Services
294 State Street
Hackensack, NJ 07601
(201) 928-1000
help@ios.com

New Mexico

Computer Security Consulting
P.O. Box 5178
Santa Fe, NM 87502-5178
(505) 984-0085
info@spy.org

DBA Southwest Cyberport
2712 Texas NE
Albuquerque, NM 87110
(505) 271-0009
info@swcp.com

VII

Zynet Southwest
3308 Valley Haven Court NW
Albuquerque, NM 87107
(505) 343-8846
zycor@zynet.com

New York

Blythe Systems
235 East 87th Street, #12J
New York, NY 10128
(212) 226-7171
infodesk@blythe.org

Echo Communications
97 Perry Street, Suite 13
New York, NY 10014
(212) 255-3839
info@echonyc.com

InterCom, Inc.
1412 Avenue M, Suite 2428
Brooklyn, NY 11230
(212) 714-7183
info@intercom.com

Tinkelman Enterprises, Inc.
82-04 218th Street
Hollis Hills, NY 11427-1416
(718) 776-6811
sales@new-york.net

Interport Communications Corporation
1133 Broadway Avenue
New York, NY 10010
(212) 989-1128
info@interport.net

North Carolina

Creative Cybernetics
8307 University Executive Park Drive, Suite 253
Charlotte, NC 28262
(704) 549-5553
info@cybernetics.net

North Dakota

Red River Net
P.O. Box 388
Fargo, ND 58107
(701) 232-2227
info@rrnet.com

Ohio

Exchange Network Services, Inc.
27050 Drakefield Avenue
Euclid, OH 44132
(216) 261-4593
info@en.com

Ohio Supercomputer Center
1224 Kinnear Road
Columbus, OH 43212-1154
(614) 728-8100
info@oar.net

Oklahoma

Internet Oklahoma
9500 Westgate, Suite 120
Oklahoma City, OK 73162
(405) 721-1580
info@ionet.net

Questar Information Systems, Inc.
5900 Mosteller Drive, Suite 1500
Oklahoma City, OK 73112
(405) 848-3228
info@qns.net

Oregon

Hevanet
25-6 N.W. 23rd Place, #231
Portland, OR 97210-3534
(503) 228-3520
info@hevanet.com

Open Door Networks
110 South Laurel Street
Ashland, OR 97520
(503) 488-4127
info@opendoor.com

Teleport Corporation
319 SW Washington Street, Suite 803
Portland, OR 97204
(503) 223-4245
info@teleport.com

Pennsylvania

Prometheus Corporation
583 Shoemaker Road
King of Prussia, PA 19406
(610) 337-9994
info@pond.com

MicroServe Information Systems
222 Temperance Hill
Plymouth, PA 18651
(717) 779-4430
info@microserve.com

SSNet, Inc.
1254 Lorewood Grove
Middletown, DE 19709
(302) 378-1386
info@ssnet.com

Rhode Island

InteleCom Data Systems
45 Hamilton Drive
East Greenwich, RI 02818
(401) 885-6855
info@ids.net

South Carolina

Global Vision
102 East North Street, Suite C
Greenville, SC 29601
(803) 241-0901
info@globalvision.net

S.I.M.S. Internet Matrix Southeast
1209 Midvale Avenue
Charleston, SC 29412
(803) 762-4956
info@sims.net

South Dakota

Dakota Internet Services, Inc.
3404 South Bahnson Avenue
Sioux Falls, SD 57103
(605) 371-1962
info@dakota.net

Tennessee

ISDNet, Inc.
5115 Mayland Way
Brentwood, TN 37027
(615) 377-7672
jdunlap@rex.isdn.net

Gold Sword Systems
917 Danville Circle
Knoxville, TN 37923
(615) 691-6498
info@goldsword.com

ERC, Inc.
P.O. Box 417
UTSI Research Park
Tullahoma, TN 37388
(615) 455-9915
staff@edge.ercnet.com

Texas

DFW Internet Services, Inc.
204 East Belknap, Suite 200
Fort Worth, TX 76102
(817) 332-5116
info@dfw.net

Texas Metronet, Inc.
860 Kinwest Parkway, Suite 179
Irving, TX 75063
(214) 705-2900
info@metronet.com

Real/Time Communications
504 West 24th, #7
Austin, Texas 78705
(512) 451-0046
info@realtime.net

Zilker Internet Park, Inc.
1106 Clayton Lane, Suite 500W
Austin, TX 78723
(512) 206-3850
info@zilker.net

USIS
Suite 351A
Houston, TX 77092
(713) 682-1666
admin@usis.com

Utah

XMission
P.O. Box 510063
Salt Lake City, UT 84151-0063
(801) 539-0852
support@xmission.com

Infonaut Communication Services
992 Cinnamon Hills Road
Provo, UT 84606
(801) 370-3068
info@infonaut.com

Vermont

Vermont Internet System and Technology Access Network, Inc.
c/o Applied Telecommunications, Inc.
95 St. Paul Street
Burlington, VT 05401
(802) 660-9190
lisa@vistanet.com

Virginia

Virginia Education and Research Network
c/o University of Virginia
Academic Computing Center
Gilmer Hall
Charlottesville, VA 22903
(804) 924-0616
jaj@virginia.edu

Washington

Northwest Nexus, Inc.
P.O. Box 40597
Bellevue, WA 98015-4597
(206) 455-3505
info@nwnexus.wa.com

Object Software Development
Columbia Seafirst Center
701 Fifth Avenue, Suite 6801
Seattle, WA 98104
(206) 343-7828
info@seanet.com

West Virginia

West Virginia Network for Educational Telecomputing
837 Chestnut Ridge Road
Morgantown, WV 26505
(304) 293-5192
cc011071@wvnvaxa.wvnet.edu

Wisconsin

Fullfeed Communications
359 Raven Lane
Madison, WI 53704-2488
(608) 246-4239
info@fullfeed.com

By Country

These service providers are located throughout the world and specialize in providing connectivity to organizations with long distances between locations.

Australia

Australian Research Network
Computer Science
University of Melbourne
Parkville, Victoria 3052
Australia
+61 3 287 9110
kre@munnari.oz.au

Austria

ACONET Association
c/o Vienna University Computer Center
Universitaetsstrasse 7
A-1010 Wien
Austria
+43 1 43-61-11 ext. 227
Peter.Rastl@cc.univie.ac.at

Belgium

Katholieke Universiteit Leuven
Department of Computer Science
Celestijnenlaan 200A
B-3001 Leuven
Belgium
+32 16 327566
admin-be@cs.kuleuven.ac.be

Bulgaria

Digital Systems
Neofit Bozveli 6
Varna-9000
Bulgaria
+359 52 234540
dhs@digsys.bg

Denmark

DKnet (EUnet Denmark)
Fruebjergvej 3
DK-2100 Copenhagen Oe
Denmark
+45 39 17 99 00
shj@dknet.dk

England

University College London
Department of Computer Science
London
England
+44 71 380 7286
kirstein@cs.ucl.ac.uk

Finland

Tampere University of Technology
P.O. Box 527
SF-33101 Tampere
Finland
+358 31 162111
fi-domain-admin@tut.fi

France

Institut National de Recherche en
   Informatique et en Automatique
Domaine de Voluceau, Rocquencourt
BP 105, F-78153 Le Chesnay CEDEX
France
+33 1 39635405
fr-domain-admin@inria.fr

Germany

Universität Karlsrühe
Rechenzentrum/DE NIC
Postfach 6980
D-76128 Karlsrühe
Germany
+49 721 608 4030
lortz@rz.uni-karlsruhe.de

Greece

Insitute of Computer Science
P.O. Box 1385
71110 Heraklio, Crete
Greece
+30 81 221171
stelios@csi.forth.gr

Hong Kong

University of Hong Kong
c/o Computer Center
Pokfulam Road
Hong Kong
+852 8592491
hcxcnng@hkujnt.hku.hk

Iceland

SURIS/ISnet—Association of Research Networks in Iceland
Taeknigardi
Dunhagi 5
107 Reykjavik
Iceland
+354 569 4950
hjons@rhi.hi.is

Ireland

University College Dublin
Computer Centre
Belfield, Dublin 4
Ireland
+353 1 706 2375
noreilly@ucd.ie

Israel

The Hebrew University of Jerusalem
Department of Computer Science
91904 Jerusalem
Israel
+972-3-5450610
hank@vm.biu.ac.il

Italy

GARR Network Information Service
c/o CNR-Istituto CNUCE
Via Santa Maria, 36
56126-Pisa
Italy
+39 50 593246
bonito@nis.garr.it

Japan

Japanese Network Information Center
c/o Computer Center, University of Tokyo
Yayoi 2-11-16, Bunkyo-ku
Tokyo 113
Japan
+81 466 47 5111 ext. 3330
jun@wide.ad.jp

Netherlands

Center for Mathematics and Computer Science
Kruislaan 413
1098 SJ Amsterdam
The Netherlands
+31 20 5924112
hostmaster@cwi.nl

New Zealand

Waikato University
Hamilton
New Zealand
+64 71 384 069
j.houlker@waikato.ac.nz

Norway

Norwegian Telecommunications Administration
P.O. Box 83
N-2007 Kjeller
Norway
+47 7 592991
Petter.Kongshaug@delab.sintef.no

South Africa

Foundation for Research Development
UNINET Project
P.O. Box 2600
Pretoria 0001
Republic Of South Africa
+27 11 841-3542
mlawrie@frd.ac.za

Switzerland

SWITCH Teleinformatics Services
Limmatquai 138
CH-8001 Zurich
Switzerland
+41 1-268-1530
Brunner@switch.ch

Ukraine

Communication Systems Ltd.
app. 94, 108/2 prospiekt 40 liet
Oktyabrya, 252127, Kiev
Ukraine
+7 044 4345460
oleg%elvisti.kiev.ua@ussr.eu.net

Index

O

Q-R

X–Y–Z

Complete and Return this Card for a *FREE* Computer Book Catalog

Thank you for purchasing this book! You have purchased a superior computer book written expressly for your needs. To continue to provide the kind of up-to-date, pertinent coverage you've come to expect from us, we need to hear from you. Please take a minute to complete and return this self-addressed, postage-paid form. In return, we'll send you a free catalog of all our computer books on topics ranging from word processing to programming and the internet.

Mrs. ☐ Ms. ☐ Dr. ☐

(first) ☐☐☐☐☐☐☐☐☐☐☐ (M.I.) ☐ (last) ☐☐☐☐☐☐☐☐☐☐☐☐☐☐☐

ess ☐☐☐☐☐☐☐☐☐☐☐☐☐☐☐☐☐☐☐☐☐☐☐☐☐☐☐☐☐☐☐☐☐

☐☐☐☐☐☐☐☐☐☐☐☐☐☐☐☐☐☐☐☐☐☐☐☐☐☐☐☐☐☐☐☐☐

☐☐☐☐☐☐☐☐☐☐☐ State ☐☐ Zip ☐☐☐☐☐ ☐☐☐☐

☐☐☐ ☐☐☐ ☐☐☐☐ Fax ☐☐☐ ☐☐☐ ☐☐☐☐

any Name ☐☐☐☐☐☐☐☐☐☐☐☐☐☐☐☐☐☐☐☐☐☐☐☐☐☐☐☐

l address ☐☐☐☐☐☐☐☐☐☐☐☐☐☐☐☐☐☐☐☐☐☐☐☐☐☐☐☐

ease check at least (3) influencing factors for rchasing this book.

or back cover information on book .... ☐
al approach to the content .... ☐
oleteness of content.. ☐
or's reputation .... ☐
sher's reputation .... ☐
cover design or layout .... ☐
or table of contents of book .... ☐
of book.. ☐
al effects, graphics, illustrations .... ☐
 (Please specify): _____ ☐

ow did you first learn about this book?

n Macmillan Computer Publishing catalog .... ☐
mmended by store personnel .... ☐
he book on bookshelf at store .... ☐
mmended by a friend .... ☐
ved advertisement in the mail .... ☐
n advertisement in: _____ ☐
book review in: _____ ☐
 (Please specify): _____ ☐

ow many computer books have you rchased in the last six months?

book only .... ☐   3 to 5 books...................... ☐
ks .... ☐   More than 5 .... ☐

4. Where did you purchase this book?

Bookstore .... ☐
Computer Store .... ☐
Consumer Electronics Store .... ☐
Department Store .... ☐
Office Club .... ☐
Warehouse Club .... ☐
Mail Order .... ☐
Direct from Publisher .... ☐
Internet site .... ☐
Other (Please specify): _____ ☐

5. How long have you been using a computer?

☐ Less than 6 months   ☐ 6 months to a year
☐ 1 to 3 years   ☐ More than 3 years

6. What is your level of experience with personal computers and with the subject of this book?

	With PCs	With subject of book
New	☐	☐
Casual	☐	☐
Accomplished	☐	☐
Expert	☐	☐

Source Code ISBN:

7. Which of the following best describes your job title?

Administrative Assistant .... ☐
Coordinator .... ☐
Manager/Supervisor .... ☐
Director .... ☐
Vice President .... ☐
President/CEO/COO .... ☐
Lawyer/Doctor/Medical Professional .... ☐
Teacher/Educator/Trainer .... ☐
Engineer/Technician .... ☐
Consultant .... ☐
Not employed/Student/Retired .... ☐
Other (Please specify): _____ ☐

8. Which of the following best describes the area of the company your job title falls under?

Accounting .... ☐
Engineering .... ☐
Manufacturing .... ☐
Operations .... ☐
Marketing .... ☐
Sales .... ☐
Other (Please specify): _____ ☐

Comments: _____
_____
_____

9. What is your age?

Under 20 ....
21-29 ....
30-39 ....
40-49 ....
50-59 ....
60-over ....

10. Are you:

Male ....
Female ....

11. Which computer publications do you read regularly? (Please list)

_____
_____
_____
_____
_____
_____
_____
_____
_____
_____

Fold here and scotch-tape